T0330079

Cities in the Anthropocene

'This thought-provoking book brings an exciting, young voice to contemporary urban planning. Jon proposes that pragmatic urban policy must factor in respectful, more-than-human relationships. Her message of hope in the possibilities of the unknown should shape critical discussion in urban planning and geography seminars.'
—Jean Hillier, Professor Emerita at the Centre for Urban Research, RMIT University, Melbourne

'Theoretically-informed and practically-engaged, Ihnji Jon has written a thoughtful and compelling argument for an anti-essentialist ecology that links environmental concerns with inequality and centers the necessary political action in the fertile complexity of cities.'
—Robert A. Beauregard, Professor Emeritus, Columbia University

'A must-read – a carefully crafted account that unsettles wide-ranging expositions of the unfolding present of perilous uncertainty. Extremely important, both theoretically and from a policy perspective.'
—Prince K. Guma, Research Fellow and Assistant Country Director, British Institute in East Africa

'Shows with nuance and care how cities can provide a platform for politics in the midst of ecological crisis. An essential book for thinking, teaching, and taking action in the Anthropocene.'
—Derek S. Denman, Postdoctoral Fellow in the Department of Political Science, University of Copenhagen

'Engaging with contemporary urban existence in creative and subversive ways, this inspiring book opens new avenues for scholars, activists and professionals to advance an environmental politics appropriate to the Anthropocene.'
—Dr Kevin J. Grove, Associate Professor of Human Geography Department of Global and Sociocultural Studies, Florida International University

'Jon's insightful research shows how place-based urban practice can connect with green theory and community activism to affirm the global role of cities as drivers of positive equity-based ecological and social change with imagination, hope and soul.'
—Dr Paul Downton, author of *Ecopolis: Architecture and Cities for a Changing Climate*

Cities in the Anthropocene

New Ecology and Urban Politics

Ihnji Jon

First published 2021 by Pluto Press
345 Archway Road, London N6 5AA

www.plutobooks.com

Copyright © Ihnji Jon 2021

The right of Ihnji Jon to be identified as the author of this work has been asserted
in accordance with the Copyright, Designs and Patents Act 1988.

An earlier version of Chapter 2 was published as "Scales of Political Action in the
Anthropocene: Gaia, Networks, and Cities as Frontiers of Doing Earthly Politics,"
Global Society 34, no. 2 (2019): 163–85.

British Library Cataloguing in Publication Data
A catalogue record for this book is available from the British Library

ISBN   978 0 7453 4149 1   Hardback
ISBN   978 0 7453 4150 7   Paperback
ISBN   978 1 7868 0754 0   PDF eBook
ISBN   978 1 7868 0756 4   Kindle eBook
ISBN   978 1 7868 0755 7   EPUB eBook

Typeset by Stanford DTP Services, Northampton, England
Printed and bound by CPI Group (UK) Ltd, Croydon, CR0 4YY

Contents

Figures and tables

TABLES

Acknowledgements

I would like to express my deepest gratitude to interview participants and others who provided assistance during my fieldwork research in Darwin, Tulsa, Cleveland, and Cape Town. Their insights inspired and motivated me to write this book. I thank Michele Acuto, Director of Connected Cities Lab, and Ken Barlow, Associate Commissioning Editor at Pluto, for believing in this project before it was fully developed. I also thank Melanie Patrick, Design Manager, for the beautiful cover design that inspired me to write better. Thank you to the anonymous reader, too, whose critique on the previous manuscript made this book better than it would have been otherwise. Special thanks to Ajay Jennings, an artist in Melbourne, for granting me the rights to use his pictures taken in Merimbula, New South Wales, during the 2019–20 devastating summer bushfire season in Australia.

Every day we encounter different people in our life paths. What we read and what we write are inevitably affected by these encounters and interactions. This book is no exception; it is a collection of ideas that I have heard and learned from different sources, peoples, and their stories. For that, I would like to thank everyone that I shared momentary instances with, whose names are too many and definitely not limited to: Mark Purcell, Sarah Elwood, Branden Born, and Mike Lindell in Seattle; Isabelle Steichen, Noah Ennis, Robert W. Lake in Brooklyn; Elanna Nolan, Stephanie Butcher, Irene Håkansson, Kathryn Davidson, Jessie Briggs, and Crystal Legacy in Melbourne; Marie-Aleth (Kéké) Hanrion and the family in Paris, Chrishny Kangatharan in Kettering, Yuree Noh and Bo Yun Park in Boston, Bo Kyung Kim, Eun Jin Kim and Ji Eun Lee in Seoul; Mathilde Lecler in Paris and her family in Caen, and Mr Evrard and the family, including Isabelle and Violaine in Paris, who helped me and watched me grow into an independent thinker. I wish Mme Evrard was still with us to read this book.

I dedicate this book to my dad, who sacrificed his own artistry to financially support other artists in his family. Before the 38th parallel border was drawn, my grandfather and the family fled to South Korea from the North. Growing up in Seoul, I was repeatedly told of the difficult journey that my family had to make. I also dedicate this book to my mom, who survived traumatic brain injury for the love of her daughters. And of course, also to my unni, Ihnmi, with whom I share my existential anxieties. My dream of becoming a writer, which this book symbolises, would not have been possible without my family's sacrifice, support, and love.

Figure 0.1   Merimbula (New South Wales, Australia), during the catastrophic fire season in Summer 2019–20. © Ajay Jennings

1
Introduction
Environment politics beyond environment

To express is always to sing the glory of God. Every stratum is a judgment of God; not only do plants and animals, orchids, and wasps, sing and express themselves, but so do rocks and even rivers, every stratified thing on earth.
– Gilles Deleuze and Félix Guattari[1]

This book is *about* cities and *for* cities as enablers of what I call 'environment politics beyond environment'. Please bear with me if the statement 'one should take care of the environment' feels old to you. Despite the lengthy history of environmentalism, let alone the outpouring of scientific facts that insist upon the urgency of action, we still constantly hear the voices of climate change deniers, as well as those who think that our actions are unrelated to the atmospheric change. Maybe, just maybe, our approaches have been wrong. At least that's what 'new ecology' writers have been saying. My argument for 'environment politics beyond environment', which this book is all about, draws its philosophical groundings from this 'new ecology' literature.

What then is 'new ecology', and how is it different from 'old ecology'? The standard criticism of 'old ecology' unfolds in three main questions:

1. On its human/nature division: In proclaiming the norm 'we have to protect nature', aren't we normalising the human/nature dichotomy – as if environmentalism is something that we do as charity, independent from sustaining our everyday life?
2. On its top-down moral grounds: Is an apocalyptic moral imperative – 'we have to do something, or we will all die' – an effective way to garner a wider audience for environmentalism?

3. On its over-reliance on 'logical thinking': Aren't humans material beings – i.e., isn't it wrong to rely solely on cerebral or 'rational' decisions for inducing an action or a desire for change?

What I refer to as 'new ecology' in this book is the recent literature on anti-essentialist environmentalism, which defies the essentialist dichotomy between human and nature, as well as the essentialist morality of the norm 'we *have to* protect nature'. Often also referred to as 'posthumanism' or 'affirmative ecopolitics' in the Anthropocene, 'new ecology' literature is 'new' for the following reasons.

Above all, 'new ecology' literature fundamentally questions the essentialist division between human/nonhuman or culture/nature, highlighting how they are intricately intertwined with one another through co-development/co-evolution processes.[2] New ecology writers argue that the story of 'how humans came to become what we are today' cannot be told without the roles of nonhuman agencies. Our material being itself is a product of historical evolution from micro-organisms; in a more contemporary context, no one can deny that our everyday cognitive decision-making is constantly influenced by different 'nudges' from nonhuman agents, either atmospheric weather patterns or digital gadgets that we interact with from the moment we start our day.

Second, 'new ecology' does not impose environmentalism on us as a top-down moral imperative; rather, it focuses on demonstrating how much we are dependent on ecosystem functions and all the nonhuman 'ancestors' who render possible the material world in which we inhabit. We *learn to be*, rather than have to be, response-able to the feedback, reactions, and voices from the nonhuman world, as we start becoming more aware of the fragility and materiality of our bodily existence – the destiny of which is entangled and interconnected with the density of other species (who are at the brink of disappearing precisely because of our irresponsible interventions).

Finally, inspired by pragmatic empiricism that rejects any a priori conception or values, 'new ecology' emphasises the empirical and sensory experiences of our immediate surroundings – arguing how our pro-environment actions should be fuelled by (and cannot be disconnected from) our everyday experiences of the world or 'what surrounds us'. This implies that 'love for nature' is something to be learned and cultivated, starting with appreciating our everyday interaction with local surroundings.

In short, 'new ecology' tries to go beyond the kinds of environmentalism that relies on the fetishised understanding of 'nature' or 'the environment' that unnecessarily creates the boundaries between our everyday living (human needs) and ecosystem functions (ecological needs). Adopting this 'new ecology' attitude to further environmentalism – especially in today's world of social and political division – this book proposes how cities can perform 'environment politics beyond environment'.

Why cities? On what grounds am I proposing that 'cities' would be an adequate scale for environmental action? Indeed, 'global city' scholars have already noted the rising influence and power of cities in the global economy and politics. They have highlighted that cities, as global economic power-houses and concentrated human settlements, are now important figures driving policy trends or more progressive political agendas. Think of American cities' mayoral statements on welcoming international refugees, for instance. Baltimore Mayor Stephanie Rawlins-Blake has stated that: 'There are few among us who can claim that their ancestors were indigenous to the United States. The welcoming of immigrants and New Americans is a critical part of my strategy to grow Baltimore, and I hope that refugees from Syria will look to our city as a potential place to call home'.[3]

Further, political actions on climate have been led by several international networks of like-minded cities, who together hope to start a global movement and culture that normalises 'pro-environment' ideals. The examples of such city networks include but are not limited to: C40 Cities Climate Leadership Group, United Nation's Cities for Climate Protection Campaign, and Local Governments for Sustainability (ICLEI)'s Cities With Nature. In short, transcending ideology or partisan politics at the national scale, cities have been playing an instrumental role in promoting human societies that are socially and ecologically responsible.

Adding to this existing dialogue on 'why cities matter', this book provides another rationale on why cities would be a particularly 'good scale' for enacting and leading global environment politics. This discussion goes beyond the conventional global cities literature, which has mainly paid attention to the 'intensity' of cities, instead emphasising the advantage of 'complexity' that cities possess, arguing that this can help cities advance 'environment politics beyond environment'. With this complexity in mind, I ask: How could we engage with those who are not particularly interested in nature or the matters of 'the environment'? How could 'the environment' be deeply situated and integrated into our (humans') everyday socioeconomic affairs – to the point where we cannot simply imagine any politics or policy decisions without factoring in our relationship with the environment? The book tries to address these questions by drawing examples from cities that have been under-researched on that front.

The book unfolds as follows. First, in 'Why Cities? Towards a New Theorisation of "Scale"' (Chapter 2), I theorise what a 'good scale' for enacting environment actions should/would look like, especially given that the impacts of environmental degradation are local (as in actual households are affected) and global (as in climate change happens everywhere in a ubiquitous manner) at the same time. Who can say for sure what the reason, or the 'root cause' is when it comes to ever-more-frequent tornado events in the USA, severe bushfire season in Australia, or severe droughts in South Africa? We can blame the world, global capitalism, and every decision related to climate crisis, but we can also blame the regional and local, for their inability to act promptly within their capacity and jurisdictional boundaries. By exploring the tension between 'ever-expanding' versus 'ever-narrowing' notion of scale in environment politics, I identify the characteristics of what could be considered an adequate or ideal scale for pro-environment initiatives. Next, I use the ideal aspects of 'city-scale' as a demonstrative example that captures these characteristics, arguing that cities can be frontiers of doing environment politics thanks to their physical graspability ('small enough'), the degree of influence and leadership that cities possess ('intense enough'), and the extent of complexity that allows cities to take on a more holistic approach to governance – taking account of the interaction effects ('large enough').

After the theoretical explorations as to why cities are a good scale for action in environment politics, I move on to discussing different cities' empirical experiences of engaging with citizens who often brush off the 'green agenda' as a partisan shibboleth. In 'Darwin vs. Tulsa: How Cities Talk About 'Nature' Without Saying the Word' (Chapter 3), I investigate the specific strategies of how cities re-articulate environment politics without saying the word 'nature' or 'the environment', in attempts to reach out to a broader audience who are often put off by the ideological claims associated with 'green agenda'. Especially in the current divisive political climate, I ask: how do cities still manage to pursue pro-environment actions, and what are their strategies for working with those who may or may not be interested in nature in the first place? Based on interviews with urban planners and environmental activists in Tulsa, Oklahoma (USA) and Darwin, Northern Territory (Australia) – whose regional economy is largely dependent on dark energy resources – I discuss the practices, strategies, and visions of what I call 'pragmatic environmentalism'. Focusing on tangible material objects and everyday surroundings, pragmatic environmentalism prioritises concrete actions over ideological agreements, and presents a speculative hope that we might be able to link immediate benefits (of whatever feels good to us for now) and long-term benefits (of our sustainable future).

The book then goes further to understand the positions of cities who often suffer from chronic socioeconomic precarities that require immediate attention, and how they try to balance competing ideals between 'green' and 'equity'. In 'Cleveland vs. Cape Town: Can a City Aspire to be Green and Inclusive?' (Chapter 4), I explore how cities – particularly those who are under the stress of addressing poverty and inequality – attempt to effectuate a marriage between 'green' and 'equity' agendas. The ethics of 'protecting nature' may be widely accepted in affluent cities, which have the resources and means to pursue green-only initiatives without further justification. But that is not necessarily the case for cities that suffer from chronic poverty and inequality; it can be considered a luxury for a city to think about nature or the environment, if its constituents cannot imagine a future beyond the next few months. What is it like to pursue pro-environmental initiatives in a context where addressing poverty and social inequality have to come first? How can cities advocate for longer-term green agendas when the socioeconomic challenges of 'right now' remains unanswered? Based on interviews in Cleveland (Ohio, USA) and Cape Town (South Africa), this chapter addresses these questions by studying how the convergence between the green and equity agendas could occur. The chapter concludes that hope lies in the willingness and capacity of social actors who create public dialogues, mainstream narratives, or policy articulations that proclaim the pragmatic benefits of environmentalism – effectively harnessing the local social, political, and economic contexts produced by each of their unique territorial experiences and histories.

In 'Cities and Complexity: Linking "the Social" with "the Environmental"' (Chapter 5), I return to the theoretical starting points outlined in Chapter

2, weaving together experiences from each of the cities visited in Chapters 3 and 4 to animate the empirical advantages of 'city-scale'. More specifically, in an attempt to extend the argument that I have made in Chapter 2 – the point that cities are an ideal scale of environment action thanks to their 'complexity' – I explain what we can learn from the social assemblage theory literature, which views social entities as 'complex systems'. What does it mean for a social entity to be a 'complex system'? I define 'complexity' by explaining three key aspects of complex social entities: intense interaction effects, unpredictability of emergent qualities (that rise out of those effects), and respecting the radical heterogeneity and difference among their constituents (which produce those effects). Based on this definition of 'complexity', I demonstrate how cities can capitalise on their 'complexity' as a way to develop more concrete and creative linkages between 'the social' affairs and 'the environmental' affairs.

In the concluding chapter (Chapter 6), I disclose my main motivation for writing this book, which was fuelled by my desire to imagine another 'reality' that casts hope in the possibilities of the unknown, for the unknown.

In today's world of political and social division, it has become increasingly difficult to arrive at a wider consensus on 'why the environment matters'. Terms such as 'nature', 'ecology', or 'the environment' are often dismissed as left-leaning political discourse, while the matters of the environment affect all of us. But let me play a devil's advocate: who is anyone to judge different people's life choices and paths? Who are we to impose an essentialist moral standard against people's lives? According to Dewey, recognising the uniqueness (or 'singularity') of individuals is what differentiates today's world from ancient culture, whose customs, traditions, and rigid conservatism tries to vilify individual characteristics as deviations from normal, or as 'dangers against which society had to protect itself'.[4] However, at the same time, celebrating the radical plurality of unique individuals can be at odds with creating a collective vision for our society, which may ask individuals to sacrifice their selfhood for the pursuit of common good. This tension posits a difficult riddle especially in the context of global climate crisis where cities and localities are obliged to mobilise themselves in the face of extreme weather events.

If the urgency of climate crises calls for more swift and immediate action, we should find more creative and inventive ways of engaging with those who do not necessarily share our ideological viewpoints or philosophies on life. This book is a testament to that very quest of how we can 'mainstreamise' environment politics and its movement, while at the same time radically embracing the differences (or 'singularities') that render societies complex, unpredictable, and hence exciting.

2
Why cities? Towards a new theorisation of 'scale'

Climate change is real, and extreme weather events are its physical manifestations. A growing literature in political theory, anthropology, and geography is embracing the concept of 'Anthropocene', which refers to the current ecological crisis physically affecting our everyday lives – in the form of urban flooding, heat waves, tornadoes, and cyclones.

The scale of political action, or the main political actor who should be responsible for dealing with this ecological crisis, is now in question. Who can really say the real reason, or the root cause, of ever-more-frequent tornado events in the US Midwest, urban flash flooding in Paris, or severe droughts in Cape Town? While we can attribute it to the umbrella-like existence of neoliberalism and its harmful effects everywhere, we can also turn our blame to local politicians and institutions for their inability to take action within their assigned boundaries of control.

I would like to show, in this chapter, why cities are an adequate scale for doing 'earthly politics'. Here, 'earthly politics' refer to pro-nature or pro-environmentalist initiatives that are motivated and driven by our attachment to local territorial experiences. 'New ecology' writers such as Bruno Latour,[1] Donna Haraway,[2] and Anna Tsing[3] argue that the motivation behind any pro-environmental political action should be connected with our empirical, physical experiences with our immediate surroundings, or our everyday relationship with nature/environment. In the era of Anthropocene, where we feel the consequences of climate change in a more tangible manner, the importance of local action is clear: several surveys, polls, and studies have found that the more we physically experience extreme climate events or weather patterns locally, the more we're likely to admit to the reality of climate change and become more engaged with pro-environmental political actions.[4]

But why cities? Why is 'urban scale' an adequate scale for enacting on pro-environment politics? In this chapter, I propose a new theorisation of 'scale' in doing earthly politics (i.e., who is acting, who should be responsible for addressing planetary environmental degradation). In order to situate my proposal within the existing scholarship, I consult with the 'politics of scale' literature in urban theory and geography, as well as the renewed attention on 'scale' issues raised by now-fashionable 'new ecology' literature.

While the decades-long theorisation on 'politics of scale' in geography have made an excellent contribution on performative aspects of scale, they have failed to respond to the affirmative politics movements in which scholars and policy makers attempt to theorise scales as ranges in which political action can be mobilised. On the other hand, the recent rise of the 'new ecology' movement often fails to move beyond the romanticisation of the local, which is easily subject to criticisms, such as 'local trap' where the small is not always intrinsically 'good'. As an alternative, I theorise 'scales of political action' that can be simultaneously both materially situated (local) and ubiquitous (global), mainly using Gaian ecology and complex theory. Finally, as a concrete example of 'scales of political action', I propose cities as frontiers of doing earthly politics, focusing on the characteristics of urban conditions that match our new theorisation of scale.

THEORETICAL IMPASSE OF 'POLITICS OF SCALE'

'Politics of scale', 'politics about scale', 'scalar politics', or simply, 'scale', were at the centre of urban theory between the late 1990s and 2000s, especially in the field of geography and international urban politics.[5] Especially in the literature's latest developments, writers were particularly committed to dismantling or de-essentialising a priori notion of scale, using the examples in which scales can only be understood in relation with one another under the all-pervasive influence of neoliberal power dynamics.[6] A decade on, the scholarly attention on such political theorisation of scale has declined. This is partly because there was already enough research and writing on how scales are a product of naturalising global capitalist social relations; we have reached a general agreement that scale is a relative concept, and that the idea of fixed, essentialist scales is more or less outdated.[7] On the other hand, the decline of work on 'scalar politics' can also be attributed to this tradition's failure to accommodate the rising needs for a more affirmative conceptualisation of scale.[8] Scale, in the context of global urban politics, was often discussed as either (a) an utterly relative concept that is only useful for scholarly analysis;[9] or (b) utterly subject to neoliberalism, different scales performing as its mere puppets.[10] The discussions around 'politics of scale' were mostly comprised of how the urban scale, or cities as agglomerated zones, are serving the global flow of capitalist economy and its resulting socio-political relations. For instance, 'scalar politics' was often used in the context of explaining 'spatial fix', where cities and urban spaces are physical manifestations of how global capitalism (and neoliberalism) operates in reality (e.g., gentrification, or inhabitant interests being pushed out by the interest of capital).

In other words, it can be said that while the efforts to tear down the fixed/essentialist categorisation of scale in politics (e.g., local, regional, national) has largely been successful, most of them have been unable to theorise a 'successful progressive reconfiguration of scale'[11] that can challenge the status quo. This eventually resulted in 'so what' questions: you understand how political concepts are constructed through repeated social processes and performances,[12] and yet you fail to re-invent these concepts in a way that can initiate a new tradition or concoct a social change. Hence, the dominant literature on 'politics of scale' faced an impasse, as it is unable to articulate scale as concrete ranges in which political action can be mobilised. The idea of 'performativity' of scale has always been there, but only in the sense of acting under the script already written by capitalism, rather than writing a new script entirely. This is one of the most acknowledged criticisms made on 'politics of scale', which points out that its theoretical obsession with all-pervasive neoliberalism often strip localities of their agency.[13]

In short, there has been a deficiency in the existing paradigm of 'politics of scale' in addressing how scales can be framed as active entities that prompt political actions. This deficiency has become ever more visible today in the context of affirmative environment politics (or 'new ecology' movements), in which the arrival of Anthropocene is often translated into pragmatic possibilities for action. Scholars in this context[14] have effectively exited the 'everything neoliberal' dialogue by focusing on imagining everyday alternatives or 'whatever action'[15] at the arrival of Anthropocene. The uncertainty is finally accepted as a part of living reality, which then leads to a courage to take actions that are possible for here and now – actually becoming comfortable with not-knowing what will come next: 'Precarity means not being able to plan. But it also stimulates noticing, as one works with what is available.'[16] 'Scales' in this context are not only just subject to neoliberal social relations, but also perform as important boundaries in which political actions can be mobilised – which can be understood as a transition from passive understanding of scale (as an analytical category) towards more affirmative understanding of scale (as an entity of action). This chapter aims to recognise such shift in the literature; going further, it also aims to provide a more concrete theoretical framework through which scales can be theorised as an active source of enacting affirmative environment politics.

THE SCALE PROBLEM IN ENVIRONMENTAL GOVERNANCE

The limits of national scale in tackling climate governance have been well noted by the environmental politics literature.[17] The gist of this literature underlines (1) a 'spillover' problem of biodiversity, where the mismatch between ecosystem boundaries and political boundaries necessitates collaboration across different localities; and (2) a 'tragedy of the commons' situation in which each state's selfish pursuit of its national interest can ultimately doom the entire planetary ecosystem. These two main issues render environmental governance a 'collective action problem'[18] where the accountability, or who should be responsible for taking action, cannot be limited to specific borders or boundaries – which is precisely what makes 'the environment' a difficult object of governance.

Identifying the scale of political action to tackle planetary environmental degradation is a highly contested issue; no one can truly have the final say in defining its physical/territorial boundaries, because it is simultaneously local and planetary. Who can really say the real reason, or the root cause, of flash flooding in Paris or severe droughts in Cape Town? The answer is likely to be 'everyone' – the world economic system and every conforming decision that led to global warming, especially the countries with advanced economies that have been major perpetrators of climate change. But that doesn't mean that it should only be about some abstract notion of 'everyone'. Local governments, institutions, and social actors are also responsible for this, as they have failed to take on immediate regulatory measures that can make concrete changes to our everyday environment. When the source of the problem is unclear – as we see in environmental governance, where local actions are intrinsically connected to the functioning of the planetary ecosystem (and not exclusively confined to its territorial limits) – the arena for political action (i.e., its boundary or scale) can never be definitely fixed and is continuously reshuffled and redefined, oftentimes between the local and the global. Local, because the common territorial condition – which is explicitly and concretely attached to the everyday lives of the population – is indeed a source of political solidarity and action.[19] Global, because in the end, we all acknowledge that what we are experiencing locally is fundamentally and inevitably related to the planetary environmental degradation, which requires us to behave as a part of 'the whole' (i.e., the earthly ecosystem). Environmental governance is one of the specific occasions in which a political issue does not correspond with its territorial boundary, causing states (as a scale of political action) to lose their legitimacy to govern.[20]

This situation is well articulated by Dyer, who coined the term 'climate anarchy', underlining states' inability to cope with climate issues effectively (e.g., states' failure to reach an inter-state agreement on carbon emission reduction targets).[21] Climate anarchy refers to 'a divergence from established mechanism of global governance', a new (dis)order that poses a 'challenge to national governmental perspectives on world politics'.[22] The tension between ecological responsibility and territorial jurisdictions[23] lies at the heart of this anarchy, resulting in the collapse of a state-driven governance logic: sovereignty. '[C]limate anarchy emphasises human survival and ecosystem stability', Dyer notes, and '[s]overeignty, even territoriality in a literal sense, will be difficult to maintain under conditions of climate change'. However, despite the potential negative connotation of the word 'anarchy', climate anarchy, according to Dyer, is an opportunity for new social coordination and action, rather than a source of paralysis: '[i]t is a positive and creative anarchy rather than the negative and defensive anarchy',[24] where the agency and initiatives of local/municipal governments can flourish in the absence of state-level action. For instance, local governments – through transnational municipal networks, such as ICLEI,[25] the Climate Leadership Group (C40), and EUROCITIES – are now taking matters into their own hands, without waiting for states or inter-state agreement.[26]

Such frustration around the state's inability and the subsequently emerging landscape of local leadership is essentially tied to the increasingly popular proposition of 'new ecology' literature,[27] which highlights how our empirical relationship with our immediate surroundings and environment should be the driving force behind any pro-nature initiative. The fundamental limitation of state-driven environmental politics comes from the fact that 'nature' or 'the environment' becomes an abstract concept (as opposed to a physically concrete local problem) that leads to ideological debates – often ending up as a 'left or right' partisan issue.[28] The recent federal election in Australia revealed this particular symptom,[29] in which the state-driven pro-nature argument, devoid of any empirical local experiences, fails to forge a true sense of connection between our everyday living and the environment. It is not an exaggeration to say that pro-ecology movements are often dismissed as an idealistically normative, or 'too radical' argument that only makes sense within the left-wing political propositions, while in fact the matters of the environment affect all of us without discrimination.

While the limits of state-level action are well noted, and the rise of new localism in global climate politics is now evident,[30] it is still unclear what 'scale' should be identified as the most appropriate range for mobilising political action, especially in terms of which scale should be accountable or responsible for tackling environmental degradation. Currently, the general agreement is that it should be (1) simultaneously local and global and (2) not fixed to a territorial boundary and yet with a concrete political entity for action (e.g., municipal governments). This conundrum of 'beyond territorial' (and thus global/planetary) versus 'realistically located somewhere' (and thus local) is the most critical problem I identify in theorising scales of political action. I explain this as the clash between two theoretical issues: the 'ever-expanding' and 'ever-narrowing' notions of scale.

EVER-EXPANDING VERSUS EVER-NARROWING NOTIONS OF SCALE

Ever-expanding notion of scale

What we can learn from the latest developments in politics of scale literature[31] – related to other poststructural efforts to dismantle a priori categories – is that scale is a social construct, and therefore we need to pay attention to how it is constructed through repeated sociopolitical processes.[32] Despite those processes being almost always subject to neoliberal social relations, we can also extend this idea in a different direction: precisely because scale is something that is constructed, it can also be *undone* by new practices. The question, then, becomes not merely about the meta-purposes and intentions of neoliberal social order, but more about how we can constitute a 'positive reconfiguration of scale' that is not confined to essentialistic labelling or categorisation.[33]

For that very reason, in the context of global environmental politics and governance, the actor network theory (ANT) approach to scale seems to be taking hold as a new way to acknowledge the agency of localities,[34] following the poststructuralist tradition of the politics of scale discourse.[35] Because the politics of scale literature has educated us on how scales are constructed and thus how 'spatiality is not synonymous with one which is territorially bound', we can now study how localities and subnational governments (e.g., cities) can engage with new political spaces that move beyond their territorial spatialities of governing and regulation.[36] Such an emancipatory reading of the politics of scale is possible in the perspective of network theory governance,[37] which underlines how social networks, developed well beyond territorial constraints, can be influential for governance at all scales, acknowledging the roles and initiatives of nonhierarchical actors at play. For instance, Bulkeley's example of the Cities for Climate Protection programme was the epitome of an affirmative 'glocal' governance in that local authorities can initiate and play a central role in tackling an environmental problem, which is inevitably an object of global governance.[38] Acuto's example of the C40 follows a similar narrative, where cities have 'a key stake in creating alternative paths for international policy making',[39] which is well exemplified in the context of environmental politics. With a network theory approach to governance, cities are not only being liberated from the constraints of national politics, constitutional barriers, and state bureaucracy, but also creating and reconfiguring 'spaces of engagement'[40] through which local institutions and practices can influence global environment governance on their own.

However, while network theory provided an effective way to free scales from the pre-existing, territorial structure, a radical extension of this logic can also be problematic due to its inability to draw realistic boundaries that define the extent to which an entity or an acting agency does not lose touch with explicitly territorial issues and interests. The cosmopolitan, or post-territorial, political subject, in its radical pursuit of freedom from any political framework, often finds itself deprived of territorial relevancy, a focal point around which a collective solidarity can be constituted.[41] The scholars working on new localism in environmental governance (e.g., 'cities as climate leaders') are essentially positioning their scale or boundaries of political mobilisation within each municipal government or city-region (which eventually becomes 'global' via their linking up with one another), and yet they often do so without a careful inquiry into or articulation of the territorial relevancy or material reality of scale. The critique of network theory and its constructivist/relational understanding of scale has always existed, especially from those scholars working through the ecological aspects of scale – which cannot lose territorial relevancy precisely due to the ecosystem functions that are materially situated. The scale of ecological functions, or the operational scale of ecosystems, is inevitably territorial, going from a smaller-scale territory (up to 10^6 m^2), where inseeding and tree replacement occurs, and slowly shifting towards a larger-scale territory (up to 10^9 m^2), where disturbance regimes and long-term climate change occur.[42] The ultimate quest for ecologists is to ask 'which scale' should be accountable for its actions and 'to what extent': '[h]ow can we measure the contributions of a particular region, or city, or smokestack, to global climate change?'[43] Similarly, Manson also called for more attention to a 'realist' understanding of scale; arguments over who should reduce carbon emissions cannot escape the question of the material impacts of each scalar element, in order to emphasise the culpability of certain localities.[44]

Hence, the adoption of a network theory governance model, despite its empowering and constructive reinterpretation of the existing 'politics of scale' dialogue, can be problematised for its lack of acknowledgement of the territorial relevance or materially situated aspects of scale. This results in an ever-expanding notion of scale, where scholars – especially those who focus on the relational understanding of scale – often fail to theorise scales as the boundaries or ranges within which a political action (i.e., a collective expression of interests/purpose in the public sphere) can be initiated and mobilised. In the context of environmental governance, it is easy to imagine that the policy actions or pro-environmental movements are more likely to occur in places where populations have physically experienced the impacts of global warming (e.g., tornadoes or extreme climate irregularities) or other environmental issues resulting from human interventions (e.g., pollution, decreased water/air quality). Several researchers have noted that public perceptions of climate change are influenced by people's physical experience of extreme climate irregularities and thus that these events can become catalysts or windows of opportunity to build support for policy action.[45] In fact, the concrete examples of scales in environmental politics, or the actual functioning of scales in environmental governance, cannot escape the discussion of territorial relevancy, especially concerning the initiation of a collective/political action.[46] The nongovernmental organisations' ecological movements, such as 'Earthjustice',[47] were fuelled by an environmental problem specific to the territory (California), which created a moment of 'shared reality' or shared territorial condition that ignited a political movement and collective action. Such territorial aspects of scale are evident in the legitimation of a political action: Earthjustice argues that environmental hazards, in particular, are best addressed 'at the scale where their effects are felt most'.[48]

Ever-narrowing notion of scale

Precisely in relation to Earthjustice's argument that political actions are best mobilised at the scale where the effects of environmental degradation are felt most, the 'down-to-earth' approach to ecopolitics has increasingly come into fashion, especially led by the affirmative Anthropocene (or what I call 'new ecology') literature.[49] This trend is best captured by scholars such as Chandler[50] and Bargués-Pedreny and Schmidt,[51] who provided a synthetic account of the origin and implications of the relevant literature. Their discussions mainly concern how these affirmative new ecology writers try to imagine and constitute 'affirmative environment politics' in an era where everything seems to be falling apart, since it might sound superficially counterintuitive to think that one can still remain motivated to act when there is nothing one can do to 'fix' the situation.

The 'down-to-earth' approach to ecopolitics is born from the new ecology literature, partly as a fundamental critique on 'the Moderns', who have lost touch with the Earth while chasing after the stars (i.e., the pursuit of indefinite 'progress'), and partly as a grand comeback of empiricist pragmatism that prioritises sensibility and bodily experience with one's own surroundings. This return of empiricism, they argue, is effectively triggered by extreme climate events and natural disasters, which now command us to 'pay attention'[52] to our surroundings, to listen to and feel the feedback from nature. The novelty of this down-to-earth approach lies in this argument that what we do 'for the environment' should not be considered a global order to be mindlessly followed; the logic of *why* we do it is fundamentally

derived from our everyday experiences and senses of our immediate surroundings, or the territory where we belong.

Being sensitive to our surroundings and response-able to what nature
tries to tell us is the main message that the new ecology literature tries to
convey. When it comes to translating that lesson into the context of doing
ecopolitics, we encounter the problem of scale, especially with regard to
the 'localisation' of our political actions. For our 'sensibilities' and 'empirical experiences' to become a source of collective action for environmental
politics, they have to be materially situated somewhere. But to what extent,
and within what scale, could they be situated? Could that be an individual household scale that has strongly 'felt' the impacts of flooding and so is
re-realising its relationship with environment? Or should that be at least a
block or neighbourhood scale, for a collective action to become more politically viable in terms of its representation in the public sphere? How can
we really 'collectively determine' the borders of subunits, in order to give 'a
realistic vision of our belongings'?[53] New ecology writers' frequent mention
of 'feedback loops' may imply that the boundaries of these scales should be
based around ecosystem functions.[54] However, whether that is to be done
to the extent that the existing geopolitical boundaries have to be completely
discarded is unclear, and this is perhaps unrealistic in actual political practices.[55] Furthermore, the idea of collectively deciding the boundaries of a
territory – through discussions among the locals who believe they belong to
a certain territory – remains theoretical or practically naive, since, in reality,
it would mean that the scale of these territories should remain small enough
for direct democracy to be operationalised. In fact, the success stories of
place-based environmental politics – which are driven by the empirical
experiences of inhabitants and their contextually competent knowledges –
seem to exist only within a scale in which direct democracy can properly
function.[56] Furthermore, the concrete examples of down-to-earth environmental initiatives are often 'micro-projects' that are limited to a very small
geographical scale.[57] Similarly, UNDP's development practices now centre
on the projects that are 'located at a very local, very immediate and everyday
level'.[58] This, I find, is the critical problem of the ever-narrowing notion of
scale that the new ecology literature faces, especially in its ardent defence of
relocalising environmental politics.

The ever-narrowing notion of scale can be problematic, as noted by early
geographers' work on the politics of scale. The most featured problem is

the 'local trap',[59] where small is not always beautiful or intrinsically 'good'. Small-scale, or 'bottom-up', direct democracy practices – often executed at a neighbourhood level – can bring about consequences that are negative at a larger scale, especially if the decisions are inconsiderate towards neighbouring communities. Consider the 'not in my backyard' (NIMBY) phenomenon: a small-scale group decision, despite its process being perfectly democratic and ethical at that level, can have unintended outcomes that can be detrimental to the entire community at a larger scale. This is especially problematic in the context of environment governance.[60] The failure to see the long-term consequences of our actions, trapped in the bubble of a small world that we can physically grasp, was probably the main reason that we created this problem in the first place. Not being able to see the connectedness, or how our decisions might directly impact the larger-scale system (e.g., ecosystem) in the long term, was the failure of modernist, silo-framed thinking that was unable to address the holistic challenges of environmental issues. In other words, new ecology writers' emphasis on relocalising environmental politics – how our motivation for 'protecting nature' should be driven by our attentive care for our immediate surroundings, or empirical experience of our world – is certainly an important contribution; however, when it comes to applying that lesson to environmental politics in practice, its theoretical perception of the local scale rarely reaches beyond local-fetishism ('small is beautiful'), often failing to address systemic issues at a larger scale.

THEORISING SCALES OF POLITICAL ACTION IN THE ANTHROPOCENE

The debates between the ever-expanding and ever-narrowing notions of scale demonstrate how difficult it is to frame scales in the context of addressing environmental degradation, cause and impacts of which are simultaneously local and planetary. The main question is: How can scales – as ranges in which a collective, political action can be mobilised – be simultaneously local and global? We should not think of scales as fixed or trapped within predetermined scalar structures, especially when environmental issues 'leak' or 'spill over' geopolitical boundaries. Yet, at the same time, we should acknowledge that the source of any political action cannot be entirely free from territorial relevancy, specifically in the context of environmental politics where the spatial and material aspects of ecosystems' scales should be considered. At first glance, this seems to be an unresolvable dilemma; meeting both conditions – local and global – sounds self-contradictory and improbable. However, I argue that scales of political action, especially in the context of environmental governance in the Anthropocene, can be both materially situated and global, if a careful theorisation of such a scale can be articulated – which has been missing in the current literature on the politics of scale. To construct this argument, I use theoretical insights from Gaian ecopolitics and complex theory to establish three characteristics that should be considered when discussing the scales of political action in the Anthropocene. The three characteristics of 'scales of political action' are: (1) they are materially situated, or subject to their territorial conditions which helps a formation of solidarity based on collective empirical experiences; (2) they possess a degree of intensity that allows them to be influential across different scales (e.g., scale jumping); and (3) they are large enough to retain a degree of complexity that renders them to account for interaction effects.

Characteristic 1: Scales of political action are materially situated (i.e., subject to their territorial conditions)

Scales of political action are materially situated or subject to their specific territorial conditions, however this 'materially realistic' aspect does not negate the 'globality' of scales. In order to explain how scales can be both materially situated and global at the same time, I would like to introduce a theoretical standpoint proposed by 'down-to-earth' ecopolitics – which interprets 'global' as ubiquitous. In essence, the down-to-earth/new materialist ecopolitics writers argue that nature is 'global' not because it can be summed up into one, graspable globe (like the one we have in our offices), but because it exists everywhere in a ubiquitous manner that is inseparable from our everyday life (like the air we breathe). Let me discuss in a little more detail why this theoretical standpoint is so critical for the rise of down-to-earth/new materialist ecopolitics.

The real point of departure for down-to-earth ecopolitics writers – from the same old 'sustainability' politics – is their way of questioning 'nature' as an abstract figure entirely detached from our everyday socio-economic issues. Latour[61] has claimed that the very first thing we should do to revolutionise our approach to environmental politics is to secularise the notion of one, holy Nature. For a long time, nature, or what we commonly refer to as the 'environment', has been considered something that exists external to us that should be studied by objective, scientific laboratories and completely separated from our daily activities. In this framework, what humans do for nature is a chivalric act of benevolence that has nothing to do with our everyday lives. A perfect example of this approach is setting up a series of 'greenbelt' areas (as our 'service' to nature) while still maintaining the same polluting lifestyles and interventions that disregard ecosystem functions (e.g., use of plastic bags, unsustainable waste management). The end result of this approach is a default perception that the environment is external to our daily activities, and we are completely oblivious to the fact that our material existence is entirely dependent on what we are provided by the eco-system. Therefore, to move beyond the 'sustainability' politics that considers environmental friendliness a tertiary option, we must discard this notion of Nature and the environment that has been externalised from the core functions of our socioeconomic activities.

For us to avoid confusing the secular version of nature with Nature, we needed a new name for the former, which is now being referred to as 'Gaia'.[62] What differentiates Gaia from our conventional notion of nature is that it does not belong to the world of scientific labs and microscopes, where identifying the 'true' version is often taken for granted. When it comes to Gaia, there is more than one true, objective version or perfect representation. Gaia is the 'localised, historical, secular avatars of Nature'[63] that are intrinsically plural, as plural as our actual experiences of the world – despite being shared by all of us, the way it is experienced varies across different collectives inhabiting different territorial realities. As opposed to Nature, which can be perfectly summed up in a single entity via unilateral consensus from scientists (as guardians of 'truth'), Gaia is continuously disputed and can never be moulded into a single comprehensive being, because it is an actual habitat where people live rather than an object to be studied. It exists through divergent 'situated knowledges'[64] that are a product of lived experiences – which differ depending on where they are physically located, or the territorial conditions within which they occur.

This in fact inspires a new interpretation of what we actually mean by 'global'. The word is often perceived in conjunction with the image of the globe, an all-inclusive object subsumed into a shape of sphere. This image of the globe essentially follows the reductionist logic that a 'bird's-eye view' can offer a good representation of 'truth'. Nature, as noted above, has been perceived the same way; it is often believed to have an ultimately 'true' version, which could be grasped comprehensively via an objective, all-knowing eye.[65] What down-to-earth ecopolitics is trying to demonstrate is that nature is not 'global' because it can be summed up in a sphere; rather, nature is global because it is everywhere in the sense of ubiquitous – permeating every second of our daily functioning. Think of digital networks and technologies, which are often examples of what it is to be ubiquitous; they are global in that they are everywhere, internalised into our daily activities – which is different from the idea of 'global' meaning reduced to a single, objective entity (the globe).

Reinterpreting the 'global' this way maintains the logical consistency of what is seemingly a self-contradictory statement: 'the most local experience is the most planetary experience'. Precisely because the universality of nature is sustained by its ubiquitous presence – rather than the objective 'truth' – the qualitative, in-depth experience at a specific location can be a valid representation of our relationship with nature. For instance, those who cultivate a close relationship with nature via gardening in the backyard can probably produce a very good narrative of how the ecosystem functions on their land, which is as valid as what a scientist or chemist can 'objectively' explain. It is not surprising, then, that there have been various collaborations wherein different localities share and learn from their unique experiences with nature (e.g., impacts of climate change or natural disasters) even though each of their experiences is subject to their specific territorial conditions. For instance, the transnational experience-sharing networks, such as *100 Resilient Cities*, transmit exemplary or flagship local initiatives, from which cities try to learn from one another how to navigate common environmental challenges. This learning effort, especially in the context of tackling environmental issues, works well despite each instance having inherent territorial specificities. This is because they all concern learning to interact with nature, which is present everywhere and is an essential part of being a 'human' (can we even imagine a second without oxygen?). A logical flaw in the human-centric interpretation of Darwinian evolution – which might conclude that 'humans' are here on their own merit – is that it is simply not possible to separate the human from nature;[66] humans are a material product of mobilised micro-organisms, and if there can be anything essential about human life, it would be nurturing a relationship

21

with nature, from which we are constituted. As a Zadist[67] slogan says, 'we do not defend nature, we are the nature which defends itself'.[68]

In Gaian ecopolitics, the 'materially situated-ness' of a political action does not contradict the idea of going global; in fact, the more situated an action is, the deeper and more concrete its experience is, which makes it even more 'representative' or valid in explaining how our relationship with nature works in reality – the ubiquitous presence of which effectively overrides the need for reductionist, quantitative generality. Gaia is everywhere, and its ubiquity cannot simply be grasped or reduced into a single globe; for this reason, the face of Gaia has to be constituted point by point, feedback loop by feedback loop, in plural dimensions – as a collective, 'compositionist' effort.[69] Once we let go of the idea of 'global' associated with the image of the 'globe', the materially situated (or 'territorial') character of political action is not a stifling cage to escape but an advantage to render us more profound – producing a more valid and perhaps more planetary account of our experience with nature. Such collective empirical experience is in fact indispensable for the formation of solidarity that can enact a political action within the given territory.[70] Following this logic, we can draw the first characteristic of scales of political action in the Anthropocene: they are inevitably territorial, in that they have to be physically located somewhere; however, that does not mean that they will lose their global implications – because 'global' here signifies a *collage* of ubiquity, rather than a unilaterally wrapped-up comprehensiveness.

Characteristic 2: Scales of political action possess a degree of intensity that allows them to be influential across different scales

Another important characteristic of scales of political action is that they possess a degree of intensity that allows them to be influential across different scales. They have the capacity to 'scale-jump' in the sense that it can bypass some hierarchical structures thanks to their collective concentration of power and resources. Such 'scale-jumping' is evident in the global urbanism literature,[71] which has documented the important role of cities in international diplomacy as representatives of agglomerated regions. However, these discussions have not been well connected to the works of scholars trying to reconcile 'constructivist' (adopting from social sciences) and 'realist' understandings (adopting from ecology/environmental sciences) of scale, especially in the context of environmental action.[72] Scholars such as Sayre, Manson and Neumann have been trying to resolve the mismatch between political and ecological scales, and have been largely inspired by complex theory in advancing 'politics of scale' discussions in environment politics. As a continuation of this dialogue, I demonstrate below how complex theory can help us theorise scales of political action as simultaneously both 'local' and 'global'.

Above all, complex theory emphasises the *nonlinearity* of scalar effects, pointing out the cases in which the effects at a lower-level scale do not automatically add up to the effects viewed from a higher-level scale; this thesis is based on the argument that 'a collection of small-scale observations is *not* predictive of larger-scale outcomes' (e.g., butterfly effects).[73] What happens at a small scale cannot necessarily be extrapolated up, and vice versa, because results are nonlinear across scales.[74] This aspect of nonlinearity noted by complex theory is useful for understanding how scales of political action can be theorised to be simultaneously local and global. What was intended to be local cannot always remain so, as its impacts can influence larger-scale functions in a way that is not necessarily calculable or predictable. As Cox[75] noted two decades ago, the 'territoriality' of a local action cannot be confined to its geographical boundary, due to the connectivity among the locals that amplify the intensity of their impacts: 'the world is far more complicated than an easy equation of state-defined territorial scales . . . Local governments may form part of networks that bring together not just local interests but agents which have a degree of locational discretion between one local government jurisdiction and another'.

Similarly, Manson[76] also argued that complex theory can help understand how 'a local action may directly affect those at a larger scale *without* moving through intermediary scales' (emphasis added). For instance, social movements/protests against environmental damage caused by globalisation (or the global unfolding of the capitalist economy) can create international coalitions that bypass regional or national scales and leap onto the global stage.[77] Furthermore, with the ever-improving communication technologies and resulting global connectivity, a wide mediatisation of 'local' events – such as tsunamis in Tohoku, earthquakes in Christchurch, or hurricanes in Florida – can easily influence policy agendas globally.[78] In short, depending on the intensity of an action, what was executed at a smaller scale can lead to

exponential effects at a larger scale, even though the initial action was physically located within a particular territory.

The condition that allows scales to be simultaneously both local and
global is the degree of intensity. The effectiveness of an initiative does not
depend on its geographical scale but on its ability to spread out its impacts
by creating coalitions and partnerships. The network theory understanding of city climate leadership[79] clearly becomes relevant here, not merely
because it acknowledges cities' agency (that bypasses national political
scales) but because these transnational coalitions can intensify the impacts
of local actions by connecting with one another. If cities are to be the leaders
of political actions against global environmental degradation, this becomes
possible via creating networks and avenues for working together – precisely because, by doing so, they can enhance the impacts of their actions.
There is ample evidence of such phenomena where a local action spirals
into a global movement due to its intensity, quantitatively or qualitatively
defined.[80] Hence, the second characteristic of scales of political action that
are simultaneously materially situated and global is that they should possess
degree of intensity sufficient to augment the influence of their actions (and
produce impacts at a larger scale), which is often effectively done via linking
with other peer scalar entities.

*Characteristic 3: Scales of political action are large enough to retain a
degree of complexity that renders them to account for interaction effects*

The nonlinearity or intensity of scalar effects, noted above by complex
theory, are in fact closely related to the interaction effects among the components that constitute a complex system, as such nonlinearity itself is driven
by the 'friction'[81] of a series of incidents in the long term. Thus, the ultimate
scale question is: how do we define the 'threshold' of *when* (or at which
point) such incalculable, unpredictable outcomes spring from a local action
– disrupting linear patterns or relationships? Sayre,[82] drawing from complex
theory in the field of ecology, argued that a major topic for theorising scale
would be defining the 'thresholds' or 'breakpoints' of nonlinear or qualitative change across scales (in complex systems). The threshold problem is
born from a practical need in ecological research, especially in terms of the
moment at which a concrete action should be taken: 'at what concentration
does a contaminant become dangerous to humans or other organisms? How

much habitat loss will result in extinction of a species?'[83] Most importantly, the idea of thresholds accounts for the time scale, to underline the interaction effects among constituents that occur over time. Once the temporal aspect is factored in, we are bound to think more about the changes and evolutional aspect of scalar effects and how they are shaped by the interactions amongst the agencies located within each scale. What makes it especially challenging to determine thresholds is that these changes are often non-linear, abrupt, or sudden, which is hard to predict or calculate through statistical correlations.

The concept of 'threshold' – where interactions amongst the parts result in a qualitative change whose effects reach beyond the designated scale – certainly helps in theorising the scale of political action in the Anthropocene, where we are often required to define which scale should be considered responsible for pro-environmental initiatives. For instance, a collection of LEED-certified[84] 'green' buildings does not automatically qualify as an 'ecological neighbourhood',[85] in which the utilities, water, and waste management would be orchestrated in conjunction to reduce ecological footprints at a neighbourhood scale. Similarly, a collection of several ecological neighbourhoods cannot automatically become a 'resilient city', because a resilient city has to reflect the relationships and interdependencies across different neighbourhoods, as well as their roles and functions within the city scale that influence cumulative environmental impacts at a broader level (e.g., transportation, industrial exchanges, land use allocations). Here, the geographical thresholds are assumed to be 'neighbourhood' and 'city'. As interactions between local agencies continue for a certain period, we anticipate unpredictable outcomes that spill over past the agencies' very local scale: 'neighbourhood' is a threshold where the interaction effects amongst buildings can start to be noticed, whereas 'city' is a threshold where the interaction effects amongst neighbourhoods can be considered. In fact, the larger the scale, the easier it is to take these interaction effects into account. For instance, cities, compared to neighbourhoods, can attend to the issues that are intrinsically systematic; governing the interaction effects of different neighbourhoods – via organising the energy effectiveness of land use designs or transportation layouts – is better addressed at a larger scale, or a more 'scaled-up' perspective.

This can lead to an understanding that the scales of political action, or an appropriate range for an initiative, should have a territorial anchor somewhere and yet still be *large enough* to retain a degree of complexity that allows them to account for interaction effects (which cannot be perceived at a smaller local scale). This mirrors the material aspects of ecological scale, which is tied to some territorial relevancy and causality (e.g., 'feedback loops' that respond to human interventions), and yet its complexity still remains. This is because there will be no perfect mathematical formula that can explain every aspect of how these feedback loops would function in reality – calling for a more holistic, or systematic, approach that oversees different interaction effects amongst the constituents. Accordingly, a scale of political action, specifically in the context of the Anthropocene, should be conceptualised as a unit that is big enough to be a system within itself, where *governing* the complexity of interactions amongst its parts implies more than the collection of simply *managing* those parts. This idea is subject to different interpretations; one can say that an apartment building is a systemic scale in itself, as it implies more than a collection of households because of the building-wide management of interaction effects between households; similarly, a neighbourhood can claim to be a systemic unit, as its governance requires reflection on interactions amongst the buildings as well as single family homes. Obviously, the question of what should be the most appropriate, operationalisable, or efficient 'local' scale for governing environmental issues should be open to debate and discussion, allowing different stories and experiences to unfold. The point, however, is that this aspect of complexity – which requires a qualitative, nonreductionist, holistic approach – should be an integral part of characterising 'scales of political action' in the Anthropocene, precisely because an environmental problem, as a product of complexity that is inherent in ecosystem functions, cannot be reduced to a simple calculative logic. Hence, the third characteristic of scales of political action: they are, despite having a territorial anchor, large enough to consider interaction effects that cannot be addressed by scales that are *too* local.

PROPOSITION: CITIES AS FRONTIERS OF DOING EARTHLY POLITICS

Following the three characteristics of scales of political action that I have outlined above, I make a case for why city-regions, or the 'urban scale', are a good choice for doing earthly politics in the era of the Anthropocene. Given that the scales are essentially unfixed entities whose boundaries are contested and contextually dependent, my argument should be considered a proposition rather than a definite imperative. This effort is a response to the increasing discussion of which scale is 'good' for addressing environmental issues the causes and impacts of which are intrinsically both local and global. The majority of academic discourses on politics of scale often neglect its operational aspects, and there is an urgent need for propositions on scales as ranges in which a political action can be engaged and activated. In my argument for why cities can be frontiers of doing earthly politics, I touch upon some pragmatic implications of the politics of scale, which can offer insights to applied research without having to adjust its theoretical depth for applicability.

Small enough to be graspable

The first rationale comes from the first characteristic that I highlighted above, especially with regard to Gaian ecopolitics' defence of the 'materially situated' character of the local. As I noted in the 'ever-narrowing notion of scale' section, a blind belief in 'the local' can lead to a local-fetishism that fails to realise why small is not automatically beautiful or ethical – which becomes clearer when we start to zoom out to the 'big picture'. However, Gaian ecopolitics' theoretical emphasis on the local moves beyond the romanticisation of the local, because it primarily concerns reframing the notion of 'nature' *not* as an external object *but* as an internal, localised part of us. Hence Gaian ecopolitics' defence of the local is an argument that what we do 'for nature' should be driven and *motivated* by what localities actually experience, whether that is the impacts of climate change (e.g., extreme climate events) or environmental degradation (e.g., pollution) in general. Essentially, it is an attempt to move past environmental politics as a moral obligation, leading towards more democratic or bottom-up initiatives that are informed/triggered by our actual empirical experiences. If it is impossible to sum up what 'nature' really is – because it is so inextricably entwined with our everyday activities and experiences – that would also mean that the way we do earthly politics should also be a *collage* of locally driven (or 'feedback-loop-based') activities that are tied to territorial anchorage.

Cities are, essentially, materially situated entities that are subject to territorial conditions, in terms of not only their cultural/political contexts but also their environmental conditions and challenges specific to their territory. As per new ecology writers' emphasis on how governance schemes should match the feedback loops and material aspects of scale – to the extent that we can physically experience the repercussions of our actions – cities are, compared to other larger political scales, one of the 'graspable' ranges in which collective action can be mobilised based on those repercussions. For instance, awareness of climate change can be more widespread in the cities that physically experience the impacts and consequences of environmental degradation, and it is likely that collective, city-wide policy initiatives can be launched based on those very experiences.[86] This point is in line with the first characteristic of 'scales of political action', theorised above; their territorial specificities (especially with regard to environmental conditions), in the context of the Anthropocene where ultimate/true/objective 'nature' does not exist, are an advantage in producing more concrete (or qualitatively rich) accounts about our relationship with nature, based on the empirically experienced and thus more 'graspable' shared realities.

Intense enough to be influential

My second rationale is connected to the classic 'global cities' literature – where cities, as global economic powerhouses and concentrated human settlements, rise as internationally relevant actors.[87] Within this tradition of 'why cities matter', cities should be frontiers of environmental politics for the following reasons. (1) Cities, as sites of production and physical manifestations of the global political economy, have political influence and power on the global stage – and thus their pioneering actions can be models for the remaining localities; (2) Cities, housing concentrated human populations, are responsible for the majority of greenhouse gas emissions – and thus changes in them will bring about more significant positive outcomes; (3) Cities, 'the most networked and interconnected of our political associations',[88] are powerful agencies of pragmatic and collaborative politics (that states cannot achieve) – and are thus more equipped to launch more progressive political initiatives, including pro-environment actions. Especially in the context of environmental issues, where nation-states lose the legitimacy to govern and act – since the 'root cause' of the problem lies well beyond state boundaries – the rising power of localities in global climate politics makes even more sense. This is certainly in line with the conventional critique of a fixed notion of spatial categories, as the political power and influence of cities exceeds their predetermined geographic boundaries. As Doreen Massey highlighted:

> Cities are social relations, OK, dead obvious, everything is social relations, so what is different about cities? And what we decided was that the crucial word for us over and over again was *intensity*, that cities were actually intensities, spatial intensities of social relations, compared with less intensive areas which are beyond the cities.[89]

In fact, as noted above, there is also a theoretical explanation for such phenomena in complex theory, where the nonlinearity of scalar effects – produced by the *intensity* of local actions whose influence exceed the designated material scales – is a key aspect of how complex systems work in reality.

An important continuation of the 'global cities' discourse is the changing paradigm of urban architectural inventiveness in the face of ecological crises. Taking a cue from Turner's work[90] on how built environments are the 'extended organisms' for how our bodies function and strive to adapt in the given climate, Downton[91] argues that cities should also be considered our 'adaptive modification' of the environment at the (human) species level, which is subject to its surrounding conditions rendered by the feedback from nature: '[t]he way we envision, design, and fabricate our built environment can be theorised as our efforts to survive and extend our physiology as human species; then, it is logical to derive a conclusion that cities and architecture should be sensitive and responsive to the feedback from nature'.[92] It is the *intensity* of cities as historical centres of human communication and social exchange that qualifies them to be the frontiers or 'transformative agencies' of redefining our relationship with nature: '[cities'] built environments are the most visible physical manifestations of our role as conscious agents of change . . . It is through our cities that we not only act on earth but can best understand that action because our cities are centres of communication and culture. As historical centres of social change, cities are best placed to be primary agents of conscious environmental change'.[93] This new interpretation of the role of built environments effectively establishes another rationale for 'why cities matter' arguments in doing earthly politics. If we consider cities to be habitats for human survival – whereby concentrated human populations 'adaptively modify flows of matter and energy through the environment'[94] – urban architecture and city-making processes inevitably lie at the heart of the kinds of planetary environmental politics that stress a more coexistential relationship with ecosystems.

Large enough to be complex

The final rationale is based on the notion that the appropriate scale should be *large enough* to oversee the interaction effects and produce the kinds of interventions that can address them, which cause unpredictable and sudden outcomes that cannot be perceived within the scope of 'too small' scales. The arrival of the Anthropocene marks our increasing attention on the unpredictability and uncontrollability of how nature (finally) responds to our actions, which has now become ever more visible, with extreme climate irregularities and natural hazard events. What these events cause us to realise anew is the precarity of human material existence and the limits of our human-centric, short-term 'problem-solving' approaches that ultimately prevent us from developing a more sustainable, coexistential relationship with nature. In this context, the increasing attention paid to complex theory and its emphasis on the unpredictability and nonlinearity of scalar effects become highly relevant, as it guides us beyond short-term, fragmented thinking towards more holistic, systematic thinking. Especially in dealing with natural disasters and their unpredictability, scholars have called for more 'scaled-up' perspectives that incorporate more systematic and coherent governance approaches.[95] Such approaches include considering ecosystem dynamics in stormwater management and land use designs in flood-prone area developments.[96]

Cities, packed with diversity and a multiplicity of social and historical layers, are complex systems within which a variety of agencies and their interactive relations come into play.[97] Playing host to different kinds of populations, in terms of cultural, economic, and vocational status, cities constantly strive to balance conservation and progress, protection and inclusiveness, and resource allocation and pursuit of inventive spirit. There is no simple solution to these problems, given that it is never really possible to fully represent and address divergent interests and concerns. Governing this multiplicity requires approaches that are *sensitive* to the complexities and unpredictable events, essentially caused by the reality of divergent agencies and interactions amongst them. For this very reason, city governments are bound to think through the unintended consequences that local decisions can bring about, being attentive to the interconnectivity of the parts and the long-term effects of local decisions on the city as a whole. I argue that this orientation of city governance is generally advantageous for pioneering a more sustainable relationship between human settlements and ecosystem functions. Scholars such as Wilson[98] have noted how the complexity and nonlinearity of *urban* systems can inspire novel ways of interpreting complex ecosystems: 'urban systems have contributed significantly to complexity theory in the past – because they are complicated enough to be interesting but simple enough to be solvable'.[99]

Compared to neighbourhood or village-level scales, cities are larger systems which are better equipped (in terms of being 'large enough') to observe the outcomes resulting from interaction effects that cannot be identified within smaller scales: '[t]o define the city one must look for its organising nucleus, trace its boundaries, follow its social lines of force'.[100] Environmental issues are more likely to face the dilemma of the 'local trap' – where locally made decisions have negative impacts on larger-scale operations – because ecosystem functions usually cannot be divided into smaller geographic boundaries. Furthermore, as noted above, cities can also offer more holistic solutions, which can more systematically reduce our ecological footprints; designing a city-region-wide transportation network to better connect different suburbs and neighbourhoods can cut down on individual car use and carbon emissions, perhaps more effectively than the 'small wins', such as turning parking lots into green spaces.

CONCLUSION

The main purpose of this chapter has been to theorise scales of political action in the Anthropocene, with regard to who should be responsible for addressing planetary environmental degradation. The major challenge I have embarked on is setting up a transformative reconfiguration of scales for political action. For a long time, scales have been considered passive entities subject to the global power/influence of neoliberalism; they act, perform, but only in the service of naturalising the capitalist social order. However, this notion of invincible neoliberalism is now being challenged, perhaps more effectively by the new ecology literature, which regards the fragility of our material existence, underlined by the unpredictability of natural disasters, as an opportunity to rethink and reframe our relationship with nature. In this context, proposing a positive reconfiguration of scale is needed more than ever, especially for the environmental issues that are intrinsically both local and global. Continuing in the tradition of the literatures on how local initiatives, in collaboration with one another, can influence the global,[101] I have aimed to provide a theoretical framework that underlines the theoretical characteristics of those 'locals'. This work is a preliminary effort to become more theoretically engaged with the political concept of 'scale', which I believe should be reflected upon *before* claiming why certain scales (e.g., neighbourhoods, villages, or cities) should be the 'leaders' in tackling the issue of planet-wide environmental degradation. Accordingly, I invite other propositions and discussions on the question of which scale should be responsible, or, more practically, operationalisable, for governing environmental issues the causes and impacts of which are intrinsically both materially situated and planetary. Given historical arguments on why a 'fixed' notion of scales is not quite adequate, it is theoretically challenging work. However, proposing and debating on scales as entities for political action can have important practical and policy implications, and this is urgently needed to activate our collective will to reframe and re-establish our relationship with nature.[102]

3
Darwin vs. Tulsa: How cities talk about 'nature' without saying the word

One of the most divisive topics of the 2019 Australian election was climate change and the environment.[1] During the election campaign, several political parties argued that it was time to consider the economic consequences of environmental degradation, such as its impacts on public health and the resulting cost of hospitalisation. Public perception also seemed aligned with that sentiment: more than 60 per cent of voters identified climate change as the most critical threat facing Australia today, with about the same number arguing that the government is not doing enough to curb global warming.[2]

However, Australia's choice as a nation was geographically divided over the issue of withdrawing from the coal industry, which the Australian rural economy largely relies upon. The urban educated left fiercely insisted that the environmental impacts of coal should be urgently addressed now, whereas the rural towns – suffering from a slowing economy, empty houses, and crime – saw the short-term economic gain (e.g., immediate job creation) as a more urgent issue. This debate about jobs versus the environment is not unique to Australia; the question of which should be prioritised has increasingly been at the centre of global political discussion, with the consequences of climate change no longer merely abstract or far-fetched prediction modelling. Today, the impacts of climate change on our everyday lives are undeniable, often physically experienced through extreme weather patterns, such as heat waves, storms, and precipitation irregularities. The severe bushfire season in the Australian summer of 2020 reaffirmed the tangible impacts of climate change, achieving heightened public attention and awareness of the topic (see Chapter 5 for the influence of bushfires on the mobilisation of environmentalism in Melbourne).

While social divisions on the issue of the environment seem to be further aggravated in national politics across the world, cities have been referred to as leaders in instigating more concrete and sincere engagement with climate change. As noted in Chapter 2, local governments – through transnational municipal networks, such as Local Governments for Sustainability (ICLEI) or the Climate Leadership Group (C40) – are now taking immediate action for change, without waiting for state- or international-level agreements.

It is now evident that cities, as local sites physically experiencing the impacts of climate change, are better suited to the kinds of political solidarity or collective sentiment that speak to the urgency of pro-environmental action. The question remains, however, of how cities can actually operationalise pro-environmental agendas that are not necessarily consistent with national-level political decisions. Especially in today's global political climate, where economic discrepancies and resulting social divisions are ever more present, it would be an exaggeration to say that all urbanites automatically support pro-environmental politics. Despite the smaller scale, urban politics is still politics, caught between the values, interests, and ideals of divergent groups. More often than not, words such as 'environment' or 'nature' have failed to bring together those from different political stances. Such words are often associated with left-leaning political discourses or are considered to be the ideas of 'greenies', which, to those on the other end of the political spectrum, are considered idealistic if not unrealistic. How, then, are cities still managing to pursue the kinds of collective actions that address environmental degradation and climate change, successfully persuading those who may not be interested in 'nature' in the first place?

In the context of the current divisive political climate, I demonstrate how cities are addressing a pro-nature agenda without using the word 'nature'. This, I argue, is essentially associated with the kinds of ecopolitics that Bruno Latour claimed since the 1990s, where what we do for the environment is not a separate chivalric action but something to be incorporated into our everyday socioeconomic functioning. I call this phenomenon 'pragmatic environmentalism', through which cities seize any opportunity to take environmental action without idealising nature at all. In this new paradigm, nature or the environment is no longer an abstract, holy figure detached from the functioning of the urban; it is fundamentally intertwined with our everyday surroundings and the operations of economic and social life in cities. Pragmatic environmentalism benefits from 'the material turn' in planning,[3] where planners utilise site-specific and tangible objects as a way of depoliticising an environmental issue, often successfully thanks to the shared physical conditions that are experienced by local inhabitants in their daily encounters.

DARWIN V TULSA

In this chapter, I make my case for 'pragmatic environmentalism' through the cases of Darwin (Northern Territory, Australia) and Tulsa (Oklahoma, USA) – where I conducted in-depth interviews with 24 environmental activists and planning practitioners (eleven in Darwin, 13 in Tulsa). These two sites were chosen for their territorial (i.e., state-level) economic dependency on extracting natural resources (e.g., the oil, natural gas, and mining industries). Such an economic dependency creates a specific political context wherein it is not easy to initiate a conversation using words such as 'the environment', 'nature', or 'ecology'. My study revealed that urban planners and environmental activists in these two cities – who fundamentally acknowledge the impacts of climate change on the economic and social functioning of their cities – developed a set of strategies to engage with audiences across a drastically varied political spectrum.

Tulsa finds itself in a 'red state',[4] its economy constructed by the oil industry and the resources that flow from it. As a result, terms such as 'climate change' and 'environmental sustainability' are often perceived as divisive political topics rather than an accepted social norm. However, the city suffers from the consequences of climate change in the form of extreme weather, such as heat, flooding, and ice storms, which affects the everyday aspects of urban living.[5] Located in tornado alley, the city is subject to various environmental hazard risks, notably urban flooding issues. As a result, the city possesses one of the most exemplary stormwater management systems, which not only protects communities from excess water but also respects natural waterways and the ecological functioning of natural systems.[6] For instance, especially after the severe flooding in 1984, the city embraced the concept of Ian McHarg's 'Design with Nature',[7] where stormwater detention ponds and flood-prone zones are turned into ecological parks and habitat protection areas (e.g., River Parks, Centennial Park, Mingo Creek). In addition, recent philanthropic investments in public space are also shaping the city's goal of attracting young professionals and young families, to whom walkability, sustainability, and environmental responsibilities are important elements in choosing the location of their nests. Public green space and park projects, such as Gutherie Green or Gathering Place, contribute to the idea that promoting sustainability and urban green space is essential for attracting young professionals who can bring in new industries and businesses. This constitutes an interesting moment in terms of how the sustainability agenda serves the city's growth ambitions, as pro-nature or pro-ecology ideas now coincide with what Millennial culture normalises as the 'cool' or 'trendy' thing to follow. Non-profit environmental organisations, often led by these early creative-class settlers, work with the city government to make the most of this cultural moment in which the attractiveness of green agendas is actually something that works for – and not against – jobs, economy, and urban growth.

Darwin is located in a region where the mining industry and natural gas production draw the federal government's attention and investments. The Northern Territory has recently been part of the controversy around whether the federal government's extra funding – which includes more investments in the Territory's capital, Darwin – had anything to do with the Territory government's recent decision to lift its fracking moratorium.[8] Darwin enjoyed an energy boom in the early 2000s after building its first LNG (Liquefied Natural Gas) plant, although it is currently looking for more sustainable economic forces for urban growth and development. Despite its desire for development and growth – even if that means tapping into 'dark' natural resources, such as by fracking – the particularity of Darwin's extreme climate and the region's 'outback' lifestyle are inducing the city to be conscious of climate change and its impacts. Darwin has historically been subject to tropical cyclones, storms, and heat waves; notably, Cyclone Tracy in 1974 was a deeply traumatic experience, and its impacts are still discussed as critical elements of Darwin's identity as a tropical city. However, more recently, the city has been experiencing more extreme weather patterns, especially heat waves and cyclones. In 2018, it was hit by Cyclone Marcus, which caused US$75 million damage. This experience played an important role in pushing through pro-nature or more long-term environmental initiatives, such as increasing the tree canopy and establishing a more resilient urban forest. In the new framework of urban forest planning, 'establishing a resilient urban forest for Darwin', trees have become more than decorative objects, through learning from indigenous knowledge/care practices on what flora and fauna are resilient to cyclones. In addition, the Darwin City Deal, launched in November 2018, plans to transform Darwin into a model for global tropical cities, especially with its place-based 'Urban Living Lab', which aims to test the latest heat mitigation technologies and energy-efficient building design.

Table 3.1 Comparison between city contexts between Tulsa and Darwin.

	Tulsa, Oklahoma, USA	Darwin, Northern Territory, Australia
First Nations context in the region	The 'Great Plain' region is the last area to be developed in the US; Strong presence of indigenous tribes as they were relocated to Oklahoma (e.g., Cherokee Nation, Creek Nation)	The Northern Territory ('Top End') was the last area to be developed in Australia due to its tough climate; Strong presence of aboriginal communities (e.g., Larrakia Nation) as traditional owners of the land
Regional economy	Dependence on oil industry	Dependence on natural gas/mining industry, significant defence force presence
Climate particularities	Tornadoes, Severe flooding, Heat, Irregularities in precipitation	Cyclones, Droughts, Heat, Irregularities in precipitation
Nexus between extreme weather and environment planning	Historically: Severe flooding in 1984 leading to beautifying stormwater detention area for general landscaping, public amenities (trail), ecological benefits	Historically: Cyclone Tracy experience in 1974 leading to general awareness in natural functions and their unpredictability, some attention on how aboriginal communities historically survived the cyclones
	More recently: Ice storm in 2016 led to establishing Urban forest masterplan; Flood buffers are turned into bike trail developments; Extreme heat leads to landscape ordinances	More recently: Cyclone Marcus in 2018 led to establishing Urban forest masterplan; Major heatwaves and drought issues led to Darwin City Deal's 'Cooling the City', as well as interests in tropical design

Figure 3.1   City of Darwin is famous for its unique landscape with beautiful mangroves in the region, in addition to the rich presence of First Australians culture. © Ihnji Jon.

'SECULARISING NATURE' AND PRAGMATIC ENVIRONMENTALISM

New ecology literature, as discussed in Chapter 2, asks us to *secularise* nature. 'Secularising nature' means that we should acknowledge how what we often idealise as 'the environment' is inseparably intertwined with and infiltrated into our daily life (i.e., the physical surroundings that we interact with every day, such as air and water quality, parks, and amenities) or the economic costs of sustaining our daily living (e.g., energy bills, home insurance, public health). What we often forget is how our everyday life choices and conveniences, such as buying a plastic bottle of water, have critical impacts on the environment when accumulated over time, which affects our own quality of life in the long term. The practices of pragmatic environmentalism, as I discuss in detail below, fundamentally demonstrate this aspect of *demystifying* 'nature'; in attempts to reach out to people across as wide a political

Figure 3.2   City of Tulsa, previously known as the 'oil capital of the world', has an abundance of art-deco architecture and historical buildings that serve as a unique city-identity – attracting Millennials and young families to take root in the area. © Ihnji Jon.

spectrum as possible, environmental activism is now being repackaged and operationalised as relevant to ordinary city living.

This aspect is more clearly observable in cities such as Tulsa and Darwin, the regional economic structures of which are largely dependent on the oil and natural gas industries. This condition generates a specific political climate in which 'the environment' or 'nature' become divisive words or concepts, as they are perceived as something opposed to job creation or the financial source of a standard of living. The bottom line is that the majority of the population would not wish to jeopardise the sustainability of their financial means – which provide concrete benefits to their day-to-day life – for the sake of chasing after an abstract vision that is hard to materialise in a short time frame. What pragmatic environmentalists do, therefore, is come up with strategies of linguistic articulation to avoid drawing unnecessary attention to the political nuance of these potentially divisive concepts. By refusing to engage with these words and instead *recoding* their pro-environmental vision with more concrete, materialised objects – such as air/water quality, civic amenities, or landscaping – pragmatic environmentalists establish themselves in typical urban life as a new social identity. Such infiltration of a particular vision into our daily living – like 'a drop of wine falls into water'[9] – demonstrates an essential element of assemblage theory, where words and narratives constitute the coding of a political entity.[10]

Another characteristic of 'new ecology' is its emphasis on empirical and physical experiences as the basis of formulating a political solidarity or mobilising for action. Latour[11] argues that the obligation to protect nature cannot be handed down from above as a moral imperative; it should be motivated and triggered by the feelings and physical experiences of our immediate surroundings. However, while Latour's (and Stengers's[12]) down-to-earth approach focused on *negative experiences* – such as feeling the repercussions of our actions (e.g., heat waves as punishment for our polluting behaviours) – as a major reason for change, pragmatic environmentalists take the opposite route: the path of Spinozian ethics, where what is good is what feels good, or what brings 'joy', 'joyful passions', and 'active feelings'.[13] Spinoza was particularly critical of 'sad passions' or 'resentful men', often caused by an act of sacrifice for something considered to be a 'noble cause', such as choosing to die due to a false zeal for religion, or forgoing the inherent ironies and contradictions of the human condition itself: 'They are like boys or young men who cannot bear calmly the scolding of their parents, and take refuge in the army. They choose the inconveniences of war and the discipline of an absolute commander in preference to the conveniences of home and the admonitions of a father; and while they take vengeance on their parents, they allow all sorts of burdens to be placed on them'.[14] What Spinoza really warned against was the danger of homogenous, transcendent values imposed from above (e.g., good vs. evil), since their simplistic and totalising dichotomisation fundamentally negates the possibilities of action or pursuing joyfulness in life – leading to sadness, suffering, and, worst of all, inaction; in that scenario, 'we can only think of how to keep from dying, and our whole life is a death worship'.[15]

Hence, Spinozian ethics tries to go beyond a top-down, imposed version of morality, or the essentialist judgement of what is good or evil; instead, there are collectively decided, historical notions of good and bad. The criteria for deciding what is good or bad – in that historical moment – depend on the particular action's ability to spread the nature or 'essence' of the system (e.g., body, organisation, the acting entity) through productive power and energy. For instance, as Deleuze explains, food is good for us, as it increases the energy of our body and allows us to extend the essence of our intentions; poison is bad for us, as it 'do[es] not correspond to our essence' and suspends our energy. A 'good' individual – equated with being free, rational, or strong – is the one who is capable of linking up with others who share the same nature and goals, hence increasing the power to spread his/her essence; 'for goodness is a matter of dynamism, power, and the composition of powers'.[16] In the end, Spinozian ethics works by the function of 'speculative affirmation',[17] or the possibility of our willingness and power to act.

Pragmatic environmentalism shares this stance on anti-essentialist goodness. Instead of emphasising our bad behaviours and their consequences – or the logic that we should now clean up our act because we are being admonished by Mother Nature – pragmatic environmentalists talk about how trees, landscaping, and nature-based amenities make us feel good in our everyday urban environment (e.g., pedestrian experience) and about the economic and health benefits of pro-environmental choices (e.g., linkage between health and air/water quality, as well as energy efficiency and electricity bills). Environmental activism is no longer something that is ethically/morally good; it is good in the sense that it helps the pragmatic aspects of our daily lives, such as reducing energy bills or enhancing quality of life with parks, trails, and amenities. At the end of the day, pragmatic environmentalism is a speculative hope that we might be able to find a method through which whatever feels good to us (pragmatic benefits in daily life) is also good for natural systems (helps ecosystems' healthy and sustainable functioning).

PRAGMATIC ENVIRONMENTALISM AND THE 'MATERIAL TURN' IN PLANNING

Pragmatic environmentalism is related to the rise of the material turn in planning,[18] especially its emphasis on the use of specific material objects as a strategy to depoliticise environmental agendas. The role of materiality and specific objects has been well noted by the recent post-humanist (or more-than-human) as well as material shift in social and critical theory. Influenced by such theoretical developments, urban planning theorists have also embarked on the challenge of how planners can actually capitalise on the neutrality of objects as a way to advance certain urban agendas, especially those concerning the human–nature nexus.

This material turn in planning engages with the materiality of urban design and objects, or the role played by the physical fabrics of the built environment (e.g., buildings, parks, streets, lanes) in shifting our ideas or the way we perceive the world. Marres's *Material Participation: Technology, the Environment, and Everyday Publics*[19] is particularly relevant in the context of using material objects to advance a pro-environmental agenda. Marres specifically addressed the potential of material things in shaping environmental politics, as they become micro-influencers, seeping into our subconscious or conscious daily-life decision-making processes. The examples include the installation of everyday carbon accounting devices or artistic interventions in public space that prompt awareness of sunlight, trees, or natural surroundings that we often take for granted.

Pragmatic environmentalists' strategies operate in a similar way. More often than not, the pro-environmental or climate change policy agendas have become a divisive topic in partisan politics, linked to ideological associations that are not necessarily helpful in advancing actions in the here and now. To detach pro-nature actions from the philosophical/ideological conflicts associated with climate change, pragmatic environmentalists repackage their agenda with 'innocent' or 'neutral' common urban objects. Such strategies were particularly apparent in the political contexts of Tulsa and Darwin, the regional economies of which are largely dependent on oil industry and natural gas extraction. Although more direct opposition against this economic structure (e.g., anti-fracking movements) was indeed present, the pragmatic environmentalists' activism was mostly concerned with communicating the benefits of pro-environmental choices. They avoided such terms as 'climate change', 'nature', 'ecology', or 'the environment', as these contain normative nuances that can provoke reactionary objections to the abstract ideal of protecting nature. To bypass such immediate rejections, pragmatic environmentalists purposefully inserted the vocabulary of ordinary material objects, such as weather, energy bills, water/air quality, or street landscapes. This approach is essentially linked with the recent material turn in planning, which aims to go beyond the limits of discursive consensus by actively embracing the role of nonhuman objects and their physical, empirical impacts on everyday urban life.

PRAGMATIC ENVIRONMENTALISM: STRATEGIES TO TALK ABOUT 'NATURE' WITHOUT SAYING THE WORD

Pragmatic environmentalism focuses on discussing the everyday benefits of specific material objects. Its main strategy is, rather than talking about an abstract notion of 'the environment', to engage the public with common objects, such as water, air, fish, butterflies, flooding, energy bills, and trees, nudging people to think that environmentally friendly choices are actually pragmatically 'good' choices that are useful (or cost efficient) in their lives. It distances itself from a normative or judgemental tone that we should 'do the right thing' – that attitude, according to pragmatic environmentalists, only attracts criticism or ideological conversations that often lead to disagreement and inaction. Pragmatic environmentalists focus on finding the common objectives and language that can connect with the widest public possible. As one interviewee puts it:

> We focus on personal and financial benefits of these 'eco-friendly' choices, not really environmental benefits . . . You have to be very pragmatic and find a common ground with people with different interests and political agendas, because if you don't do that, it's just not going to happen at all.

In this section, I lay out the strategies that pragmatic environmentalists use to talk about nature without using the word or even evoking aspects of ecology or the environment.

Water quality, air quality, health and wellness

One of the easiest selling points of environmentalism is air and water quality and how this affects our health and wellness. It is undeniable that air and water quality affect every household, and the specificity of materiality being 'air' or 'water' can easily neutralise the ideological association of pro-nature arguments. A prominent urban planning example in the American context is low impact development (LID), which promotes on-site stormwater treatment or a net zero increase in impervious surfaces. LID requires that site owners/developers compensate for impervious surfaces, caused by developing the site, through creating bioswales and rain gardens that facilitate the infiltration of excess water. LID practices help water quality and the general

health of streams by allowing the water to be absorbed on-site, going directly
to an aquifer rather than collecting and transporting pollutants and parti-
cles (on the street) to the stream. While this technical practice is inherently
a pro-environmental action, it is promoted in a way that places emphasis on
water quality rather than the abstract idea of nature. A LID brochure (distributed by the department of stormwater quality in Tulsa) advertises LID's
positive impacts on stream health and its pragmatic benefits for the household: 'Harvesting rain water runoff from home is a win-win situation. You
save money on your utility bill while helping your community achieve the
common goal of clean water in our rivers, lakes, and streams'.[20] As an interviewee working in the field of environment and water quality says:

> It is about finding the right language to use, finding something that
> connects with them. Recreational boating and fishing are pretty frequent
> here; for someone who boats and swims in a lake, they would know that
> we have lake closures when water gets polluted – due to the develop-
> ment of particular algae that actually make people sick. We talk about
> how these things can also happen in town, to get people's attention on the
> practices that can prevent polluted runoff. It's about finding something
> that clicks in their heads.

Health and wellness at the individual household level are popular topics,
which pragmatic environmentalists often use to introduce water and air
quality topics at a community scale. The non-profit organisation 'Sustainable
Tulsa' hosts a monthly workshop on sustainable living and environmentally
friendly business practices (e.g., energy efficiency and waste reduction).
One workshop primarily focused on the health impacts of the environment,
starting with air quality issues at home, before expanding into more generic
discussions on environmental awareness and reflection on daily practices.
The argument *for* green space is also tied to its positive impacts on mental
health, or the pragmatic benefits that people can feel and experience.

What is clearly observable here is the emphasis on the economic and
lifestyle benefits of pro-environmental choices, which are no longer good
deeds conducted out of courtesy or moral value judgments, but are contextually rational choices involving feedback that is direct and tangible.
Furthermore, the notions of 'the environment' or 'nature' do not exist as
an abstract background to our daily lives – whenever the environment is

mentioned, it is always empirically situated within the context of everyday living, such as water management or air quality issues that people collectively experience in the community. Given that pragmatic environmentalists aim to gain a wider audience and engagement, they often work with businesses and private entities, which may lead to traditional environmentalists criticising them for being a 'sell-out'. However, with pragmatic environmentalists' un-assumed approach to introducing the environment as a material element on which we all are inseparably dependent (e.g., water, air), isn't this

Figure 3.3 The exhibition booth of Department of Stormwater at one of the Sustainable Thursday events in Tulsa. The department advertises rain barrels and low impact development under its programme 'Save Our Streams'. © Ihnji Jon.

really about nature being secularised to the extent that it becomes the pre-condition for our socioeconomic activities, rather than idealised as a holy figure to be treated separately? In political contexts where concepts such as ecology, climate, or the environment are often shrugged off as far-fetched ideals, conversations about the environment often begin with our relationship with our immediate surroundings. This is invariably in line with the new materialists' emphasis on tactile/empirical experiences[21] or their discourses on 'feel it to act'.

Extreme weather, heat waves, flood management

Another effective topic to introduce how nature affects our everyday living is extreme weather and environmental hazard risks. Tulsa and Darwin are both subject to extreme weather and the subsequent public safety risks, notably heat waves (Tulsa and Darwin), drought (Darwin), severe flooding (Tulsa), cyclones (Darwin), and tornadoes and ice storms (Tulsa). Talking about these natural hazards, risks, and mitigation strategies has become a good way of engaging with a public not initially interested in 'greenie' issues. Several researchers have already noted how climate irregularities and extreme weather events influence public perception on climate change.[22] Most recently, the results of the poll conducted by the National Opinion Research Center at the University of Chicago indicated that 74 per cent of Americans said extreme weather in the past five years – hurricanes, droughts, floods, and heat waves – has influenced their opinions about climate change, concluding that 'personal observations of real-time natural disasters and the weather around them have more impact than new stories or statements by religious or political leaders'.[23] If, as new material environmentalists argue, experiencing the consequences of climate change can drive interest in environmental issues.[24] The pragmatic environmentalist approach of utilising local disaster experiences to introduce a pro-nature discourse is an actual manifestation of such a strategy.

Several interviewees in Darwin noted that extreme heat is associated with climate change in the Northern Territory, especially with more consecutive days of high temperature (e.g., above 35C):

Heat is a big issue here, and with climate change, it's becoming more and more apparent. Especially for people like me, who've stayed here more than 20 years, we notice the change – we have historical experiences to compare back to. The days with 35 degrees [Celsius] in the wet season only lasted about five days or so in 1992; now that's becoming ten days or longer, and now the scientists predict it to become 190 days. On average, that's only a one-degree difference per year, but when you think about having consecutive days of such high temperature, it simply becomes unliveable.

To mitigate heat in the city, urban planners are working on planting more trees and creating cooling stations landscaped with vines, plants, and shrubs – at the cost of parking lots.

We've been trying to do more landscaping around CBD for a long time. But a lot of traders here were afraid of losing car parking, so they were opposed to the idea. But now they finally turn around as they see that

Figure 3.4 The shade structure in Cavanaugh Street in Darwin CBD. The extreme heat – with temperatures exceeding 60 degrees – is pushing the city to develop more public awareness on climate change and infrastructure responses to such change. © Ihnji Jon.

landscaping and cooling the city is in fact good for their businesses, because people simply don't come out to CBD when it's too hot and there's no shade. They finally agree with the loss of parking for more landscaping.

What can be observed here is how experiencing the impacts of climate change – collectively felt within a certain geographic area – can influence public support for environmentally friendly decisions, such as sacrificing parking lots to make more room for trees. There is almost no argument for or mention of pro-nature discourse or its associated ideological debates. Instead, what is on the table is how people feel about the weather, how the heat affects businesses, and therefore pragmatic solutions (to that problem) that coincide with what 'greenies' would argue for – 'fewer cars, more trees'. Pragmatic environmentalism works in these specific moments in which decisions made purely on the basis of pragmatic benefits – cooling the city, more pedestrian traffic, more economic activities – conveniently fall in the realm of a pro-nature agenda as broadly defined.

In Tulsa, on the other hand, heat is often normalised as the usual summer weather in the region, and so is not necessarily associated with climate change. Severe urban flooding or precipitation irregularities are more apparent forms of extreme weather. The level of precipitation is becoming harder to predict year after year, and the extreme irregularities are becoming the trend. One of the interviewees mentioned that: 'Weather variabilities do seem to have become a trend; for instance, we had extreme drought a year ago, which killed a lot of trees, but then, this year, we had a historic flooding in 30 years, affecting communities in the northeast'. Tulsa is also at risk of tornadoes and ice storms each year, which result in power outages and home damage, provoking people's general awareness of weather patterns and their impacts on everyday living. Extreme weather often results in high electricity prices, with humid weather, a high heat index and volatile weather conditions frequently requiring the operation of peaking power plants (peaker plants; power plants that serve as backup and are only called into action during peak periods), driving up electric bills.

As a result, in Tulsa, 'flooding' or 'extreme weather' have become major currency words for talking about the environment, its changing trend, and how communities should prepare themselves in response to the unpredictable nature of their surroundings. Pragmatic environmentalists, working in this particular weather context, capitalise on how such extreme weather

Figure 3.5 In Darwin, the experiences of extreme heat and the resulting decrease of foot traffic in the CBD area persuaded the traders to give up car parking spaces for more trees and landscaping. Cavenagh Street and Knucky Street are selected to be tested for a pilot programme on cooling the city and influencing microclimate via more tree planting. © Ihnji Jon.

events draw attention from the public, redirecting it towards the path of sustainable development and green infrastructure. As one planning practitioner puts it,

> When I talk about these [environment-related] things, I talk about disaster preparedness. We always start the conversation with extreme weather impacts and how they affect us. Everybody agrees with this. Then we talk about building homes that are resilient to wind and hail, together with the green aspects that would help them deal better with flooding issues, such as green infrastructure, LID, rain barrels, bioswales, and permaculture.

Especially in Tulsa's context, the phrase 'climate change' often elicits scepticism, denial, and avoidance, however extreme weather and flooding – things that people can actually feel and experience the impacts of – are becoming the major trigger for perception shift and behavioural change.[25] Flooding and stormwater management have traditionally been a good medium to execute

Figure 3.6   Centennial Park in Tulsa is practically a stormwater detention pond (a version of green infrastructure in preparation of severe flooding). But it is landscaped well enough to serve also as a public park/green space. © Ihnji Jon.

some of the pioneering nature initiatives in this conservative oil town back in the 80s; Tulsa is home to an exemplary stormwater management model wherein urban green spaces are designed to both protect human settlements and preserve natural habitats.[26] As a continuation of this trend, the flooding event in May 2019 proved to be an opportunity for pragmatic environmentalists in Tulsa to provoke more public interest in green practices. And when they do so, it is often in association with the dollar values of these practices:

> They may not care about the environment, but they may care about how their home could have been flooded or the potential impacts of these extreme events in general. Especially right after the storms, tornadoes, or flooding like this year is a good moment to talk about these things. When we talk about resilient homes, this could positively lead to insurance premium reduction. We directly go to the dollars and talk about significant savings upon the installation of green infrastructure or energy efficiency features.

The professional liability of architects and urban planners in private firms is also another element through which resilient design features are enforced, especially in the uncertain climate conditions of Tulsa:

> You can't know exactly what will happen with Tulsa's climate. This affects the notion of professional liability. You can't deny that as architects and planners, we do have a responsibility to anticipate and address the issues to come. Energy and climate concerns are out there; even though the building code is to meet the minimum, you are still responsible for introducing the ones that can address the potential issues in the long term. We actually anticipate lawsuits in case of our failure to do so; we recently had a training session with lawyers about our professional liability and responsibility.

This question of expert liability – that urban designers and planners, who work closely with the impacts of climate change in their specialised professions, now have the *legal responsibility* to introduce, inform, and guide more future-oriented practices – is a concrete manifestation of how Anthropocene or the physical consequences of our actions are affecting or necessitating additional green practices.

Caring for nature is no longer a chivalric moral obligation but a survival
strategy that is inseparable from our daily socioeconomic activities.
Although people may not be initially interested in the idea of ecology or
environmental thinking – because of their political associations or other
reasons – when it comes to adopting environmentally friendly features in
the house you live in or the building where you work, it is no longer a matter
of choice. In the current era of the Anthropocene, where the impacts of
climate change aggravate the uncertainty and risks of our living conditions,
there are pragmatic obligations behind these pro-nature options. The professional liability of architects and planners specifically demonstrates how
close climate change is to our lived reality and how it is shaping the environments of even those who disagree with the idea of it. At the same time,
it also demonstrates the pragmatic advantage of emphasising the *material
aspects* of pro-environmental practices, which extends 'material participation'[27] in environmental politics, where the availability of technology can
shape our behaviour *without* affecting our conscious decision to take part in
(or renounce) a pro-nature ideology.

Energy efficiency, renewable energy, innovation

Energy efficiency, renewable energy, and innovation are also popular topics
for pragmatic environmentalists when introducing environmental sustainability ideas as part of a trendy and exciting global movement that we do
not want to lag behind. In Darwin, in the face of fracking and increasing
economic dependency on extracting 'dark' natural resources (e.g., shale
gas), environmental organisations are translating a pro-environmental
agenda into a pro-renewable-energy and pro-innovation agenda. A notable
example is their active advocacy for a renewable energy industry (e.g., solar,
wind, hydrogen), such as '10 Gigawatt Vision', which aims to generate jobs
and economic revenue by 'building over 10 gigawatts of clean, renewable
energy generation by 2030'.[28] As a professional working in the field of environmental activism observes:

> Jobs, economic development, energy . . . we need to speak to these issues
> to get more attention from politicians and policy makers. That's why we're
> now mostly working on renewable energy as a solution that can substi-
> tute [for] fracking and gas dependency. Words like 'jobs' and 'economy'

can reach a broader audience, and we can engage businesses, industries, and citizens for the kinds of things that we believe in.

As a main selling point, the 10-Gigawatt Vision report highlights the geographic advantages of the Northern Territory – especially the abundant solar energy and climate conditions that particularly *make sense* for this region to pursue renewable energy. One key argument frames this pursuit as a 'global trend'. For instance, 10-Gigawatt Vision notes that: 'some of the world's leading companies aim to source 100 per cent of their electricity from renewable sources. Apple, Google, and Microsoft have already achieved this goal. More than 500 global corporations have joined Science Based Targets initiative which requires them to set emissions reduction targets in line with the Paris Agreement'.[29] The ultimate question then becomes less an environmental issue and more whether we will miss out on this timely and important economic opportunity, which is seemingly tailor-made for the Northern Territory and its climate conditions.

Redefining what is essentially a pro-environmental initiative as a fashionable global trend is also highly prevalent in Tulsa, which even goes a step further by trying to link renewable energy with innovation and excellence. 'It's all about the future', says a PowerPoint presentation during a meeting of the 'Chamber One Voice – Environment and Sustainability Taskforce', a policy advocacy meeting for regional sustainability/pro-environmental initiatives in Tulsa. The presentation, made by the Oklahoma Center for the Advancement of Science and Technology (OCAST), effectively repackaged electric vehicles (EVs) and other related pro-environmental technologies (e.g., recycling fracking water) as being the result of inventiveness and human endeavour associated with 'pursuing excellence'. Its discourse about advocating for EVs mentions CO_2 emissions and other environmental benefits last. Instead, what is presented as the main motivation for supporting the EV industry is its future-forward potential as a job generator and economic opportunity that all the global companies are now a part of. 'Global carmakers to invest $90 billion in electric vehicles', says another slide in the presentation, noting how international companies, such as Ford, Volkswagen, and Toyota, are competitively spending billions of dollars on EVs.

Especially in Tulsa, where oil or 'dark' energy sources can be found relatively cheap, pushing for EVs is not always easily accepted.

People here earned their living through the oil industry . . . so when I talk about my job as an advocate for EVs, some of them feel personally attacked by it. I always try to frame EVs as 'being prepared for newest technology' or a 'cheap, fun, exciting consumer choice' rather than a pro-environmental choice. In fact, I don't talk about environmental benefits at all – instead, I talk about pragmatic benefits that comes with it, such as their low operational cost and less maintenance issues.

When asked whether their personal motivation is pro-nature/pro-environmental activism, they replied in the affirmative:

Absolutely. Climate change is real, and I worry about the future of my family and my children; that's why I do what I do. But I don't necessarily talk about that with other people, because I try to respect others' personal upbringing and background that don't allow them to see it that way.

This interview illustrates how pragmatic environmentalists shape and transform their pro-nature dialogue into a personally beneficial, rational choice that makes sense even to those who do not think about or believe in climate change.

Such a diffusion of pro-environmentalism through technological objects, such as EVs – without challenging people's personal beliefs or perceptions of the world – has been also noted by Marres's *Material Participation*, where the programmed objects, such as energy-conscious buildings, make people participate in environmentalism without necessarily realising the positive pro-environmental impacts of their behaviour (e.g., temperature-controlled buildings or reuse of rainwater in toilets). Material participation in this sense is not an environmentally conscious choice/act but an occurrence that happens to be aligned with the green agenda. Pragmatic environmentalism goes a step further in that it capitalises on the moment in which 'what works for people' intersects with 'what is good for the environment'. While material participation does not necessarily need to engage with people's consciousness (because the functioning of the buildings itself can be programmed by designers and engineers without informing the users), pragmatic environmentalism introduces a new *culture* to the public by conveying certain implied messages: (1) environmentally sustainable choices are also 'smart' and rational choices (what 'makes sense') that could render one's life easier and more affordable, so pro-environmental actions are no longer a nuisance or an accessory act of charity but an edge for more convenient and resourceful living; and (2) environmentalism is not necessarily going back in time; we have arrived at a moment where the pursuit of innovation, efficiency, and excellence can be dedicated to imagining a more sustainable relationship with nature. In that sense, pragmatic environmentalism is not necessarily technology-driven material participation, as it is activated by a group of people with the purposeful intention of concocting a linkage between everyday (pragmatic) benefits and long-term (environmental) benefits.

Terms such as 'net zero', 'off the grid', or 'cutting edge' are often used to introduce a pro-environmental agenda as a pioneering futuristic vision that the existing system supports. An excellent example of how this reframing of a green agenda into an innovation agenda works is 'The Joinery: Living Building Challenge' project in Tulsa. The Joinery project is a process of building the first house (which is to serve as a community centre) in Tulsa that can qualify under the *Living Building Challenge* by the Living Future organisation. The challenge is essentially about minimising the carbon footprint during the construction *and* maintenance of the house. All building materials have to be locally sourced and sustainably managed, and its functioning should achieve *net positive* water and energy, using rain barrels and solar panels. Going further, the house should also apply biomimicry elements in its landscape design, an innovative and creative approach that emulates 'nature's time-tested patterns and strategies'.[30] Launching this 'eco-building' in Tulsa entailed a long process of persuading the city council and local politicians to come on board. One major hurdle was trying to get permission from the Department of Environment Quality (DEQ) in Oklahoma to allow the building site to be water independent (not connected to the city sewer system). To achieve net zero water management, let alone net positive, the house should be able to create and treat water *on-site*. The city council and planners worked together to obtain approval from DEQ for the Joinery to be a special project that could be exempted from the central sewer connection requirement. As a result, Tulsa became the first city in Oklahoma to actively engage with a net zero water policy.

Framing this undeniably pro-nature project as cutting-edge innovation – and potentially a rare destination for young families and Millennials – was crucial:

Politicians here in general tried to stay away from nature-driven topics, because those were often associated with the realm of 'politically left'. So then I just talked about how this is a good thinking for Tulsa to put us on the map, to attract young people to Tulsa. Tulsa is trying to draw more young professionals and families; this is now a big thing here. In city council meetings, I asked them: Don't you want Tulsa to be seen as a thriving city that attracts young people? Wouldn't it be great to have a house like this in every neighbourhood, as a community centre that can be especially useful in times of disasters? Looking back, the best way to push this project forward was probably that, pitching it like a unique project that will draw young minds to Tulsa – creating a kind of destination that makes Tulsa an attractive place for young people.

Living Building certification is difficult and rare – there are fewer than two dozen certified projects in the world, and the Joinery, if successful, would be the only one in Oklahoma. Although the motivation and driver for doing this project were genuinely green, its advocates used different strategies to offer hooks that could work with the existing system. Tulsa tries to grow and attract more young families and professionals; pragmatic environmentalists capitalise on this to interject how their green initiatives can work synergistically with the city's growth aspirations, *essentially because* 'green culture' or 'green destinations' are what draws young professionals. Should this be framed as a green agenda being co-opted by global capitalism? Or can it be framed as an agency or intention trying to recode the existing system in a way that allows it to pursue a pro-environmental agenda? While pragmatic environmentalists can easily be characterised as 'sell-outs', I would like to challenge this conventional framing and shed light on their techniques for recoding the system.

Trees, aesthetics, landscaping, amenities, destinations, quality of life

One of the most popular 'objects' in mediating the relationship between the urban and nature is trees. Trees are essentially neutral objects which people have positive relationships with, without involving any grandiose admiration of nature. It is not surprising that more and more cities today are now engaging with 'urban forest plans' as a way of attaining a broader consensus on the positive impacts of 'greeneries' in urban spaces. In these plans, trees, shrubs, and parks are almost discussed as *technical objects* that can provide cheap solutions to many urban problems, such as cooling down the city (e.g., trees help address urban heat islands), facilitating the natural water cycle (e.g., tree roots absorb water and help replenish the aquifer), providing a pleasant environment for people to enjoy, and reducing neighbourhood violence and crime. The positive impacts of trees are often immediate and empirically felt, and no one can really deny the functional benefits they can bring. As one person in Tulsa put it:

> It simply has the impact that we can feel. If you go out in the woods, and compare that with just outside of the building [on] a day like this today . . . it's hot and steamy. There's definitely a difference that we feel. If you know that you feel that difference, imagine if our planet was green every-where; it just has to be cooler. How can you not think that what we can experience locally doesn't have impacts on the global? If you're bicycling, if you're riding under the trees, under the shaded canopy, the experience is way different. It just has to matter.

In this context, trees are simply pragmatically beneficial objects beyond the elements of nature: 'Trees simply make us feel good . . . we plant trees not just for nature but also for shade, urban cooling, pleasant urban environ-ment, and breeze'.

Darwin and Tulsa both have urban forest plans that were established *in the aftermath of* natural disasters. 'Once you lose something, then you finally see the value of it', describes an interviewee in Tulsa, explaining how its urban forest plan came about:

> What really triggered all of this was the horrible ice storm in 2007. There have been trees that were not native and had shallow roots that couldn't withstand ice storms. After the storm, 30 per cent of our urban forest was gone. After such repetitive natural disasters, studies had to be done on the status of urban trees, and then [the non-profit organisation] Up With Trees came in and start planning for replanting trees that could be resilient in the local climate, promoting for citywide urban forest strate-gies . . . it was a big deal for the planning scene here in Tulsa.

The story of Darwin is surprisingly similar. Cyclone Marcus wiped out the non-native trees with shallow roots (e.g., African mahogany trees), which inspired the city to embark on its urban forest plan, entitled 'Establishing a Resilient Urban Forest for Darwin'.[31] The plan addresses why so many trees were uprooted by the cyclone and lists strategies for maintaining trees as 'a valuable community asset'. The advocacy for 'why trees matter' often begins with their functional value: 'It is true, that planting a tree is an investment in the future . . . In our developing cities, trees provide multiple benefits and recent studies indicate that their value to society can be significant. Preliminary research for the Darwin CBD trees undertaken in 2016 valued trees at $2.4m . . . studies have shown that this cooling effect [of trees] can reduce air-conditioning costs for adjoining properties by thousands of dollars per year'.[32] It can be observed that, in both cases, it became easier to derive a shared sentiment around the value of trees and their everyday benefits in the aftermaths of disasters, when people experienced what it felt like to be without trees. A planner in Darwin remarked that: 'It was sad to see the trees fallen down everywhere, quite frightening and devastating, but because of that, we received a lot of response and enthusiasm from communities who wanted to volunteer for replanting efforts'.

Especially in Tulsa, where the political climate is less forgiving when it comes to the topics of the environment or climate change, trees and landscaping are serving as an effective material medium through which certain pro-environmental actions can be activated. What is especially important for understanding pragmatic environmentalists is their ability to reconfigure unlikely associations, connect different points of interests, and eventually work out a way to implement a pro-environmental agenda *without* imposing their primary pro-nature motivations or principles. The trick is to first find out what really drives people to do what they do, then think of a segue that can connect their interests with environmental actions. An environmental organisation representative explained that:

> We make it about what's important for them. For instance, some elected officials are interested in education, especially improving public schools. We then talk about the impacts of trees and landscaping to education. It has been proven that if kids have more frequent access to green space, they show up more, leading to higher attendance, higher standardised scores, and higher graduation rates. For large philanthropic foundations,

whose primary interest is often addressing social inequality, we talk about the social benefits of trees, especially in reducing vandalism and crime . . . So you see, we kind of sell it backward, by starting a conversation that can pull them in, and then show benefits of trees that match their different niches.

Whatever the driving motivation may be, if the action itself can support what they do, pragmatic environmentalists will take it:

It's your money, and you may not be interested in trees or the environment, but you may want to buy a picket sign that comes with trees because you want to advertise something . . . the end result is a community getting the trees that it needs. So I don't care what your motivation is; whatever that is, what we get to do is the same: planting trees that have impacts on the city.

'Quality of life' is also a popular language and currency for pragmatic environmentalists attempting to introduce more 'green elements' in urban built environments. The actors working in the field of urban planning and design often frame the pro-environmental aspects of their initiatives as amenities that enhance quality of life. Planting more trees and landscaping are go-to solutions for the aforementioned 'creating a destination' that can attract young families and professionals who are largely interested in a green, walkable downtown. Ultimately, the culture and trend of young professionals – who often equate quality-of-life factors with the presence of green spaces and walkable cultural/programmed destinations – actively informs the future vision and planning of the city:

Sometimes it's not driven by the actual desire to be energy efficient. It's more about what's trendy and cool: what makes it special, local, unique, and fun. The younger generation doesn't buy the cheapest product; they are more interested in what's unique about the story of the product and the place where it's sold. So we try to capitalise on 'making it cool and trendy', such as place-making strategies and creating photographic moments. And, as you know, all of these now require green space, reuse of materials, and sustainable practices.

The popularisation of new urbanism – which advocates for a dense, walkable town-centre model of urban design that discourages car use – is no longer a moral ideal of sustainability for the sake of sustainability; it is essentially a good business plan that works well for attracting targeted younger demographics:

> Millennials, people of 35 years and under, love their cities and walkable downtown. They don't want to own houses or big lands. We have seen the comeback of downtown and reoccupation of buildings, mostly due to the influx of young professionals. They like living in densely populated areas and look for shared, public green spaces. Our projects respond to such a change in trend and audience; planning for parks, green spaces, and walkable communities has easily become a major element of what we do.

A similar trend is occurring in Darwin, where the city reinvests in a downtown with green infrastructure and integration of nature in the built environment.

> We're trying to create [a] more pleasant environment in the city for people to roam around and hang out more, which could help the economy of our city. 'Creating a pleasant condition', or 'creating a destination', has become the motivator for planners to be engaged more with nature and the environment in general.

What we see here is the piggybacking of pro-environmental initiatives on the discourse of enhancing quality of life in cities, which is particularly effective as the current mainstream culture of Millennials takes a particular interest in what is local, unique (i.e., story-worthy), *and* green.

The influence of a mainstreamed 'coolness factor' can also be observed in the aesthetic details of landscaping practices; the sudden legitimisation of native plants, shrubs and a more 'bushy' look of garden design – as opposed to the conventional manicured lawns – is essentially the result of this change in trend and culture, led by young professionals who value something reverential in the area (this phenomenon was predominant in both Darwin and Tulsa). What you realise, eventually, is that despite all the ironies and superficialities that Millennials might project to some, the permeation of their culture is what facilitates the pursuit of the green agenda, especially in places where climate change or environmental issues are hard to prioritise. By stating this, however, one does not condone the negative impacts of gentrification. Instead, what I am striving to point out here is how the cultural shift and change in mainstream perception (of what is cool, trendy, and up to date) can play an important role in assisting the operation of this green agenda. This is especially true in devising ways to engage the widest possible political spectrum. To secularise 'nature' and draw the everyday relevancy of why the environment matters, the role of culture – which penetrates into our consumption habits and common behavioural choices – should be acknowledged and strategised for its *potential purposeful use.*

Figure 3.7 RiverParks in Tulsa is a flood buffer along the river which also serves as bike and walking trails during the dry season. © Ihnji Jon.

Species extinction, conservation, and stewardship

Another popular engagement strategy in both Darwin and Tulsa is to talk about species extinction, mentioning how the existence of certain specific

Figure 3.8   Gathering Place, a brand-new park that promotes pro-ecology imageries and landscaping using indigenous plants, is an example of how mainstream culture and interest in green urbanism as 'quality of life' factor can be used for pushing through pro-environment urban politics. © Ihnji Jon.

species is currently threatened. However, the particularity of pragmatic environmentalists' approach is that they focus *less* on the negative impacts of human intervention and more on its potential positive impacts – the kinds of things that we can do in the present moment, in daily choices and our usual environment. This approach is similar to the recent literature on a more 'affirmative' understanding of the Anthropocene,[33] where writers discuss the potentialities of everyday alternatives or 'whatever action' in the arrival of the Anthropocene. If the reality of the Anthropocene forces us to reflect on the fragility of our planet (and our own existence), the result need not necessarily be despair, but may be an opportunity to draw attention to what can be done here and now. In relation to this 'casting hope in the Anthropocene', pragmatic environmentalists attempt to draw attention to nature and the environment by proposing what we can do to protect 'little critters' from extinction, with simple, doable, ordinary choices.

Figure 3.9   Crow Creek Meadow advertises easy ways of achieving win-win condition in which households benefit from 'flood mitigation' or 'simplified lawn care' while at the same time protecting water quality and contributing to biodiversity. © Ihnji Jon.

A good example is Crow Creek Meadow in Tulsa, a citizen-led community garden in a residential neighbourhood that experiences frequent flooding. Its purpose is to normalise the aesthetics of native plants and their disorderly appearance, by showcasing how wildflowers and native plants can also be an excellent option for individual household gardening. To promote this new beauty standard, the dedicated task force focuses on communicating the pragmatic benefits of native plants, such as their efficiency in managing rainwater (e.g., their deeper roots absorb more water) and simplifying lawn care (e.g., less maintenance compared to standard manicured lawns). They also widely advertise that native plants provide shelters for endangered species in the region, such as monarch butterflies. Tulsa is a migration gateway for monarch butterflies, and milkweed, a plant native to the Oklahoma region, is the only plant that these caterpillar babies can survive on. 'Everybody loves monarchs; there's simply no debate about that',

Figure 3.10 Crow Creek Meadow, with its milkweed planting, also serves as a 'Monarch Waystation', certified by Monarch Waystation Network Program.
© Ihnji Jon.

noted one of the group members leading the Crow Creek Meadow project: 'No one wants to see these little critters disappearing. Talking about butterflies is a great way to attract attention [to] native plants, environment conservation, and wider impacts of our choices'.

In fact, Sustainable Tulsa also uses endangered species and their disappearing habitats as a way to introduce how our food security is inevitably dependent on healthy ecosystem functions, notably the roles of pollinators and their habitats. Furthermore, given extensive faith-based communities and conservative political orientations, different wordings were used: '*Conservation, stewardship, legacy,* are the kinds of words that we use to safely usher in the topic, without people rolling their eyes'. Similar to this trend, Darwin's department of environment runs a voluntary programme entitled 'Gardens for Wildlife', which aims to penetrate the residential suburbs and private lands where the mainstream urban ideal of sustainability is less worshipped. The programme provides support for any household wanting to create a wildlife habitat in its garden, such as free workshops and educational events. In this context, species extinction is often put forward as an urgent topic that can entice attention from the public; 'when we talk about how specific species, especially certain birds, are at the threshold of extinction, people suddenly become very interested and willing to do what it takes, including donations or signing up for movements'.

One of the most effective strategies for communicating the topic is to reach out to the youth or families with young children: 'Children who play down in the water look for fish and crawfish, or even kayaking in the river, you would notice whether there's a fish or not. We can talk about these little critters and how their lives are affected by our daily practices'. Strategies to work with school programmes and children were also very present in Darwin: 'In collaboration with schools, we organise events that can be attractive and exciting to students, such as mangroves walking tours or bat watching nights . . . and by engaging with children, we can reach out to families and people in private residential areas that are often difficult to access, because children will start asking questions to their parents and their family members'.

In relation to mentioning specific species and animals as a way to increase awareness of environmental degradation, recreational fishing and tourism often become popular topics with which to draw people's attention to their behavioural choices: 'Fishing is a huge thing here in Darwin, a family activity and true passion for many. It is, within that dialogue, easier to talk about the negative impacts of plastic bottles, as it directly affects fish habitats and you could actually prove that in numbers . . . With the support from private citizens, we're currently pursuing a citywide plastic ban in public markets'. Tulsa also shares a similar context: 'Tulsans are passionate about fishing, camping, and outdoor activities. In terms of recreational fishing and its industry, the pollution directly affects fish population – proving the 'dollar value' of biodiversity that people can actually see and feel . . . We often use these examples to promote our "save our streams" program'. Utilising the tangible, material reality of fish, birds, and other animals and their habitats is one of pragmatic environmentalists' main strategies, which is connected to the recent wave of new materialism in environmental politics.

Table 3.2 A summary of the strategies of 'pragmatic environmentalism'.

Emphasis	Action example	Pragmatic benefits	Accompanying outcome	Implying vision
Water quality, air quality, health and wellness *'Fishes in our streams are dying'* *'Keep our lake clean'*	Low Impact Development (LID) practices, 'on-site' stormwater treatment Avoiding disposable plastic bottles, Participating in recycling programmes	Healthy everyday environment, protect property value	Protect water, reduce carbon emissions, increase tree canopy	Public health and environmental protection go hand in hand
Extreme weather, emergency preparedness, insurance premiums *'Let's be prepared for flood'*	'On-site' stormwater treatment, regulations that restrict runoffs, riverside parks and trails that serve as flood buffers	Stormwater detention, prevent flooding, decrease insurance premium, individual security and protection, protect property value	Protect water from pollutants, encourage natural treatment of stormwater, increase tree canopy	Designing with nature, or respecting natural systems, is beneficial for our own good – socially and economically
Energy bills, energy efficiency, renewable energy, innovation *'Cheap, fun, and exciting consumer choice'* *'net-zero', 'off the grid', 'cutting edge'*	Use of renewable energy for 'off the grid' maintenance (solar and wind), energy-efficient building designs, electric vehicles, and charging stations	Energy bills reduced, less maintenance, and long life of EVs, considering long-term life of site developments	Reduce carbon emissions, divert energy sources	The pursuit of innovation, efficiency, and excellence can be dedicated to imagining more sustainable relationship with nature

Quality of life, landscaping, amenities, destinations *'Trees decrease crimes'*	Focus on aesthetics, design, native plants, create more green areas	Trees and landscaping are proven to decrease vandalism and crime	Increase tree canopy	Increasing contact with nature is linked with addressing socio-economic inequality
'Young professionals love walkable and green downtown'		More agreeable pedestrian experience, high walkability factor, shoppers spend more money, increase investment return		Urban growth goes hand in hand with environmental sustainability; an 'attractive city' for Millennials is a walkable, green city that prioritises sustainability
Species extinction, education for kids, land legacy, stewards of the land	Community gardens reserved for native plants that cultivate species habitats	Education for children, community pride	Protect biodiversity	Caring for the environment is connected to caring for our children
'Let's protect monarch butterflies'	Tree planting and landscaping in public schools	More trees in schools lead to students' better performance, higher test scores		

INTERMEZZO: CAUTIONARY REMARKS ON 'GREEN + HEALTH'

Before I conclude, I would like to caution about associating green politics with individual health. The rising scholarship on the mainstreaming of green politics often uses the health impacts of pollution and environmental degradation as an important segue to introduce 'why the environment matters'. Public health issues can certainly serve as a point of interest to connect with a wider audience, with pragmatic environmentalists – as I noted earlier – capitalising on the health interests of individual households, by attempting to translate individual 'wellness' into a broader awareness of nature, the environment, or what surrounds us. Furthermore, the health implications of the environment are inevitably linked with the 'feel it to act' argument voiced by the new materialist ecopolitics, since an individual bodily response to our living condition is in itself empirical experience that can motivate pro-nature political action. However, we should be aware of how this individual wellness factor can also be used for the kinds of local politics that promote exclusivity.

For instance, there was a recent 'Not In My Back Yard' (NIMBY) movement in San Francisco, where a wealthy community opposed a homeless shelter on the grounds of its 'negative health impacts', such as drug use and crime.[34] The opponents of the shelter used the California Environmental Quality Act to pursue a lawsuit against the city, arguing that the presence of the homeless population was itself a 'health and environment hazard'. Such incidents reveal the dangerous potential of the 'green + health' argument, where the everyday aspects of appreciating the environment can be turned into selfish motivations fuelling exclusive local politics. This phenomenon has been referred to as the 'local trap' by critical geographers,[35] who noted the danger of being 'too local' – in the sense that it can undermine the wider-scale implications of democracy and citizenship. When detached from the inclusive pursuit of a pro-nature agenda that can be expanded to a wider-scale collective good, the green agenda's association with individual health is highly susceptible to a local trap endangering greater democracy in cities.

This danger particularly touches on the question of what the 'adequate scale' for pro-environmental political action should be. While an emphasis on local empirical experiences can be a strong motivation for a pro-nature agenda, a hyper-romanticisation of localism can neglect the possibility of exclusive politics being driven by fragmented local interests (i.e., local trap or NIMBY-ism). Pragmatic environmentalism, working in the space of advocating for the immediate benefits of pro-environmental choices, may be easily subject to such a local trap. Therefore, one should be wary of the wider implications of locally driven environmental actions, noting that the ideal operation of pragmatic environmentalism should be grounded on the principle of inclusive spatial governance, situated within the pursuit of greater democracy and justice.[36]

DISCUSSION: TOWARDS THE ENVIRONMENTALISM OF 'ORDINARY PEOPLE'

Pragmatic environmentalism is a strategic attitude enacted by social actors who try to interject their pro-nature values wherever they can, effectively recoding the existing system rather than trying to dismantle it all at once. In recognising human agency as doing what we can in a given context, it tries to reach out to a wider audience that may not initially be interested in nature, and, while doing so, capitalises on the neutrality of specific material objects as a way of disarming the reactive response of climate sceptics. It is especially visible in cities where the political context does not accept the pro-environmental agenda as a mainstream social norm. Its emphasis on using the materiality of specific objects, empirical experience, and hopeful sentiment (towards what can still be done) shares its theoretical stance with the rise of the material turn in planning, as well as new materialist (or 'down-to-earth') ecopolitics. On the other hand, instead of a penalising or judgmental argument ('clean up the mess, or we'll die!'), pragmatic environmentalism attracts people's attention through communicating the everyday benefits of pro-environmental choices. This anti-essentialist attitude towards normativity or what should be done – going beyond the essentialist morality of 'protecting nature' – invokes Spinozian ethics, which rejects transcendent values imposed from above (e.g., good versus evil), and instead prioritises productive power and the energy to *act*.

When it comes to pragmatism, one should be reminded of its root in anti-foundationalism.[37] As Robert Lake noted, a main contribution of pragmatism – from Dewey to Rorty – is to unveil the illusory nature of 'self-evident' foundational belief. If one relies too heavily on 'the crutch of dogma' or universal principles 'dictated from high authority', we may end up naturalising and justifying our actions that do not actually incur any form of 'change' in our everyday decision making of here and now.[38] But as a critical theory reader, one might ask: what is the value of anti-foundationalist thoughts in pursuing more just and equitable urban futures? The answer is that Dewey's prioritisation of plural democracy, which begins by valuing the everyday experiences of the public (as much as we value the opinions of 'the experts' or 'the educated'), will guide us towards the politics that meaning-fully engage with 'ordinary people'.

Who are 'ordinary people'? Recently, Pierre Charbonnier, a French phi-losopher and environmental historian, provoked a debate on whether the French intellectuals' signatures on 'The Environmental Imperative' would be really effective in terms of creating a *real* change. In his column, 'Ecology doesn't unite us, it divides us',[39] he argued that the elite-driven imposition of environmentalism is not effective in reaching out to those who are eco-nomically marginalised, as we saw in the *gilet jaune* (yellow vest) movement in France where the working class fiercely rejected the government's carbon tax initiative. For the participants of this movement, 'ecological ideals' are a luxury available only for those who have economic privilege; the 'ordinary' others are more concerned with their bills to pay and are imprisoned by cars. Bruno Latour also offered a similar sentiment, pointing out the limits of the universal imperative of 'protecting nature' that fails to consider the geopolit-ical diversities. Concerning the Citizens' Convention for Climate, a French assembly consisting of 150 self-selected and randomly chosen citizens who are to lead the national ecological transition, Latour noted that: '[t]he 150 people of the Citizen Climate Convention have done an admirable job and have all become certified ecologists, but the idea that their solution will be followed by 66 million French people because they are representative of the population is naïve . . . It's just the opinion of 150 people who were sub-jected to admirable and very expensive procedure, who were made aware of things. But it's 150 out of 66 million! What do we do for others?'[40] Here, 66 million people are the 'ordinary people' who may or may not be auto-matically on board with ecological ideals – depending on their everyday livelihood concerns that often dictate their philosophical ideas on life.

Going back to answering the question of 'why anti-foundationalism matters' in the critical approach to the urban, one could pay more attention to the real reason *why* Dewey was an avid advocate for 'embodied intel-ligence driven by actual experiences' over the essentialist moral standards legislated by the philosophers, experts, or 'educated'. Alice Kadlec, in an attempt to resuscitate the critical value of Deweyan pragmatism, argues that Dewey's commitment to place ordinary people's 'everyday lived experiences' at the centre of science and politics is indebted to his activist position *against* the elitist-driven ideological abstractions.[41] More specifically, in *Reconstruction in Philosophy*, Dewey tried to dismantle the ancient Greek's bifurcation of 'reason vs. experience', which saw *reason* as the only power of 'enlightened', 'educated' choice – dismissing *experience* as 'marginal', 'unenlightened' particularities that need intervention from the elite.[42] Dewey's effort therefore focused on recovering the power of everyday lived experience which will, after repetition over a certain period of time, eventually become nourishment to the future critical reflections and reason. And this is one of the radical aspects of Dewey's philosophy that democratises knowledge, philosophy, and science *beyond* the reach of the elite few.

In order to uphold the values of radical and plural democracy, which *never* disregards the opinions of the public as dismissible voices coming from the 'uneducated mass', it became cardinal for Dewey to attend to everyday experiences that gradually *but* democratically deliberate social norms from the ground up. This approach is indeed slower, and could be perceived as 'less radical', but avoids hammering down the imperatives from above, which could be considered undemocratic.[43]

In attempts to imagine a future of environmental politics that goes beyond the essentialist morality of 'protecting nature', my proposition of pragmatic environmentalism is committed to creating a 'soft momentum' that reaches out to unlikely audiences. The ultimate objective of pragmatic environmentalism is to prompt a voluntary change in people's behaviour by creating 'the right kind of mood' for environmental action – rather than relying on a universal imperative that still remains too abstract for the mainstream public. This approach prioritises the values of pluralism in radical democracy that attend to the opinions of the public as much as the opinions of the elite few. Pragmatic environmentalists believe that a concrete engagement with the public, no matter how creative they would have to be in finding a common ground, will eventually bring about an evolving collective understanding about the natural world. It is patient, for it attempts to build a slow momentum for environmentalism from the ground up, without rushing to impose it from the top. But for that very reason, it is radical, for it values the everyday experiences of the 'ordinary people' as much as the educated 'reason' of the intellectuals or experts. As Lake notes, a radical realignment of planning practice is possible under Dewey's pragmatic ethos, since it engenders a shift 'from a stance of distanced objectivity to an engaged attitude of solidarity and empathy'.[44] While the history of Western democracy – originated from the Platonic ideal – has retained its dismissive attitude towards 'the incompetent and ill-informed mass',[45] Dewey's creative democracy is radical because of its unwavering belief in the public's (or 'ordinary people's') capacity to participate in common goals and forge a collective alliance *without* aristocratic rule.[46]

CONCLUSION

Based on 24 interviews with environmental activists and urban planners in Tulsa and Darwin, I demonstrated more specifically how pragmatic environmentalism operates in reality. Essentially, it contributes to the current debates on city leadership in the global climate crisis by answering a specific question: in the current divisive political climate, where referring to 'the environment' or 'nature' is often dismissed as purely left-leaning political discourse – thus failing to forge a broader audience and inspire collective action – how do cities still manage to pursue pro-environmental actions, and what are their strategies for working with those who may not be interested in nature in the first place?

This investigation revealed that there are five main trajectories for how pragmatic environmentalists link the issues of 'nature' with the mundane everyday surroundings that people may care more about, going from a very simple object to a broader concept and vision. The first strategy is emphasising water quality, air quality, and health and wellness, which captures the neutrality of objects, such as 'water' and 'air' as a way of introducing our inevitable dependency on nature for our basic conditions of existence (specifically manifested through the health impacts of environmental degradation). Its implied vision notes how public health and environmental protection issues go hand-in-hand, and that the matters of 'the environment' affect us all without discrimination. The second strategy is to capitalise on the local conditions of extreme weather and emergency preparedness, through which people can acknowledge the agency of nature and start questioning what could be done to tame its potential aggressiveness. The implied vision of this strategy notes that 'designing with nature', or respecting natural systems, is beneficial for our own good – socially and economically. The third strategy highlights the monetary benefits of energy efficiency, extending that dialogue towards the advocacy of renewable energy as a strand of pursuing innovation and excellence. The implied vision of this strategy is particularly interesting, as it tries to deliver the message that environmentalism is in fact a future-oriented agenda (and less about going back in time), and how human efforts to strive for betterment can be dedicated to imagining a more sustainable relationship with nature. The fourth strategy focuses on the 'feel good' factors of green urbanism, such as the positive impacts of landscaping and green destinations on quality of life. The role of mainstream Millennial culture – which particularly considers the local as unique, and green as cool and trendy – is important here, as cities try to attract young minds and professionals with their desire for growth. Finally, the fifth strategy entails talking about species extinction and educational programmes for children, implying that what we do for nature and the environment may be akin to caring for our children and their interactions with the world surrounding them.

One might argue that pragmatic environmentalism is the programme of sell-outs who are already submissive to the system before even fighting. To this, I would point out that it may be the slowly permeating impacts of these 'soft' strategies that will allow us to build a political project of empathy and respectful engagement with others. As DeLanda notes, the possibility of collective agency and change can only be accessible through a shared belief, gradually cultivated through constant human interactions, the circulation of ideas, and repeated empirical actions.[47] Dewey also described the permeation of new values that occur *democratically* over a period of time; as Lake[48] cites Dewey:

> As the new ideas find adequate expression in social life, they will be absorbed into a moral background, and the ideas and beliefs themselves will be deepened and be unconsciously transmitted and sustained. They will color the imagination and temper the desires and affections. They will not form a set of ideas to be expounded, reasoned out and argumentatively supported, but will be a spontaneous way of envisioning life.[49]

Pragmatic environmentalism in this sense is a strategy 'to keep the conversation going'[50] rather than hammering down with what the elites know 'better' than ordinary people. By focusing on what can actually be enacted here and now, pragmatic environmentalism is 'radical' in the sense that it (1) prioritises concrete actions over ideological agreements; (2) effectively secularises nature/the environment by showing how it is ubiquitously present in (and inseparable from) our everyday (socioeconomic) life; and (3) imagines and presents a speculative hope that we might be able to link immediate benefits (of whatever feels good to us for now) and long-term benefits (of our sustainable future). In the world of social and political division, coupled with global climate crisis, we are in dire need of radically reconfiguring environmentalism as a mainstream culture and way of life that *goes beyond* the enclave politics of those who accept 'protecting nature' as an unquestionable norm. If the idea of the 'radical' essentially symbolises shattering the status quo, pragmatic environmentalism does exactly that by tearing down the elitist wall of green idealism and reaching out to an unlikely audience.

4
Cleveland vs. Cape Town: Can a city aspire to be green and inclusive?

To many cosmopolitan cities around the world, the concerns about the current ecological crisis seem 'natural'. In the city visions of Paris, Barcelona, New York, and Melbourne it is common to observe these global cities' sincere commitment to climate crisis and their concrete plans for actions, through for example, 'Superblocks' (Barcelona), '15-minute city' (Paris), or going carbon neutral by 2020 (Melbourne). But for cities that are subject to chronic social inequality and poverty, matters of the environment often come second. It can be considered a luxury to think about nature or the environment, if one cannot imagine how to sustain one's household beyond the next few months due to homelessness and joblessness, and the crime and violence often associated with these issues.

The conflict between the green and inequality agendas is not a new topic in the field of urban studies, especially with regard to reconciling social and environmental 'sustainability' goals. The green gentrification literature[1] also provides a trenchant critique on how unreflective coalitions between environmental sustainability and profit-driven urban planning are likely to generate the kinds of physical outcomes that are detrimental to the poor. On the other hand, the possibility of green activism competing with other social movements has also been noted. Several scholars discussed how some green-only movements find themselves in a privileged space, neglecting urgent issues of inequality and social justice affecting immigrants and historically marginalised communities.[2]

What has been less explored, however, is what it is actually like to pursue a green agenda in a city context in which issues of poverty and social development have to come first. How do cities like Cleveland (Ohio, USA), the poverty rate of which is over 33 per cent (fourth highest city in the country), pursue a green agenda ahead of what is considered to be more urgent by the public, that is poverty and crime? How do cities like Cape Town (South

Africa), where historical social inequality permeates all aspects of planning and development, introduce the importance of caring for nature – when at least one in five (20 per cent) of its residents live in informal settlements without basic amenities, including sanitation and clean water?

In attempting to address these difficult questions, this chapter focuses on the question of *how* urban planners and local environment activists navigate the pursuit of a green agenda in contexts where the urgency of addressing poverty/inequality is more apparent. Based on my survey of the existing literature, complemented by interviews with planning practitioners in Cleveland and Cape Town, this chapter discusses the realities and challenges of addressing environmental concerns alongside social inequality/development concerns. Going further, I offer the promise of localised, *place-based* environmental politics, by exploring how local historical contexts and place-specific elements can help advance the convergence between green and social equality agendas.

How do cities, as local sites activating more tangible politics, explore the negotiation and convergence between green and equity values? What are the historical contexts and elements that influence the kinds of efforts that respond to these two competing ideals? At the same time, what kinds of positive articulation and narratives are being used by environment planners and activists who are striving to broaden their policy audience and go beyond the 'green-only' agendas? In attempting to answer these questions, I pay particular attention to how environmentalist ideals (or advocacy for 'protecting nature') can be communicated and pursued in a context where the argument for addressing 'human needs' (e.g., inequality, poverty, or violence) is more predominant.

CLEVELAND V CAPE TOWN

This chapter compares the cases of Cleveland and Cape Town, focusing on how these two cities are coping with the tension between green and equity agendas. Despite vastly different political contexts, Cleveland and Cape Town share important characteristics that can reveal the realities of what it is like to pursue pro-environment initiatives *especially under* the heightened pressure of urban poverty and inequality. Above all, both suffer from high poverty rates, which obliges them to chase after further economic development and investments. Such aspirations for economic boosts (for the purpose of job creation) are also embedded in the two cities' efforts to be more 'green' (e.g., going carbon neutral or adopting nature-based solutions to flood mitigation).

Secondly, both cities suffer from the spatial segregation of poverty and unequal disinvestment. As one of the major 'rust-belt' cities, Cleveland had to endure a drastic economic downturn after post-industrialisation, including an exodus of manufacturing jobs and population. The financial crisis in 2008 also had drastic impacts on the city's housing market, resulting in foreclosed homes and vacant lots, especially in historically distressed areas (mostly African American neighbourhoods in the east side of the city). Similarly, Cape Town carries the historical legacy of apartheid in its physical form, with its white inhabitants occupying the scenic hillside areas along the coastline in the west, while the majority of non-white citizens reside in townships in the east (often known as 'Cape Flats' from the 1950s when the apartheid government forcedly moved non-white residents into informal settlements in the flatter areas away from mountains). This aspect of spatial segregation (or urban inequality manifested in a physical form) has infiltrated the strategies for pursuing green agendas in these two cities, either through prioritising distressed areas for urban greening (Cleveland) or seeking alternative energy procurement in informal settlements (Cape Town).

This research is based on in-depth conversations with practitioners broadly working in the field of urban planning, environmental activism, and economic development. I interviewed 21 practitioners (ten in Cleveland, eleven in Cape Town) in total, based on questionnaires that specifically reflected how 'the matters of the environment' can be intertwined with more tangible local concerns, drawn from a literature review and desktop research on the two cities. In the case of Cleveland, the interviewees included government planners and non-government practitioners working on the environment and sustainable development. In the case of Cape Town, interviewees included government personnel working on environment planning and sustainable development, as well as non-government professionals working on nature conservation and water management. Based on the interview data, I teased out the main themes that respond to the question of what it is like to pursue pro-environment initiatives under the pressure of urban poverty and inequality issues. I discuss these results in detail in later sections, following the literature review on green vs. inequality.

Table 4.1 Comparison between city contexts between Cleveland and Cape Town.

	Cleveland, Ohio, USA	Cape Town, South Africa
Poverty/unem-ployment rate	As of 2018, according to the Census Bureau, a third of city residents (33.1%) live in poverty, with child poverty rate of 50.5%.[3] These rates remain worse than they were before the recession of 2007–9 (the overall poverty rate in 2006 was 27%, with child poverty rate of 41.9%). As of 2019, Cleveland metro area's unemployment is reported to be 4.3%.[4] However, the Center for Community Solutions' survey in May 2019 reported that 48.5% of local residents living in poverty were working either full-time or part-time, indicating that people who are working (even in full-time) are still unable to pay for their necessities due to low wage.[5]	According to the city's communication materials dated in 2016, the poverty rate in the city is estimated as 25.1% (without taking account of informal economy sector).[6] According to University of Cape Town's research evidence on child poverty (published in 2018), the percentage of children living below the upper bound poverty line is 35% in Western Cape region, 59% in Northern Cape region, and 80% in Eastern Cape region.[7] As of 2018, according to Economic Performance Indicators for Cape Town, Cape Town's reported unemployment rate is 23.8%, with youth (15–24 years old) unemployment rate of 45.5%.[8]
Spatial segregation	Since the financial crisis in 2007–9, Cleveland suffered from the soaring number of foreclosed homes and vacant lots especially in historically distressed areas – mostly African American neighbourhoods (in the east side of the city).	Cape Town carries the historical legacy of apartheid in its physical form, where the white inhabitants occupy the scenic hillside areas of the west while the majority of non-white citizens reside in townships in the east (often known as 'Cape Flats'). According to the 2011 Census, 20.5% of Cape Town's households live in informal dwellings, which is expected to rise continuously as more people are moving to the city-region looking for opportunities.[9]

Cleveland vs. Cape Town

History of environmentalism	Cleveland has a long history of environmental activism, which began by the Cuyahoga Fire in 1969 (resulted from rapid industrialisation). The fire catalysed the nation-wide environment movement and the establishment of the federal Environment Protection Act.	Cape Town's environmentalism has been closely linked with the region's effort to create low skill jobs in the post-apartheid era, especially via Working for Water programme where non-white populations were hired to remove 'invasive species' that soak up more water (hence harming the water reserve in the aquifer).
Nexus between extreme weather and city vision	With global climate crisis, Cleveland is more and more subjected to extreme heat (combined with humidity) and flooding. The city tries to take account of this change in addressing inequality, especially by prioritising disinvested areas for green infrastructure or pursuing manufacture/construction jobs through green technology.	With global climate crisis, Cape Town has been experiencing severe droughts and irregularities in precipitation. The historical drought in 2018 ('Day Zero') laid bare the realities of what informal settlement residents live through every day; the urgent need for more equal access to water, energy, and sanitation was able to be discussed more openly. This led to the city exploring more decentralised models of utility services and delivery via green technology.

Figure 4.1　　Cleveland City Centre. © Ihnji Jon.

Figure 4.2   Cape Town City Centre. © Ihnji Jon.

GREEN V INEQUALITY: COMPETING IDEALS
AND THE POSSIBILITY OF CONVERGENCE

Environmentalism and its overlap with addressing social inequality have been well articulated in the environmental justice (EJ) literature. Through concepts such as 'green gentrification'[10] or 'eco-apartheid',[11] EJ literature, which often stems from the Marxist political ecology tradition,[12] has made a significant contribution in unveiling how the marginalised and poor always end up in the most polluted and hazardous parts of the city.

What has been less discussed, however, is what comes after such trenchant critique on systemic injustices driven by global neoliberalism. Hence the main motivation behind my investigation was to better understand how government planners, officials, or policy advocacy practitioners strive to work within the conditions of here and now, despite the intrinsic contradictions of pursuing progressive ideals in a world shaped by capitalism. By addressing *how* cities may reconcile the tension between environmental and social priorities in their future visions, my reference to 'green versus inequality' departs slightly from the existing EJ tradition in that I am mainly interested in suggesting potential ways of enacting positive intervention (beyond critique).

In order to discuss my case studies in light of the current research trend on this topic, I surveyed the existing works on when the green (i.e., the pursuit of environmental sustainability) and equity (i.e., addressing poverty and social development) agendas diverge, as well as the possibilities for bringing them together.

Green Gentrification

Several scholars have questioned whether green cities can also be equitable and inclusive, especially in the dominant presence of market-driven urbanisation and planning.[13] 'Ecological Gentrification' or 'Green Gentrification' have become core vocabularies highlighting the potential negative impacts of pursuing *green-only* agenda, through which the city governments' ardent promotion of 'climate friendliness' may result in such inequitable outcomes as housing unaffordability for lower income or non-white residents. Notably, green gentrification literature reveals how environmental improvements (e.g., more parks, green spaces, attractive 'green' amenities) can often drive up real estate prices, causing the displacement of working class or lower income residents. In response to the rising trend of green gentrification, some scholars have advocated for 'just green enough' strategies; 'just green enough' clean-up activities *do not* automatically lead to 'parks, cafes, and a river walk' model of a green city – the area will continue its industrial use and support blue-collar work.[14] As the authors put it: 'Ideally, cleanup of Newtown Creek will be just green enough to improve the health and quality of life of existing residents, but not so literally green as to attract more upscale 'sustainable' LEED-certified residential developments that drive out working-class residents and industrial businesses'.[15]

If these literatures highlight the realities of capitalism-driven urban development – how the rich will always live in a greener/more pleasant environment, while the poor often end up in the least desirable parts of the town – the possibilities of such phenomena are greater in the context of emerging economies where social disparities are often more evident. Writers frame this tendency as 'eco-apartheid', where the increasing risk of climate-related disasters can lead to an even more inequitable urban landscape in which 'segregation' becomes a brutally Darwinian ideal (i.e., 'survival of the fittest') – with the rich living in more climate-proof areas with better access to emergency goods and services.[16]

Understanding these issues at a larger scale context – notably of city-planning and its overall future vision – the implication of these outcomes can be summed up to the question: Can a city aspire to become green *and* inclusive, or is this an unreachable dream in the context of capitalist-driven urban development? This question constantly looms in formulating visions of future cities, especially in today's era of climate emergency. The aforementioned side-effects of 'urban greening' can create antagonism against the city's focus on environmentalism, such as the rising trend of installing 'green infrastructure (GI)' or now internationally popular 'urban forest strategies'.[17]

Indeed, looking at challenges to come and preparing for climate crisis are absolutely critical. However, how can cities introduce these *longer-term* green agendas when *the present* socio-economic challenges of 'right now' remain unanswered? Since the green agenda is likely to focus on longer-term ecological solutions, it can easily be contested by the equality agenda, which is mostly concerned with providing immediate economic and social relief for marginalised groups in a much shorter time frame. If adequate government interventions are undeniably the key to a green *and* inclusive city, then the question is how the public sector, policy makers, and advocacies can articulate a compelling narrative that these priorities do not necessarily go against one another. Indeed, the challenge goes both ways: for some, the challenge is to persuade environmentalists to be more on board with creating more equitable and just urban spaces, and for others, the challenge is to persuade equity-driven activists and policy shapers to realise the urgency of pro-environment actions. Acknowledging both challenges as equally important, this chapter contributes to extending the scope of EJ literature beyond critique, by suggesting when and how environmentalism and social justice principles can be pursued as collective visions and directions of city-planning.

Green Activism vs. Social Activism

An important strand of literature on green versus inequality is the conflictual relationship between environmental activism and social activism.[18] The 'characteristically white and well-funded environmental organizations,'[19] enjoying the systemic privileges that their members have by default, often fail to recognise the interconnected nature of environmental and social justice. In other words, the green-only organisations often neglect the role played by systemic neoliberal power structures, which not only cause ecological crisis (via exploiting nature) but also close eyes to structural social injustices experienced by the marginalised. For instance, scholars have shown how the Sierra Club, as a moderate authority on environmental issues, failed to embrace the intersectionality of climate and immigrant justice. By rendering the kinds of green-only solutions that only scratch the surface, the Sierra Club failed to 'meaningfully grapple with interlocking systems of power, privilege and oppression, including colonialism and neoliberal globalisation, much less the role of US economic and political policies in creating the very conditions that compel immigration into the USA in the first place.'[20] Other authors have also noted how the mainstream green movement remains predominantly a 'white space,'[21] to the point that green activism itself may even support an anti-immigration argument.[22] Notably, Hultgren's book underlined how well-intentioned (and yet immersed in white privilege) environmental activism in the US is, in fact, reinforcing *exclusionary* forms of political community.[23]

Recognising this potentially conflictual relationship between the green-only and social justice agendas, increasing attention has been paid to the actual political realities of pursuing them simultaneously. For instance, Black et al. provide a deeper understanding of how fusions of climate change and social justice movements can occur, through an empirical case study of climate justice movements in Georgia (the US South).[24] The movement against the Keystone XL Pipeline provided an opportunity for environmental organisations (e.g., the Sierra Club and 350.org) to reach out to a broader audience, achieving more widespread political engagement on environment issues. Its coalition politics – between environmental organisations and communities of colour/frontline communities – became a symbolic moment of solidarity work that has been neglected by mainstream environmentalist movements.[25] As Black et al. notes, '[t]he Keystone pipeline issue provides an ongoing opportunity for purposeful, visible and earnest solidarity with indigenous communities and frontline environmental justice communities.'[26] They conclude that more strategic alliances, which are cognisant of historical geographies and political economies of white supremacy, are essential to formulating more meaningful inter-movement collaborations and coalition politics.

Viability of the green agenda in development-first contexts

At the same time, there have been extended debates on the question of how to make a pro-environment agenda viable for development-first (often referred to as 'emerging economies') contexts, where the attention of governments, nongovernmental organisations, and social activists – who aim to work in the interests of a wider public – is often fixated on issues of poverty and inequality. Especially for African cities, where chronic poverty and social inequality are still a major barrier for any development goals, the aspiration for green or ecological urban futures is often considered a luxury they cannot afford to pursue. Sustainable development studies scholars, particularly those who work in the contexts of emerging nations, argue that the sustainable cities discourse should be more cognizant of the realities of poverty, inequality, and resource scarcity in the Global South.[27]

For environmental sustainability to become a more feasible and operable agenda for development-first cities, it has been argued that there should be a more conscious effort to effectively link it to social development priorities. For instance, a reflection on more sustainable resource use (in terms of energy, water, waste, and sewage – often abbreviated as 'EWWS') is particularly required in meeting the demands of the ever-growing rate of urbanisation and increasing new settlements in poorer areas. Most importantly, cities in emerging economies do not share the concerns of the northern hemisphere's 'shrinking cities'; for cities such as Bangalore or Cape Town, 'growth' is not an objective or pursuit but a challenge to be faced and responded to. The question then is how to talk about the pro-environment imperatives (e.g., we have to conserve nature for its own sake) in contexts where the demand for more decent living conditions is rising exponentially (e.g., the right to water and sanitation for informal settlements). Issues of unemployment and the poor's living conditions are inevitably addressed through the modes of economic development. Under these conditions, caring for the environment is often seen as a secondary concern, or, more simply, just another constraint preventing the pursuit of a life of dignity and hope.

Economic development remains the primary means of escaping financial precarity for urbanising populations around the world. For this reason, scholars have argued it is critical to focus on the pragmatic and tangible/ monetary benefits of pro-environment actions, via considering the actual costs of environmental degradation and their negative effect on developmental growth (e.g., the cost of doing business in an area that suffers from drought will be higher than in areas with a more sustainable ecological infrastructure).[28] In relation to that, other writers have offered a list of urban planning practices where the marriage between pro-environmentalism and development priorities can occur, such as peri-urban agriculture, recycling and waste management, off-grid renewable energy promotion, and empowerment of communities to enhance their immediate environments.[29]

Possibility of convergence between green and inclusivity

In summary, the existing literature on the green versus inequality agendas – and the possibilities of convergence between the two – notes two critical aspects of pursuing both agendas together. First, the works of geographers repeatedly note the importance of a place-based approach to understanding these movements, such as studying the historical or territorial conditions that have influenced their ideological positions and visions. This emphasis is significant to understanding potential coalition strategies with other local movements – it would be difficult to understand the coalition politics behind the movement against the Keystone XL Pipeline without considering the historical background of US South, the contribution of the civil rights movement, and constant local activism against white supremacy and racial inequality. In addition, international development scholars also highlight the role of the local political economy and socioeconomic context in effecting a green agenda in development-first cities. Their argument consists mainly of how the green agenda should be able to respond to/be integrated with more immediate local priorities.

Second, the existing literature on green versus inequality implies the possibilities of linguistic articulation and discourse that accentuate a common ground across different interests and priorities. For instance, a 'jobs versus environment' narrative can effectively be dissolved if it is possible to articulate a logic that underpins the concerns of both environmentalists and social activists. The increasingly popular trend of green-equality fusion in social movements – e.g., the movement against the Keystone XL Pipeline, Blue-Green Alliances, alliance against the US-Mexico border wall, and Green

New Deal – testifies to the power of discourse and articulation that Laclau and Mouffe noted decades ago.[30] Furthermore, development scholars note the opportunities of linking ecological crisis (e.g., severe droughts, flooding, extreme climate events) with a longer-term agenda for sustainable development. Knitting together the moments that highlight resource scarcity or the limits of ecological capacity – via providing a coherent narrative and discourse relevant to the everyday realities of urban stakeholders – appears critical, especially in activating a green agenda in places where social development priorities have to come first.

This chapter responds to these two aspects in the existing literature: the importance of harnessing local historical/socioeconomic contexts to address the green and equality agendas together; and the role of positive discourse and articulation in marrying competing ideals. The chapter details the experiences of Cleveland and Cape Town, two cities that undertake environmentalism at a time when addressing poverty is considered to be more acute.

CLEVELAND: INDUSTRIAL PAST, VACANT LOTS, AND ECONOMIC DEVELOPMENT IN GREEN + INEQUALITY

What is Cleveland's major motivation to go green? Where did it begin, and how is it shaped by contextual and historical specificities along the way? In particular, now that the city aspires to move beyond its decades of economic distress and urban poverty, how do such aspirations affect the future of pro-environment politics? These were the main questions I wanted to explore via in-depth conversations with practitioners broadly working in the fields of urban planning, environmental activism, and development. These conversations led to the past, present, and future of environmentalism being identified as fundamentally a local affair. The historical water pollution concerns from its industrial past – marked by the traumatic fire on the Cuyahoga River in 1969 – resulted in the city's particular interest in and activism about protecting the river and its environment. In the present, the abundance of vacant lots and local poverty concerns are influencing environment planning, in terms of choosing the location of green infrastructure. For the future, the city's aspiration for economic development frames going green as an economic opportunity to create jobs, especially with the city-wide installation of a renewable energy infrastructure.

Industrial past and fire on the Cuyahoga River

One of the most notable features of water management in Cleveland is the Northeast Ohio Regional Sewer District (NEORSD), a regional public utility district responsible for maintaining the quality of water (stormwater runoff and sewage) that goes into Lake Erie and the Cuyahoga River. NEORSD is, as one of the interviewees noted, 'distinctive in that it is a watershed-based district – as opposed to each municipal office being responsible for water quality only within its own jurisdiction'. NEORSD was set up after the devastating Cuyahoga River fire, which was caused by severe industrial pollution. The fire sparked nationwide environmental activism in the US and instigated various federal level environment control initiatives, including the Clean Water Act and Environmental Protection Agency (EPA).

The impacts of the historic event still resonate as a traumatic memory that permeates the city's everyday relationship with water. In Cleveland, it is very common to encounter communication materials that emphasise the need to protect the river and its water (these materials are often installed in public bathrooms, waterfront areas, and stormwater management sites that are open to the public). Most recently, in 2019, the Cuyahoga River celebrated 50 years of clean water since the fire – its new campaign, 'A River Reborn', reminds people of the fire, the history of what caused it, and the need for environmental consciousness. The celebration included a public art performance/exhibition event, Cuyahoga River Lightning, which highlighted the river's role in Cleveland's history of urbanisation and environment politics. As the exhibition explains, '[w]hen an oil slick on the Cuyahoga River caught fire in Cleveland in June 1969, the outrage and soul-searching that ensued contributed to the birth of the environmental movement and the establishment of the EPA. From a nightmarish accident came political action, hope, and improvement'.[31] The exhibition framed the fire as the price that the city had to pay for its rapid industrialisation and development; this price, in the end, sparked a decades-long collective reflection on the fragility of human-nature relationship and the sense of obligation and action to care for the river.

NEORSD is a concrete institutional product of that history – an independent local agency specifically dedicated to monitoring and controlling water quality in the region. Every household in the Cleveland area has to pay sewer district fees that directly fund NEORSD's work, which mainly concerns managing wastewater treatment plants, combined sewer overflow control,[32] and a regional stormwater management programme. But beyond technical infrastructure management, what is particularly characteristic about NEORSD's work is its embeddedness within the Cleveland citizen's everyday socioeconomic affairs of urban living. The fees for an individual household are calculated based on the amount of impervious surface area on its property: those who cause less environmental impact (with fewer impervious surfaces, reducing untreated stormwater overflow) will pay less, while those who have a more developed area (with more impervious surfaces, causing more untreated overflow) will pay more. Furthermore, when building a house or redeveloping a site in Cleveland, the difference between impervious surfaces before and after is calculated and accounted for when determining new stormwater fees; a decrease in impervious surface is eligible for credits (a fee reduction). Credits can be gained for extra efforts at reducing stormwater discharge, via placing rain gardens or rain barrels. This calculation method – fees directly linked to the environmental impact that each household inevitably contributes – instils the idea that one should pay for water pollution and that personal actions will be met by monetary penalties or compensation.

Vacant lots and green infrastructure (GI) as a saviour for disinvested communities

Cleveland has been referred to as a key example of 'shrinking cities',[33] where a previous economic heyday and its subsequent downfall have resulted in an abundant reserve of abandoned houses, vacant lots, and blighted neighbourhoods. These vacant lots are sad symbols of rapid post-industrial decline and often sources of illegal littering and neighbourhood violence. The US financial crisis in 2007 further aggravated the situation, with Cleveland becoming the 'epicentre' of foreclosures in the aftermath of the subprime mortgage crisis,[34] and having to establish a land bank to manage vacant lots and properties. Cuyahoga Land Bank, a non-profit, government-purposed entity founded in 2009, works specifically on strategically acquiring blighted properties and repurposing them for productive use. There are currently 3,000 vacant lots still waiting to be reclaimed in the Cuyahoga County (100,000 vacant and abandoned homes Ohio state-wide). One key solution to make better use of vacant lots is transforming them into green infrastructure (GI) projects, which can function as community gardens, urban farms, and stormwater management sites. This not only serves ecological purposes but enhances quality of life factors through curbing neighbourhood violence and health hazards.[35] It has been empirically proven that well-maintained green spaces can help reduce crime; furthermore, several research efforts have revealed that the exposed soil (of vacant lots) can create substantial health hazards,[36] and new green space maintenance/gardening efforts can prevent this risk.

The most critical aspect of turning vacant lots into green infrastructure is their location. While properties in the traditionally well-off white suburbs (in the west side of the city) can be suitable for rehabilitation and seeking new owners, abandoned properties in the east are often subject to demolition and neglect, affecting nearby residents' financial status and safety as it inevitably attracts crime and violence. The historical disinvestment in the eastern African American suburbs is perhaps not news, but the foreclosure crisis and subsequent further blights worsened residents' resentment that their neighbourhoods had been forgotten by the government. An interviewee, a life-long Cleveland resident, explained that: 'the eastern suburbs have been economically disenfranchised for so long that they fear that the city representatives are not representing their interests ... people still feel forgotten and excluded, especially seeing the city's resources being spent elsewhere'.

Addressing this feeling of exclusion has been a central task of Cleveland's Community Development Corporations (CDCs). Particularly since the post-industrial population exodus of the 1970s, Cleveland's strong network of CDCs has played a significant role in coordinating community development and activism.[37] Between 1950 and 1990, Cleveland's population dropped by 45 per cent, from 914,808 to 505,616. This had severe and lasting economic effects, with reduced local government spending and a declining population hitting the African American neighbourhoods on the east side especially hard. In response, a network of east-side CDCs was formed with the explicit aim of improving neighbourhood conditions and negotiating the antagonistic sentiments of distressed residents. Contesting the city's primary investment in downtown renewal through the 1980s, CDCs acted directly on behalf of residents, advocating for improved neighbourhood living conditions and a renewed focus on targeted economic development.[38]

The strong presence of these CDCs – as historical institutions for grassroots organisation – has shaped the way that GI projects have unfolded in

Cleveland.[39] CDCs reappropriated the city's increasing interests in sustainability, climate change, and flood mitigation in a way that serves their own primary purpose, which is the economic development and rehabilitation of their neighbourhoods. In collaboration with NEORSD, which has consistent access to funding dedicated to stormwater management (through the mandatory contribution from individual households, as noted above), CDCs – especially those in the eastern suburbs – work specifically on maximising the economic and social benefits of the GI's physical presence in their neighbourhoods. For instance, one of NEORSD's flagship actions has been The Green Ambassador Slavic Village Demonstration Project, which is essentially about greening and beautifying an abandoned lot into a community garden with a capacity to infiltrate 200,000 gallons of stormwater per year. Slavic Village, located in the southeast of Cleveland, suffers from foreclosed houses, empty lots, neighbourhood violence, and a lack of economic activities. Slavic Village Development Corporation (SVD; the Slavic Village CDC) hence saw this GI project as an opportunity to rebrand the neighbourhood as a vibrant 'eco-district' that could attract new capital investments and economic development.[40] In return, Slavic Village's strong community engagement and SVD's established trust with local residents was seen as an advantage by NEORSD, as maintaining parcel-level rain gardens requires collective action and initiative within the neighbourhood. Similar examples include the Fleet Avenue Green Infrastructure project, Fairhill-MLK project, and Urban Agriculture Innovation Zone, all of which are located in historically disinvested neighbourhoods, in an attempt to showcase the social benefits of green urbanism.

Turning vacant lots into green opportunities has been popular in typical rust-belt cities in the US. However, what makes Cleveland particularly interesting is the active highlighting of the socioeconomic benefits of GI by CDCs. Above all, CDC participation resulted in the prioritisation of historically disinvested areas as testing sites for GI projects. Second, and equally important, CDCs have been able to capture and divert what has been designated 'stormwater funding' towards greening vacant lots that directly service neighbourhoods' socioeconomic vitality. Capitalising on the city-wide effort to mitigate climate change and NEORSD's constant funding for stormwater management, CDCs in Cleveland are going green not necessarily for the environment's sake, but due to their own internal aspirations for further economic growth and neighbourhood revitalisation.[41]

Figure 4.3 A community-led art and gardening project in Slavic Village in Cleveland. © Ihnji Jon.

Promise of renewable energy and green economy in rust-belt cities

After in-depth discussions with ten key informants working in the field of urban planning, environmental activism, and development, what stood out was how Cleveland's pursuit of a green agenda is primarily driven by its aspirations for job creation and economic growth. The 'Sustainable Cleveland' campaign started in 2009, as part of an effort to revive its economy. As one of the interviewees put it,

> Sustainable Cleveland was launched by the [then and current] mayor in 2009 in the middle of economic recession. The most important element was its piece on sustainable economy. The city saw 'sustainability' as a good foundation that could be used for different objectives, especially for economic development and sustainable water use, although now we're leaning more toward advancing equity.

It appears that Cleveland's priority cannot be addressing climate change alone, especially given that the city struggles with a high poverty rate:

> Cities like Cleveland cannot be compared to New York, which obviously has much more resources to spend on climate resilience. For us, it's more about human vulnerability and providing economic opportunities for low-income population, for their human resilience.

It is not surprising, then, to see 'local green job creation and sustainable economic development' proclaimed as one of the key benefits of taking climate action in Cleveland. In its new Climate Action Plan (CAP), pursuing renewable energy and a carbon neutrality objective is not framed as merely good for the environment; the argument is greatly weighted on the side of its economic benefits, such as manufacturing jobs for electric vehicles or construction jobs for green buildings/energy-efficiency retrofits. Climate change and the global imperative to reduce emissions are framed as an opportunity for reimagining sources of future economic growth rather than a constraint that deters business activities. As CAP specifies, '[t]he Sustainable Cleveland 2019 initiative is, at its core, focused on sustainable economic development. This plan builds off lessons learned since 2009 by prioritising actions where business and government can work together to support green job growth'.[42]

Out of necessity and the city's soul-searching effort, Cleveland's CAP is a well-articulated, all-around plan. In trying to find overlapping areas that tick all boxes, its cross-cutting priorities consider job creation, equity concerns, citizen engagement, and the environment. CAP makes a business case for the city-wide goal of energy efficiency – for instance, scaling up green building practices offers employment opportunities for contractors working in non-residential heating, ventilation, and cooling (HVAC), who can retrofit buildings and homes to save energy and the budget spent on energy. The average wages of these 'green jobs, good jobs' are specifically highlighted: HVAC contractors can earn $60,200 per year, and renewable energy sector jobs have an average annual wage of $84,500.[43] The list of potential local green industries is expansive, including manufacturing wind turbines and turbine generator set units, storage batteries, and lighting equipment. The promise of the green economy in Cleveland seems to be coming true, as the city reports that there were 1,321 renewable-energy jobs and 10,967 energy-efficiency jobs in Cuyahoga County in 2018.

As for the equity lens, the city also aims to make sure that these new clean energy jobs are available for low-income communities. An interviewee said:

> Yes, we're looking at climate, but we can't divorce that from uplifting lives of underserved communities. How to provide job opportunities, how to ensure that low-income households have the access to that power [of renewable energy], are really at the core of what we do for climate.

In a context where urban poverty and inequality pose an existential question for whatever project the city embarks on (and directs its resources towards), initiatives for the environment cannot be separated from citizens' everyday concerns. Reviving manufacturing and construction jobs through the new wave of clean energy is one of the key intersecting moments that the city tries to embrace.

In that sense, it is almost as if the global 'sustainability' mandate is giving the purpose, identity, and hope that the city needs following its lost glory days of the manufacturing economy. Or perhaps that sustainability itself can act as a catalyst for bringing those days back again. The city's nongovernment sector takes comfort in the rosy side of this, focusing on building offshore wind farms and more solar field installations. As one interview participant puts it,

> Offshore wind is going to be a big emerging industry in the US, especially in the East Coast, so we're trying to catalyse that moment with the assets that we have in the region . . . In fact, Ohio is uniquely positioned, as we already have manufacturing for clean energy component parts, for solar, for wind, and for energy-efficiency insulation; [so] it's really a matter of leveraging all of that supply chain, to advance the industry here, locally.

Cleveland has ambitious plans to install wind turbines off the cost of Lake Erie, which would be the first freshwater wind farm in North America and in the Great Lakes region. All of these pro-environmental initiatives now appear to be working in favour of city branding and marketing, repositioning Cleveland as a green city with a bright future: 'The intention is to be a demonstration to help the rest of the country and region to understand that we can position Cleveland as an epicentre of the wind industry for offshore wind generation'. While the pursuit of a green economy may be a common thing for all rust-belt cities hoping to get their jobs back, Cleveland's active communication strategy, folding these socioeconomic concerns under the umbrella of sustainability, is particularly deliberate and purposeful.

The story of Cleveland teaches us that, to achieve an effective marriage of the green and equity agendas, the motivations for environmental sustainability have to be situated within the history and particularities of local contexts. The role of linguistic articulation and creating effective narratives that justify such a marriage should also be noted, something that was effectuated by the planners and environmentalists in Cleveland. Below, I discuss how a similar argument can be made about the environmental politics of Cape Town, despite its different 'developmental status'.

CAPE TOWN: POST-APARTHEID POLITICS, DROUGHTS, AND POVERTY RELIEF IN GREEN + EQUALITY

Poverty, inequality, and the spatial segregation that systematically hides them are perhaps the most pressing challenges that Cape Town faces today. Driving around the west side[44] of the city near water and mountains, one hardly faces the reality that this is one of the most unequal cities in the world. The legacy of apartheid is not only lived through spatial form, but also through the status of unemployment and multi-generational deprivation. 'It's jobs, jobs, jobs', said Edgar Pieterse, director of the African Centre for Cities at the University of Cape Town, stressing the importance of addressing economic questions in African countries.[45] The issues of unemployment and impoverishment, especially in African cities where the public sector is often short of political and financial resources, are materialised as mushrooming (informal) settlements and lack of essential services, such as water, sanitation, and electricity. Given that more than 20 per cent of Capetonians live in these settlements, how do you even begin to introduce matters of the environment when basic living conditions are still not assured?

The recent severe drought event in 2017–18, which instigated a well-mediatised campaign ('Day Zero'), seems to have had positive impacts on advancing and mainstreaming the discourses on ecology and nature, with people having experienced resource scarcity and the value of water in their daily functioning. My visit to Cape Town and conversations with key informants were intended to better understand (1) the history of environmental activism in Cape Town; (2) the linkage between the water crisis and a more generic sustainable development agenda; and (3) the relevance of and strategies for pursuing a green economy in a development-first context.

The influence of post-apartheid politics in environmentalism

While the Day Zero water crisis has been widely covered in academic research,[46] what has been less discussed, especially in the field of urban planning, is the history of environmentalism in Cape Town and how it has been intertwined with the post-apartheid political economy. Neely's investigation on the Working for Water (WfW) programme (and the politics behind environmental activism in post-apartheid Africa) remains a pivotal work that captures what it is like to actualise pro-environmental initiatives in Africa, with an added emphasis on economic development and job creation.[47] WfW is a state-funded project that aims to preserve local biodiversity and ecosystem dynamics via clearing invasive alien plants. These plants, a legacy of colonialism and the plantation economy, are reported to be harmful not only to local species but also South Africa's water resources, as they tend to soak up/consume more water, affecting aquifer recharge and river flow. The local scientific community and biologists, concerned with the status of Cape Floristic Region's unique biodiversity, have been making a case for such programmes since the early 1990s. Their efforts gained momentum in 1995, when the newly elected post-apartheid government saw this programme as an opportunity to generate new, unskilled, labour-intensive jobs for the non-white poor. WfW received significant government funding and proved tremendously successful in terms of its positive impacts on ecosystem services and social development.[48]

What made this programme particularly well known and popular was its success in marrying ecological benefits with poverty relief. Local ecologists have been particularly strategic in the pursuit of their pro-environmental agenda, creating a well-articulated linkage and relationship between science, management, and poverty relief rather than talking about 'pure' ecological purposes.[49] In that regard, the programme's renowned success reveals how environmentalism in South Africa is newly positioning itself in the post-apartheid era. With changes in national funding priorities, which now focus more on doing justice to history (often through providing more economic opportunities for the historically deprived), aiding the environment must be integrated with socioeconomic development priorities. WfW symbolises what kind of pro-environmental initiatives can actually work in development-first contexts; with the special attention paid by scientists and research communities to issues of social justice and equity, framed in close relation to (and not separated from) ecological motives, eventually paying off in tangible outcomes.[50]

Such 'impacts of post-apartheid politics on environmentalism' – especially with regard to its pressure on creating labour-intensive jobs for the historically deprived – are still present today. The Nature Conservancy recently released a business case report for its Greater Cape Town Water Fund, which essentially argues for the financial benefits of investments

Figure 4.4 Cape Town, thanks to its unique location that allows different soil types and micro-climates, is home to distinctive sets of vegetations. The city has traditionally been deeply invested in the protection of its biodiversity and environmental systems that support it. Environmentalists in the region have found a way to link the value of biodiversity with economic benefits (e.g., tourism) as well as job-creation potentials for non-white poor via invasive species removal programmes. © Ihnji Jon.

made in clearing invasive species. At the heart of their ecologist agenda is a strenuous effort to formulate discourses around the *economic value* of nature conservation and its job-creating potential as a growing industry. Above all, there is an emphasis on the argument that restoration interventions typically require high labour work.[51] The efforts to link jobs with nature conservation go beyond removing invasive species. Especially for youth education and professional training, nature conservation is associated with the tourism industry so as to be considered part of the 'green economy' arena. The argument is that the beautiful landscapes in the Cape Town region are not only an important economic asset that attracts tourists, but are also the setting for the headquarters of multinational tech companies that value lifestyle amenities and benefits. In that sense, initiatives for conserving nature are the source of an economy that is, at its core, 'green'. The Cape Town Environmental Education Trust (CTEET), a public benefit organisation (PBO),[52] actively organises youth education and skills training programmes that usher disadvantaged youth into the field of nature conservation. 'Giving hope to Cape Town's youth to access jobs in the Green Economy', claims CTEET, in its articulation of what it does. The organisation offers nature conservation learnerships, especially for low-income youth, to address the significant skills shortage and unemployment issues in non-white communities – the products of systemic racial and spatial segregation during the apartheid era.

Drought crisis, utility provisions, and sustainable development

Cape Town has experienced consecutive droughts in the past,[53] but perhaps the most mediatised drought was the recent 2017–18 Day Zero crisis, where the city officiated the countdown towards the estimated date that its water supply would run out. There is no debate that Day Zero helped remind Capetonians of the city's resource scarcity and their dependency on the natural environment. But how did this crisis influence the conversations around the green agenda and its relationship with the equity agenda? Did it exacerbate the tension? Or could it possibly have offered a way for reconciliation? My in-depth discussions with practitioners were built around the question of whether the drought crisis can lead to more interest in longer-term sustainable development, which considers not only matters of 'the environment' but also more equitable access to resources.

Above all, it was noted that the water crisis underlined the status of inequality and the everyday struggles of the poor, a reality that the affluent Capetonians often forget due to the city's historical spatial segregation. The extreme drought event cracked open the existing legacy of deep social and racial inequalities, as marginalised communities (often living in informal settlements) fought for their right to water. The general sentiment was that the drought finally offered an opportunity for middle-class Capetonians to realise what it is like to struggle for everyday access to water, which has always been an issue for residents in informal settlements. As Rodina puts it: 'is it possible that the experience of wealthier communities in having to live on 50L per person per day (for those that did try) will engender the sense of empathy and deeper acknowledgement of the water inequality that is otherwise often unseen?'[54]

In that sense, the drought crisis brought to the government's attention the unequal access to basic infrastructure and the requirement that these urgent needs be responded to. As one interviewee noted:

> Crisis moments point out where inequalities are and where our priority should be. You can't have sustainable resource provision if you have unequal service provision. We're working on the idea of cross-subsidizing electricity and water, using the fees from high-income households or engaging with the private sector.

In the end, the drought might have had a positive impact on making everyday inequalities more visible, inspiring more government resources to address them. Cape Town recently published a new water strategy,[55] and it is clear that its vision recognises water inequities and the urgent need to work with informal settlements, especially through improving access to water and sanitation for these vulnerable communities. The strategy claims that the city's 'water will be managed in a way that is equitable, transparent, and inclusive'; to do so, it will ensure all citizens have 'the human right to water and a safe environment, including access to basic sanitation'[56] and that the city will 'work with communities in informal settlements and with other stakeholders to improve the daily experience of access to water and sanitation.'[57]

On the other hand, the shock of the water crisis also led to more general conversations around resource scarcity and how the city can prepare for such uncertainty. The crisis revealed the limits of centralised utility provisions, resulting in renewed discussions on whether the city needs to seek new ways of procuring and managing water and energy. The city is dependent on national government infrastructure to acquire and distribute water and electricity. Regarding water, three out of the six dams that Cape Town uses are owned by the national government; while for electricity, the city relies on the operations of ESKOM, the South African national electricity public utility (Electricity Supply Commission, also known by its Afrikaans name 'EVKOM'). In fact, prior to the drought crisis, the city had been experiencing several power outages (that lasted two to six hours) which negatively affected its economy and the operation of small and medium-sized enterprises (SMEs). The general unreliability of centralised energy management triggered the city's intention to explore more decentralised sources of energy and possibly achieve some degree of independence through renewables (e.g., solar, wind).

In South Africa, local governments are not permitted to pursue their own electricity procurement or distribution (they all have to rely on ESKOM); in this context, the renewable energy sector has been gaining ground especially for its direct access to energy sources and localised/shorter circuit for distribution. Overall, the underlying assumption behind these efforts was the increasing uncertainty of resource scarcity and the potential advantages of pursuing decentralised models of utility provisions. The drought crisis again strengthened this assumption and the city's motivation to lead towards renewable energy and low-impact developments. Ultimately, the Day Zero experience has become an important opportunity and useful segue for the renewable energy (and green technology) sector to proclaim and justify its relevancy. An interviewee remarked that: 'During the Day Zero crisis, people really felt the reality of resource scarcity . . . and from that angle of resource scarcity, we were able to link the water crisis with the energy crisis and talk about what green technologies can offer in times of uncertainty'.

What would be the implications of pursuing decentralised energy procurement for urban inequality? There are, in short, pros and cons to this. The debates on the city-scale promotion of an 'off-the-grid' model are instigating conversations around the intersection between green technology and its potential (positive and negative) influence on inequality. The 'off-the-grid' model – and the green technology that allows it – is 'good' in the sense that it can increase the general resource/cost-efficiency of households and businesses. They will be able to acquire and manage their own energy (e.g., via solar panels) and water infrastructure (e.g., via rain barrels and independent grey water management), and in doing so will be more conscious of how they use and treat energy and water. Furthermore, green technology promises something useful and interesting to informal settlements and their future pathways towards more accessible energy and sanitation. Especially in the contexts of new settlements in the north and east of Cape Town, where the centralised government resource infrastructure often fails to reach,[58] decentralised energy procurement and water management can actually become a more realistic alternative than waiting for an official extension of that infrastructure.[59] 'Alternative resource delivery' is increasingly becoming a trend, where a PBO, such as GreenCape,[60] finds another way to deliver key infrastructure to informal settlements via engaging with the private sector.

For instance, GreenCape worked closely with an informal settlement community in Witsand, with its survey results revealing that what the inhabitants most wanted was street lighting; as the lack of light at night attracted violence and crime. To find a more practical financial solution (without seeking direct public investment – which is often lengthy and limited), GreenCape arranged a creative financial model: a private telecom company helped build a solar-powered street lighting infrastructure, which is paid for by settlement residents through their collective mobile data plans. In the face of the rapid rate of urbanisation and growth in Cape Town's suburbs, coupled with the fact that local governments in South Africa often have limited resources and power, such alternative service provisions seem to be emerging as a new hope.[61]

However, the 'off-the-grid' model can have negative implications for the maintenance of city-wide infrastructure. During the drought, one of the interviewees noted, 'some households drilled boreholes in their backyards to access the aquifer directly, which can be detrimental to the region-wide ecological infrastructure if they occur haphazardly without a larger-scale systemic management'. Also, higher utility fees from upper middle-income households subsidise the distribution of services to lower-income households. Given that these green technologies still remain expensive, if those who can afford to install them opt out of the city-wide system, the city revenue will decline and so will its financial capacity to invest in the new infrastructure development (maintenance of old infrastructure, such as dams) it desperately needs (to respond to its urban growth rate). Consequently, the city is now trying to come up with a new financial model that can charge base infrastructure fees for all households, separate from the actual usage tariff. That way, people can stay 'on the grid' with what can be considered a backup battery cost, and the city can retain its consistent funding for managing its utility infrastructure. One interviewee asked

> How do you create a financial model that basically enables the city's revenue, while at the same time making green technology sufficiently attractive for people to take on? . . . that's the key question that the city tries to resolve. Our argument is that rather than losing all customers who will start defecting from the grid system [with solar PVs],[62] it's better for the city to embrace the new technology and mitigate its potential losses by coming up with a new financial model. Plus, 21 townships[63] [in Cape Town] now allow rooftop PVs, and the effect of such a growing market will soon help achieve economies of scale [i.e., small infrastructure fee charges will accumulate over time with the growth of users].

'Sustainable development' has always been an oxymoron in some sense, but in Cape Town this is especially so given that 'growth' is not an objective but rather the reality that the city has to face. To create jobs and be able to provide utility services for those who currently live without them, economic development and growth is an imperative. One key contradiction in pursuing sustainable development in Cape Town is navigating the tension between using resources for growth (for a shorter time frame) and being conscious of resource limits (for a longer time frame). An interviewee, an engineer and former resident of the eastern suburbs, observed:

> Environmentalism has always been a privileged, white people thing. I'm not entirely on board with the idea of leaving our aquifer alone for ecological reasons. People live without sanitation, and we need resources, and we know that we have a huge water source underneath us . . . we have to think about environmental needs together with social and economic needs. Yes, climate change is a problem, but people need to survive, and we need to use the resources to live in a decent human condition.

The clash between ecological values and the right to have an acceptable standard of living is clear; some of the direct conflicts occur in actual urban planning practices, where people try to establish new (informal) settlements directly above the aquifer, which the city tries to discourage for ecological reasons.

While such ironies of sustainable development present significant challenges for urban planning/development professionals working in Cape Town, their incessant efforts to create a new discourse of possibility deserve recognition. Capitalising on the traumatic collective experience of Day Zero, they have been able to reorient 'water' discussion to a more generic 'resource scarcity' issue, interjecting the message that the crisis was about not only water but also about balancing short-term needs (e.g., assuring decent living for all) and long-term accountability (e.g., the ecological health of the environment that assures long-term sustainability). In these dialogues around acknowledging the limits of nature and the need for collective behavioural change, the topic of 'utility provision' seems to act as a middle ground potentially allowing coalescence between the green and equity agendas. The water crisis laid bare the realities of what township residents live through every day; and the urgent need for more equal access to water, energy, and sanitation was communicated and discussed more openly thanks to the wide mediatisation of the crisis. Such discussions have led the city and other organisations to explore more decentralised models of utility services and delivery, which green technology can speak to and offer its technical advantages for. Especially when the rate of urbanisation slips out of government control – and the resulting pressure on the government to catch up on extending the remits of its infrastructure – utility service provision can become a medium through which 'equity' values (e.g., equal access to resources) and 'green' ideals (e.g., low-carbon technologies) can be reconciled.

'Going green' as a growth strategy for the historically disadvantaged?

About 45 km north of Cape Town city centre, there lies Atlantis, a planned suburban district built by the apartheid government to relocate non-white South Africans away from Cape Town. Initially designed as a 'model apartheid city' ('coloured[64] dream city'), Atlantis was a manufacturing town built exclusively for 'coloured people' to live and work. The very birth of Atlantis symbolises the ideology of apartheid, or segregated spatial development. As Cape Town underwent massive development pressure, with its growing manufacturing industry and population density, the apartheid regime, in its effort to keep Cape Town white, invented the concept of a new town with factory jobs where it could 'dump' and forget about non-white people. Due to its distance from the metropolitan area, Atlantis residents needed a source of economy within the site. Consequently, the Atlantis Development Committee offered incentive packages (e.g., low-cost loans, low company taxes, cash grants for relocation costs) to industrialists to open new factories that could pump out labour-intensive jobs.[65] With these concessions, more than a hundred factories moved in by 1980, and Atlantis grew quickly in the first ten years after its establishment in 1975.

However, these factories turned out to be primarily low-skill, light manufacturing industries (mostly textiles, clothing, and furniture), which are highly vulnerable to economic recession. Most of these companies took advantage of a seven-year concession package with minimal capital investment and could easily move elsewhere when this ran out – Atlantis without government incentives was not an ideal location for businesses. Eventually, it was no longer economically sustainable on its own. After democratisation and the beginning of the post-apartheid era, its future became even more bleak, as the very conception of this new town was funded through the apartheid regime's motivation for spatial segregation. Lacking support from the post-apartheid government, which was occupied dealing with other issues of the apartheid legacy, Atlantis was largely forgotten. By 1994, it was plagued with poverty, unemployment, and isolation.[66] The rise of Asia as the global centre of manufacturing and the global financial crisis in 2007–9 further aggravated the situation, leaving Atlantis and its surrounding informal settlements (such as Witsand) significantly disenfranchised. Today, Atlantis is the most staggering material proof of the apartheid ideology and its operation, the legacy of which still lives on in the poverty of its remaining residents (close to 60,000).

In 2017, the City of Cape Town and the Western Cape Provincial Government – with the intellectual contribution of GreenCape – finally came to a decision to turn things around, establishing a Special Economic Zone (SEZ) in Atlantis.[67] Led by Mayor De Lille, the first non-white mayor in the history of Cape Town, the project claimed to be committed to social development and job creation in the area. In this context, the green economy is being hailed as the ultimate panacea: the new SEZ aims to host exclusively greentech industries and attract *labour-intensive* and yet specialised manufacturing jobs. It is essentially about creating manufacturing jobs, but ones that are more value-added and future-forward in terms of: (1) skilled jobs that are sustainable in the long term; and (2) keeping up with the global market for going green, especially the clean technology market. Currently, the manufacturers of wind turbine towers, geotextiles (permeable fabrics used for stormwater infrastructure), and insulation products (double-glazed windows) have been involved in the development, which has created about 300 new jobs, mostly for Atlantis residents. In the future, it aims to attract more diverse green technologies, including electric vehicles, biofuels, materials recycling, and solar panels/green building materials manufacturing – with the goal of creating 3,000 direct jobs in the zone by 2030. The establishment of Atlantis SEZ and its purposeful focus on green technology has one primary objective: poverty relief, through local jobs for its residents – whose destiny has been shaped by the history of Cape Town and the legacy of apartheid. Specifically for that reason, one key function justifying the Atlantis SEZ is providing skills development training for residents, through partnerships with youth organisations, high schools, and local technical and vocational education training colleges. From the initial establishment through the continuing development, the project has been working closely with communities (Atlantis residents),[68] with the term 'inclusive economy' a key pillar of its rationale.[69]

Ultimately, the green economy serves as a beacon of hope for youth in the area, whose horizons are often limited to their immediate surroundings, which present harsh conditions. As an interviewee reported:

> Young people in this area have a very grim outlook on the future.[70] With the prospects of the green economy, we would like to offer a message of hope that there can be a way toward a better future, a kind of vision that answers to their questions. Showing that vision is very important, because hope drives so much. Hope can't feed people, but it can create the circumstances where jobs and economy can land. It feels liberating and so positive to be able to do that.

The Atlantis SEZ is still in the very early stages of development, so it is hard to know whether the rosy promise of the green economy can be fulfilled, with going green a pragmatic strategy for advancing a social development agenda for the historically disenfranchised. But the promise is there; the coalescence between the green and equity agendas made possible through the job creation capacity of green technology. And the promise feels real, because it is situated within a specific local political economy, capitalising on the specific historical, political, and economical context of that particular site.

Cleveland's journey of environment politics began with an environmental disaster after decades of rapid industrialisation. A devastating river fire left a long-lasting legacy through both an institutional structure – the establishment of NEORSD and mandatory household fees for water management – and collective memory/trauma affecting individual behaviour. The disaster helped instil the message that polluting is costly and that anyone who does so will have to pay for the environmental consequences. Building on this history and a widespread culture that understands 'the environment' as an integral element of everyday life, NEORSD has been working to preserve water through GI projects. But these efforts could not be separated from the socioeconomic dynamics that Cleveland underwent during its post-industrial decline. These environmental initiatives had to be situated within the local social needs of neighbourhoods suffering from population exodus, vacant lots, lack of economic activities, and the resulting violence and crime. GI projects, apart from their ecological benefits, can offer social and economic side benefits, which was why they were so well received and supported by the CDCs, with a strong presence in local politics of representation in Cleveland. A comparable pattern appears in Cleveland's active interest in renewable energy – wind turbines and solar panels are pursued not necessarily for the sake of the environment but because of their job-creation potential.

Cape Town's environmental politics have always been inseparable from its obsession with creating labour-intensive jobs. This is mainly because of the historical legacy of apartheid, which systematically prevented the education of 'the Coloureds', resulting in continuing social inequalities and multigenerational economic disadvantages, especially for non-white Capetonians, who often have to reside in survival-first conditions. To lift them out of poverty, creating relatively low-skill, labour-intensive jobs for the historically deprived has been the major post-apartheid policy priority.

Environmentalists and scientific communities manipulated this inclination in the 2000s by proposing that removing invasive species makes not only a good pro-ecology case but also a good business case. More recently, the shock of the Day Zero water crisis has also helped push pro-environment discourses forward. The existing sustainable development advocates were able to capture that moment as an effective segue to introduce more generic resource scarcity issues and the practical advantages of green technologies in facing them. Green technologies are not only environmentally friendly but also contribute to the city's competencies in response to increasing climate uncertainties – via more decentralised models of energy/water procurement and distribution. With the city under immense pressure to deliver utility services to informal settlements, which is fundamentally the product of social inequality and unequal access to basic resources, there are serious attempts to harness renewable energy and green technology in a way that helps the everyday lives of the poor.

In terms of how the green economy is perceived in these two cities, there is an uncanny resemblance between Cleveland and Cape Town, with renewable energy and green technology industries embraced as an opportunity to bring back *labour-intensive manufacturing jobs*. As noted above, Cape Town's history of spatial segregation has left the city with deep economic disparity and social inequality issues, which are still reflected in the everyday realities of non-white Capetonians. In that context, creating labour-intensive jobs is the government's top priority, and it appears that renewable energy and related green technology industries may offer relevant prospects. Especially for Atlantis, which used to be a strategic centre of manufacturing industries, its historical place identity and its residents' rapport with that history seem attuned to the journey towards a green manufacturing economy. A similar story unfolded in Cleveland, where the city tried to harness its past history as the centre of industrialisation (especially car manufacturing) to propose a green economy as a tailored opportunity to reviving manufacturing jobs. Its geographical location (the Great Lakes area) is also used to justify the potential growth for wind turbine energy and how this can position Cleveland as an epicentre of the offshore wind energy industry. This illustrates how the promise of the green economy feels more tangible – as opposed to an abstract political argument – when it actively harnesses a territory's specific historical backgrounds, contexts, and concerns. In short, the stories of Cleveland and Cape Town teach us that the coalescence of the green and equity agendas is possible only when the green agenda becomes a geographically grounded, politically present, place-based *local affair* that effectively responds to the socioeconomic life of everyday citizens.

DISCUSSION: POLICY LANDSCAPES
OF SITUATED ENVIRONMENTALISM

While Urban Political Ecology (UPE) tradition has accentuated how urban policies are subject to the overarching system of global political economy (i.e. capitalism), cultural geographers have introduced the concept of 'landscape' in which human agency, when enacted in conversation with the social environment that it finds itself in, can be pronounced in a way that cannot be captured by all-pervasive economic logics. Humans are economic and narrative/mythical animals, and subsequently, our will to act, as well as its meaning, have to be interpreted not in isolation but as a situated component within the surrounding landscape – continually evolving through new serendipitous encounters with technologies, cultures, and the changing physical environment.

If we could apply such concept of 'landscape' in policy studies, I would argue, we would be able to behold new political possibilities where local social actors can successfully mediate the dissonance between 'ecology first' and 'social issues first' arguments. Such landscapes would entail, as we have seen through our cases in Cleveland and Cape Town: water, plants, extreme climate events, green technologies, built environment/urban designs, political/social tensions physically present through spatial segregation, and so on. But what can orchestrate these material facets of each local landscape is cultural and political narratives, which are invented and deployed by humans, as actors of language and generators of new logics. Therefore, the studies of 'policy landscapes', as I showcased here in this chapter, have to focus on how certain policies and their discourses come to life by the practices of local actors who exercise their agency in conversation with their situated landscape – via harnessing the surrounding materiality of things and places in which they operate. Such studies would have the most significance in situated environmentalism, where the competition between different epistemologies of temporalities (i.e. immediate economic relief vs. longer-term ecological concerns) is the most acute. This contention, policy landscapers would believe, could be resolved by the creation of new narratives and cultural interventions concocted by human social actors (I delve further into this problem in Chapter 5).

What 'policy landscape' reveals then is the possibility of 'promise' that different actors are committing to one another – here, now, you and me. Hannah Arendt has famously claimed that 'making a promise' is the only thing that could help us navigate the sea of uncertainties, because of its phenomenological insertion of 'now' animated by interpersonal agreements. Such mutual promise takes different shapes and forms, either as manifestos or contracts, but the most important quality about promise is its performative capacity to deflect the linear trajectory of time – thanks to its resolute intention to incur a positive change. If 'future' is not a fixed story but a possibility of multiple storylines, their trajectories are still in the process of being contested and remade in the present. Rather than relying on existing explanatory frameworks to populate the same stories everywhere, policy landscapers would embrace such open-ended prospects of interhuman communication and their spatial potential to launch a different future through collective actions of here and now.[71]

CONCLUSION

I chose to study Cleveland and Cape Town in order to propose that the issues of 'First World' and 'Third World' cities are not necessarily different (hence no more exoticisation of the Global South). This proposition suggests that cities can learn from each other's journeys and experiences regardless of differences in overall developmental priorities. Before going into the field, I surveyed academic literature on environment politics, planning, and geography, to more broadly overview when 'green city' and 'inclusive city' become two competing ideals. In attempts to broaden the scope of EJ literature (beyond its renowned critique on capitalist-driven urbanisation processes), I focused on identifying the potential possibilities of convergence between environmentalism and social justice visions.

My field visits and interviews in Cleveland and Cape Town were designed to uncover the history of environmentalism in both cities as well as the local practitioners' perspectives on the potential marriage of the green and equity agendas. In the end, the convergence of the two pursuits can occur when they together constitute a concrete vision that is not only customised to local geographic/historical contexts but also ready to positively affect the material lives of people. Comparing these cities helps us understand the specificities of local histories and their impacts on both cities' efforts to marry environmentalism with addressing inequality. At the same time, however, similar patterns emerged. Both Cleveland and Cape Town have experienced how the impact of disasters affects social perceptions of environmentalism. Likewise, both cities have focused on developing a renewable energy sector, positioning it as a generator of jobs rather than a partisan shibboleth. These shared patterns reveal how urban governance challenges in the 'First World' are not necessarily different from those in development-first contexts. In the current globally networked system of finance and climate, there exists a range of possibilities for learning and knowledge exchange across cities that have benefited from or been disenfranchised by diverging development histories.

The major challenge for environment politics today is, undoubtedly, to narrow the *time gap* between more immediate socioeconomic concerns and longer-term ecological concerns. While this mismatch remains daunting, hope lies in the willingness and capacity of social actors who can create discourses, linkages, and articulations proclaiming the pragmatic benefits of environmentalism; effectively harnessing each of their unique territorial experiences and histories. Turning local worries into opportunities to advance environmentalism – using the power of discourse and culture – is the promise of localised environment politics. Such situated experiences manifest 'policy landscapes' in which constituting agents continually generate new realities through their everyday encounters with new ideas, peoples, and resources. These moments of policy landscapes that practitioners reinvent anew are temporary and speculative; but their everyday practices, both conceptually intentional and materially grounded, contribute to the actualisation of a 'community' with political possibilities.

5

Cities and complexity: Linking 'the social' with 'the environmental'

We cannot just be environmentalists . . . We need an integrative political thought, which necessitates a foundation in which the human and the natural are not just linked because they benefit one another, but where they share a common core and are present within one another: the human is not just a part of the nature, the nature lives interior of the human, like the individual is not just a part of the society, but the society lives interior of the individual.[1]

– Edgar Morin

The scope of 'history' is notorious: it is the deeds enacted, the tragedies undergone; and it is the human comment, record, and the interpretation that inevitably follow. Objectively, history takes in rivers, mountains, fields and forests, laws and institutions; subjectively it includes the purposes and plans, the desires and emotions, through which these things are administered and transformed.[2]

– John Dewey

In the previous chapters, I demonstrated how cities, as local sites empirically experiencing climate change, are embarking on the path towards more ecologically and socially inclusive futures. Although I was able to show how government officials and environmental activists are striving to inculcate environmentalism into those who are not necessarily interested in nature, the question remains as to whether the 'complex systems approach' can provide a meaningful advantage for cities taking on environmental actions.

In Chapter 2, I proposed the 'urban scale' as an adequate scale for taking environmental actions for three main reasons: (1) cities are small enough to be 'graspable', which allows them to develop shared material experiences of feedback from nature; (2) cities are intensive enough to possess the degree of influence and leadership, given their population size and concentrated built environments; and (3) cities are large enough to be complex, which requires a holistic and nonlinear approach to governance. I believe that I have provided some evidence for the first two. Above all, I have shown how shared experiences of climate extreme events and natural disasters help develop a degree of solidarity and collective understanding that matters of 'the human' cannot be isolated from matters of 'nature' or 'the environment'. In Darwin and Tulsa, extreme heat and tornado events are giving environmental activists an opportunity to reach out to those who are not necessarily interested in nature. In Cleveland and Cape Town, environmental disasters, such as the Cuyahoga River fire or severe drought ('Day Zero'), have helped formulate a collective culture and discourse that there are tangible material costs to environmental degradation. Second, I have shown how cities are leading an institutional form of environmental action thanks to their intensity and concentrated population. In Cleveland and Cape Town, several city-scale actions have been adopted as a part of policies and regulations, such as a mandatory stormwater management fee (Cleveland) and new water management strategies recognising natural resource scarcity (Cape Town).

However, perhaps less articulated has been my third rationale on why cities are better scales of environmental action due to their being 'complex' entities. In Chapter 2, I argued that an appropriate scale (for environment action) should be large enough to oversee the interaction effects and produce the kinds of interventions that can address these effects, which can cause unpredictable and sudden outcomes that cannot be imagined within the scope of 'too small' scales – a collection of green buildings does not become an ecological neighbourhood, nor does an aggregation of ecological neighbourhoods become a climate-resilient city. It is apparent that transportation networks (e.g., bike lanes, buses, trams, subways) or water quality management are better executed at a larger – city or regional – scale, given that their flow of movement cannot be contained within 'too small' scales.

In this chapter, I will elaborate further on how the complexity of cities gives them an edge in environmental actions. In other words, how can complex theory inspire the kinds of approaches that are environmentally normative and yet effectively tied to the everyday elements of 'the social'? Drawing from assemblage and social complexity theory, I synthesise the three core aspects of social entities as complex systems. Based on these three

111

aspects, I discuss how cities' complexity can assist them in creating effective linkages between matters of the social and the environmental.

THREE ASPECTS OF SOCIAL ENTITIES AS COMPLEX SYSTEMS

Considering social entities as complex systems has become increasingly fashionable in the social sciences, especially with recent efforts to re-establish the relationship between social systems and ecological systems. As discussed in Chapter 2, numerous scholars have attempted to tackle the mismatch between the scales of social and environmental systems.[3] The material functioning of ecosystems often defies social and political boundaries (e.g., administrative/jurisdictional boundaries of cities, localities, regions), which makes it challenging to define who is responsible for what when it comes to environmental degradation. Although this mismatch has often led to frustrations around what scale of environmental action is best, viewing social entities in light of ecological entities has allowed social scientists to see what characteristics of social systems can be considered similar or equivalent to those of ecological systems,[4] and how that comparability can inspire governance approaches in an increasingly uncertain and complex world.[5]

Reflecting this recent trend, I would like to synthesise here what it actually means to consider *cities as complex systems*. Indeed, considering cities as complex systems is not a novel idea, and can be traced back to the Chicago school of urban sociology in the 1920s. The interaction between human behaviour and the physical environment, or the role of materiality influencing the human spirit, was located at the heart of the Chicago school's thesis: buildings, streets, or spatial organisations induce the 'mood' or 'atmosphere' of a neighbourhood, dictating how humans behave and what individual agencies are capable of. Sociologists such as Anthony Giddens[6] continued this line of thought, theorising 'regionalised locals' (such as cities) as 'stations' or 'clusters' of human interaction and social practices. Building on that, Manuel DeLanda[7] discussed material aspects of cities (e.g., expressive architecture, street lighting, sewage pipes, electricity cables, and telephone wires) as concrete examples of how complexity manifests as functions of social systems, especially through connectivity or a flow of materials sustaining human life.

For the purposes of my argument on how the complexity of cities helps articulation of the social and the environment, I focus on three aspects of social entities as complex systems, mostly inspired by DeLanda's rendering of Deleuzean social assemblage theory, with which he builds social entities from scratch. How do social entities arise *from* initial interpersonal networks and friendships *to* social groups, networks, organisations, cities, and states? Rejecting *a priori* notions of state or hierarchical social structures, DeLanda's work dissects what is behind the formation of collectives or societies and then rebuilds them block by block – starting from individuals. In that sense, one may consider DeLanda's work as a bottom-up approach to understanding the social, which emphasises the value of heterogeneity over imposed unity.

However, according to DeLanda, although social entities arise from individuals and their agencies, that does not mean that groups lack a life of their own: as much as individuals form societies, societies affect individuals in terms of their perceptions, behaviours, and the exercising of agency. This is where complex theory becomes useful, that is, in attempting to articulate that *it is possible* to acknowledge the existence of a 'soul' of 'the whole' (i.e., how collectivities affect individuals/their constituencies), while at the same time respecting the heterogeneity and diversity of individuals.

Is it not contradictory to both acknowledge the 'wholeness' of groups (which affect and shape individual behaviour) and individual agency (which theoretically should give people the power to act however they want)? DeLanda proposes a solution by demonstrating the characteristics and functions of complex systems and how they may unfold in the context of social groups and their evolution towards larger entities. Here, I identify and synthesise the three key aspects of social entities as complex systems, which will be then used for my argument on how they can help link between the social and the environmental in cities.

Interaction effects

Individuals have their own agencies, and radical acceptance of their heterogeneity (or their 'singularity' as opposed to 'generalness' or 'ordinariness') is essentially the key to understanding Deleuzean assemblage thinking. Despite his advocacy on social justice values, Deleuze's work is fundamentally against totalitarianism *even if* its cause is to disseminate (or impose) social equity everywhere (see Tampio's argument on why and how Deleuze would have resisted a tyrannist appropriation of his theory).[8] Given the top-down imposition of group values/culture does not sit well with Deleuzean ontology, how do groups achieve a life of their own, their culture, or their soul – in other words, how do groups become more than the sum of their parts?

According to DeLanda, for the soul of groups to occur, three things should happen: repeated interaction amongst individuals, the intensity of these interactions through density, and physical (geographical) boundaries that allow individuals to propagate a sense of solidarity and collective spirit.[9] This encapsulates the core of complex theory. As argued in Chapter 2, complex theory is about understanding how the whole becomes more than the collection of its parts, thanks to the interactions between these parts and the effects that emerge out of them. As DeLanda states, 'although a whole emerges from the interaction amongst its parts, once it [i.e., the whole] comes into existence, it can affect those parts. Emergent wholes are real because they are causal agents capable of acting back on the materials out of which they are formed'.[10]

Placing interaction effects at the heart of understanding social entities may relieve us from the ontological contradiction between 'having a group identity (which is the soul of the whole)' versus 'respecting/acknowledging individual agency and heterogeneity', because the very wholeness of identity itself is something constituted through interactions among heterogeneous components over time – rendering these interactions a 'causal redundancy'. The soul of the whole (that arises out of interactions) is often referred to as 'emergent properties', which is an important quality of what is considered a 'complex system'. These properties are often unexpected and unintended (i.e., 'organic'), and yet this is what maintains the consistent functioning of the whole. Think of how prices are decided in traditional markets – without centralised imposition, trading practices have been established via continuous, repeated, intensive interactions over time. As Simone writes of Tanah Abang Market (a traditional marketplace in Indonesia):

> Decisions on trading practices, on who can sell what in what particular part of a market that has no clearly fixed boundaries is a matter of interweaving different times of the year, with changing compositions of sellers and buyers and producers and with differing calibrations of advantage and disadvantage . . . Here, the market becomes an occasion to reiterate memories of association and to provisionally explore new ones.[11]

In the context of cities and urban theory, the adoption of assemblage and complexity thinking offers an opportunity to explore interactions between human and nonhuman (i.e., material aspects of the city – buildings, infrastructure, everyday surroundings), and how such a 'mutually constitutive symbiosis' allows cities (or locales) to develop their own local rendition of capitalism or the logics of global order.[12] In other words, cities come to have a soul or collective identity that allows them to partake of a life trajectory of their own, which is ultimately rendered available via the accumulation of interaction effects at a micro scale over an extended period of time.

History and evolution

As noted above, interaction effects become a collective soul when they occur repeatedly, intensively, over an extended period. Ephemeral, one-time interactions will not stick; it is essentially the accumulation of different temporal/ historical layers of interactions that enables the 'wholeness' or 'soul' to emerge. In that sense, understanding social phenomena with temporal scales is key to applying complex systems thinking to social entities. Complex systems are, due to their emergent or organic properties, which are hard to predict and often unintentional, 'open' or 'breathing' systems the conditions of which are continuously changing and shifting. Hence, contingency and evolution are the main characteristics of social entities as complex systems, highlighting the fact that they are products of particular moments in time; they will emerge, they will change, they will evolve or disappear, depending on the particular historical context in which they are situated. As Bousquet and Curtis put it, 'Particular social entities, agents, or sites are viewed as historically situated and potentially transient bundles of social processes.'[13]

History also means a certain degree of stability, which cannot be easily dismantled by one revolutionary incident. This point is critical – although complex and assemblage thinking rejects any essentialist hierarchies of social structures, and despite the fact that emergent properties are at the core of how a complex system functions, that does not necessarily mean that one can suddenly overthrow the existing system and historical agencies already-in-place. Bousquet and Curtis cogently explain that assemblage theory's

> effort to move beyond essences is clear in the emphasis placed upon historical processes: each concrete social assemblage is the result of a set of

historical processes that have worked to construct a synthesis of organic, non-organic and social elements into a whole. The endurance of this whole may be accounted for by further historical processes of identity stabilisation, or the whole may eventually be destabilised by 'deterritorialising' social mechanisms that work to undermine its coherence. Through the incorporation of organic [i.e., emergent qualities] and non-organic [i.e., historically grounded social evolution] components into the theory, DeLanda aims at a synthetic account of both the material and socially constructed elements of entities.[14]

This implies that 'emergence', 'contingency', 'breathing' aspects of a complex system have to be better understood within the idea of evolution that occurs over time, although abrupt changes do happen in particular circumstances. But overall, change is something that surfaces when there have been repeated interactions among a group of people, within certain physical boundaries, over time.

For instance, the recent #metoo movement against sexual harassment was a collective awareness and effort to change the male-dominated culture that threatened the safety of women in workplaces, with the movement benefitting from communication technologies allowing rapid circulation of information and interactions. However, one can hardly say that the centuries-long patriarchy has suddenly been stripped off entirely, with women's struggles against everyday discrimination, routinised sexual misconduct, and harassment is still far from 'over and done'. It is difficult to uproot the patriarchal culture overnight, and it will take years of repeated interactions and deliberate interventions to eventually bring about a cultural shift. All of which is to say that, in analysing social entities as complex systems, it is important to understand that their emergent qualities or identities are not separate or independent from the accumulated historical layers of human interactions: 'a style is not an individual psychological creation, but an assemblage of enunciation'.[15]

Once we take account of this temporal component of how changes occur, it becomes clearer that the soul, identity, or wholeness of social entities cannot be divorced from their historical contexts. In other words, the soul of the system is deeply situated within the layers of historicity, slowly developed by years and years of accumulated interactions and behavioural changes at a micro level.

When it comes down to evolution, however, one should note the importance of chemical reactions between the old and new. Agency and initiatives for change are inevitably grounded within the historical context in which they are launched. However, what makes social entities evolve is the disturbance or turmoil these initiatives bring onto existing (i.e., old) social norms and conventions. The chemical reactions between the breath of new ideas and already-established customs and praxis gives birth to the emergence of new identities that newly define 'the whole'. In other words, the introduction of new ideas for change does not get annexed by the existing whole but 'produces an over-all change, a new configuration that alters its properties'.[16]

Introducing a new (subversive) identity while respecting heterogeneity

But, of course, deliberate intervention or planning can fast-forward these slow, accumulative processes of change. Think of social activism, such as the aforementioned #metoo movement – although there is a long way to go, it is undeniable that the widespread coverage of #metoo in social media, art, and culture has garnered radical moments of social change. Individuals, powered by intensive interaction solidarity-building with others, can instigate the start of a cultural shift. As DeLanda puts it,

> Interactions among members of these populations may sometimes lead to the formation of political alliances or coalitions among communities, alliances being the paradigmatic case of relations of exteriority in the social realm. In some cases, alliances lead to the emergence of larger-scale entities such as social justice movements . . . The aggrieved community's goal is to achieve recognition as a valid interlocutor on the part of governmental organisation, that is, to be treated as a legitimate maker of collective claims, a goal that must be achieved against strong opposition from the countermovement.[17]

While it is true that, as Butler has shown,[18] wearing drag one day will not cause the world to suddenly welcome gender fluidity, acting in interaction with others – through public parades, forums, social commentaries, journalism, documentaries, movies, books – can build a cultural momentum that can pressure institutions and the powerful for change. The power of popular media and culture cannot be dismissed, as it can normalise certain social values and ideals as something worthy of discussion, time, and resources. The popularity of Greta Thunberg in social media, which instigated global youth-driven climate movements in 2019, signifies an iconic moment of our time in which, if you can create a compelling articulation about something to the point that it becomes a 'cool', 'cultured', or 'woke' thing to follow, you can become a producer of your future. If patriarchy is a product of social construction, it can also be undone by continuous and multiple social interactions. In other words, one can introduce a new identity that counters the currently dominant culture, although, because of the historicity discussed above, it will take continuous effort and time.

In introducing a new identity – or alternatives that are considered new because of their subversiveness – it is important to note the role of 'expressive' resources. As noted above, effective social movements are accompanied by deliberate campaigns, media coverage, public marches, petitions, and pamphlets. Linguistic articulations, such as slogans or statements, together with more expressive images or films, are the 'repertoires of contention'[19] that can assemble new social movements and entities, and organisations arising out of those movements. In today's era of social media, posting statements or symbolic pictures/videos has become easier, and it is faster to circulate and interact with. Such intense circulation powered by communication technology, when compounded with physical congregations (public meetings, marches, parades), may fuel social change.

The emphasis on expressive resources is particularly important to a Deleuzean political project. As noted above, Deleuzean assemblage theory obtained its significance for its ultimate protest *against* totalitarianism and essentialism. In its radical defence of heterogeneity over forced unity/centralisation, Deleuze's vision of the postmodern left was to encourage multiple assemblages working towards liberty and equality *without* 'a transcendent organising agent' or centralised enforcement, such as the state. For within the ideals of postmodern left, where openness is a limitless possibility rather than a constraint, it would be a crime to suppress the multiplicity of identities, interests, and opinions, *even if* the cause of that suppression is to advance equity (e.g., a political programme that centralises its operation, which could oppress diversity along the way).[20] Assemblage theory's defence of 'multitude', at the end of the day, is an effort to embrace 'minorities and minoritarian becomings that do not conform to the Marxist ideal of an urban, male, heterosexual, industrial worker'.[21] It is, in a Deluzean political project, not ethical to let 'beings suffer by torturing themselves to conform to the standard'.[22] Furthermore, the essentialist category of 'proletariat' or the dichotomisation of the haves and have-nots – or us and them – does not sit well with postmodern openness and the fight against essentialism and external imposition.

How, then, do you organise a movement or political action, if your group's identity is, theoretically, eternally fluid and open to 'the other'? This is the key question for the postmodern left's continuing pursuit of liberty and equality.[23] Deleuze's proposal is for the left to become 'an abstract machine of consistency', where the value of justice and freedom becomes a sort of elixir that permeates into every segment of the 'body' or material existence of a system. While your smartphone itself has a physical presence, it is the apps that make it function (e.g., calendar, calculator, messenger, or bank). Here, an app is an abstract machine. An abstract machine, in the context of politics, is an idea or invention that is expressed through text or other symbols. A political example in *A Thousand Plateaus* was Lenin's 1917 text, 'On Slogan', which was an abstract machine that triggered the Bolshevik Revolution.[24] Abstract machines operate by function, not by form.[25]

In the end, it is all about creating compelling articulations and expressions that the public can be persuaded with, through poetic devices.[26] Another example of an abstract machine is the Pink Panther – through juxtaposition of an unlikely colour (panthers cannot be pink) onto a likely image (the character does look like panther), together with music (the groovy saxophone tune renowned as the Pink Panther theme) the rhythm of which reinforces the image of the character, Pink Panther becomes a phenomenon that is engraved in the hearts of the public, everyone and everywhere, across generations and continents.[27]

The functions of an abstract machine (of consistency) infiltrate every bit of a being – like 'when food or poison spreads through the body, when a drop of wine falls into water'[28] – so much so that it can be enacted on in a radically heterogeneous and decentralised manner (i.e., in a *constant variation*), to the point where it cannot be captured by the state apparatus or capitalist system.[29] An abstract machine does not coerce one to believe in what it expresses, but it can compel one to join its side. Such a notion of the abstract machine can be interpreted with the aforementioned expressive resources, in that both refer to a poignant and opportune articulation/expression that will be carried through by many agents, materially incarnating themselves as social movements, cultural shift, or a policy change. If the source of solidarity should not be hammered out by essentialist dichotomy and categorisation[30] or centralised enforcement/menace, the only way to introduce or pilot a new identity or vision is to use expressive mediums and abstract machines that can be popularised, vetted, and supported by the public voluntarily. This approach respects that, in many circumstances of life and the complexity these entail, it would be impossible (and unethical) to force a unilateral consensus for good, and hence pursuing liberty and equity is ultimately about *becoming* freer and more equitable, and not about arriving at the ultimate destination of 'happily ever after'.

LINKING 'THE SOCIAL' AND 'THE ENVIRONMENTAL' IN CITIES – BY CAPITALISING ON THEIR COMPLEXITY

Building from the three characteristics of social entities as complex systems, I would like to discuss how cities can capitalise on their complexity in linking the social and the environmental. To reiterate, the three key aspects of social entities as complex systems are the following. Above all, complex social systems contain intensive interactions within a physical boundary; these interactions, upon their repetition over time, give birth to emergent qualities that give identity to the whole – the 'wholeness' or soul of a system that allows it to be more than the sum of its parts. Second, complex social systems are the products of historical evolution, which occurs over an extended period. The notion of them being 'open' or 'breathing' not only highlights their unpredictable and emergent properties (that boil up out of intense interactions) but underlines the historical trajectory of how the system has evolved over time. In other words, emergent properties are always situated within the layers of history developed since the beginning of that system. Finally, complex social systems use more gentle ways of introducing new identities, which radically acknowledge, accept, and respect the heterogeneity of their components. This includes the abstract machine approach, where the components are encouraged (rather than forced) to participate in developing new identities, often through symbolic mechanisms, such as compelling arguments, opportune articulations, or provocative expressions, the messages of which can permeate the entire functioning of the system's bodily (i.e., material) existence.

Making human/nonhuman interactions as an 'everyday affair' – through the efficient flow of materials in basic infrastructure

Cities are centres of intensive interaction and circulation – through movements of goods, services, and ideas. How, then, can cities make the most of this aspect so as to support the marriage between the social and the environmental? To address this, I am going to extend the idea explored briefly in Chapter 2, about how built environments can become 'extended organisms' of our efforts to survive in a changing climate. Drawing from Turner and Downton, I talked about how cities' built environments can become physical manifestations of our role as conscious agents of change. Given that cities involve concentrated physical infrastructure (e.g., electricity, water pipes, transportation networks) and structures (e.g., buildings) – which effectively mediate 'us' (humans) and our material surroundings – cities can become representative models of what intense interaction between humans and their nonhuman surroundings should look like. In relation to that, we observed the material/posthuman turn in urban planning over the last decade.[31] Materialism-informed planning often unfolds in concert with the ecological systems of regional water courses, green infrastructure, and urban climatology, as it seeks to engage with socio-materiality, which involves detailed attention to the material aspects of sites, ecosystems, and environmental systems (see Chapter 3 for more details). There are many site- or building-scale examples that capitalise on urban infrastructure's materiality as a way of reframing our relationship with nature, which are well covered in ecological urbanism and landscape urbanism literature.[32]

But to connect human and nonhuman affairs at *a citywide scale*, in a way that highlights the inevitable interactions between these two, one needs to pay attention to basic utility infrastructure and the everyday needs of the people. The reason behind why it is so difficult for economically challenged neighbourhoods to connect with pro-ecology ideals comes from the fact that such ideals are so distant from their everyday living. As I showed in Chapter 4, this disconnection is ubiquitous in cities around the world, irrespective of their developmental status. In recent coverage on 'how to talk about environmental issues in *banlieues*'[33] (economically challenged suburbs in the outskirts of Paris), the mayor of Ile-Saint-Denis, Mohamed Gnabaly, expressed the difficulty of discussing 'ecology' when the majority of the city's residents live in day-to-day conditions of precarity – the end of the world sounds like a distant echo for them. It is not an exaggeration to say that, today in 2020, going 'eco' is still perceived to be a luxury, reserved for the privileged who have the time and resources to pursue it.

But everyone needs running water on tap, electricity generated using, or in interaction with, natural resources (water dams, coal, oil), and waste management (the end products of which need to be handled by the natural ecosystem). François Jarrige, a French historian working on energy transition as a societal choice, argues that

> energy is what connects the social world with the natural world. We used to have a very intimate relationship with energy: those who cut trees for heating should take account of the ways in which they are transformed – more than those who presses [sic] the switch to be lit. There is no society without an energy system, and each energy system determines the social and political forms of organisation.[34]

The advantage of cities as centres of material movements and interaction is to reinstate such a human dependency on nature through basic utility services and resource management, for which 'economies of scale' or 'effective circulation of materials' can be better achieved at a larger-scale view. For instance, one of my interview participants, who works for a composting and food waste collection service company, noted that the company operates at the city-region scale in order to benefit from economies of scale:

> For those who work on sustainable living and food services, we know that 20 miles [about 32 km] is more or less the threshold to be certified as 'local produce'. In economic terms, like transportation costs and economies of scale, our experience proved that the site within a 20-mile radius is a good, manageable, 'local' scale that works for our locally run family business – which covers just about the main metropolitan area. By limiting our operation within a 20-mile radius, we avoid extra packaging or far-out post delivery. Some composting companies import and export composts from other states, but I think, why can't they deal with their own food trash locally?[35]

Managing food waste gives an excellent example of what makes a good local scale. When does it become 'too far', to the extent that it discounts the benefits from economies of scale? Conversely, when is it that it remains 'too small' (or too local), to the point where it cannot enjoy economies of scale? Organic waste can turn rancid or repugnant when one takes too long to process it, so a 'too long/far' distance would not be ideal. At the same time, larger-scale processing can help more efficient distribution of compost and overall managing of excess waste. The composting company (that I communicated with) collects food waste from different locations within the city region and brings it to the processing centre, which turns the waste into odourless fertiliser. The company delivers the fertiliser to the original location (where they collected the waste from) or sells it to others in need. Restaurants are more likely to have more waste, and individual households less, and yet the pattern of demand is the reverse. Here, we can see the pragmatic advantages of the city scale in reconciling human needs (e.g., food consumption) and environmental system processes (e.g., composting) through achieving a more efficient flow of materials.

While economies of scale make a good case for centralised resource management (as in the case of composting), that does not imply that all centrally moderated utility infrastructure is ideal. As I explored in Chapter 4, Cleveland's stormwater management tried to move away from grey infrastructure (centralised tunnel networks) in an attempt to facilitate more on-site infiltration of wastewater (green infrastructure). The case of Cape Town also shows the pros of decentralised energy procurement (solar panels on-site), as this will allow more efficient distribution and use of energy, in addition to reducing cost and overreliance on state-run infrastructure.

However, a larger-scale view in resource management remains important, especially when it comes to environment system cycles where everything – consumption, disposal, and regeneration – is connected. During the drought event in Cape Town, affluent neighbourhoods drilled private water bores to get water on their own. Such haphazard usage of underground water can be detrimental to the overall health of the aquifer as a system, not to mention result in unequal access to water, as the poor would not have the tools/resources to manage such an operation.

Further, considering larger-scale dynamics can also assist in the performance of decentralised infrastructure. For instance, green infrastructure (pocket parks, decorated water detention sites), when connected with one another via existing waterways, can perform to its maximum potential of contributing to a more efficient urban water cycle. Each site can infiltrate what it can and forward to other sites when it cannot. By adding connection that facilitates water movement, networks of green infrastructure can cope with excess water in the most economical way, rendering a very short turnover period of water going back to the natural systems. Likewise, if decentralised energy procurement using solar panels is governed at a neighbourhood or a city scale via connected grid systems, each household can send back the power that it saved but does not need, crowdsourcing energy and deploying it where it is needed most. Thinking about human–nonhuman interaction through everyday infrastructure or utility networks may showcase the value of the city scale in environment actions.

These everyday materialities are a great medium or segue through which the questions of the environment can be connected with the social. 'The *banlieue* culture, that's to live on limited means, and that, is also what ecology means', said the mayor of Saint Seine-Denis, who strives to narrow the time gap between the concerns of 'the end of the month (*fin du mois*)' and those of 'the end of the world (*fin du monde*)'. Efficient electricity, water, waste, sewage (EWWS) infrastructure designs and deployment, which can minimise resource use, are of great interest to communities who worry about 'the end of the month' as these can reduce their electricity or water bills. Furthermore, pursuing efficiency can reduce cities' environmental impacts – the resource consumption of these concentrated human habitats (i.e., cities) is predominantly high. In that sense, everyday infrastructure can be framed or articulated as a point of intersection where we can clearly see how many resources we are using, how much environmental impact we are making, and how resource scarcity is the concern not just of households but of the global environment system overall.

More conscious efforts should be made to make these everyday infrastructures visible and interact-able to the extent that people can create immediate linkages between everyday human needs and their direct environmental impacts. A good example of such an approach is the North East Coastal Park project in Barcelona, which juxtaposes waste-management infrastructure with public green space on a beautiful beachfront site, with people able to see where their garbage eventually ends up. *Connection* and *visibility* – using these elements to frame everyday infrastructure in a way that highlights our ultimate dependency on the environmental – could be a pivotal step towards more response-able human civilisation; and cities, as central nodes of intensive interaction and circulation of goods and materials, will be able to lead that process.

Taking account of time and history

What makes a city a 'city'? Does 'intensity' itself define the essence of what a city is (i.e., can a city simply be equated with a sheer concentration of people or human habitats?). Urban historians would give a definite 'no' to this question – what makes a city a 'city' is *not* how many people reside in its territory *but* a 'sense of place' that arises out of the complex processes of interaction amongst its people, histories, and physical/geographical settings. This is something intangible that lasts longer than a human lifespan. Cities are historical magnets of human culture and civilisation, which often begin by being represented as holy, spiritual places that attract people from different villages and remote areas.[36] Lewis Mumford, a renowned urban historian, stated:

> In view of its satisfying rituals but limited capabilities, no mere increase in numbers would, in all probability, suffice to turn a village into a city. This change needed an outer challenge to pull the community sharply away from the central concerns of nutrition and reproduction: *a purpose beyond mere survival.*[37] (emphasis added)

The spiritual power of cities allows individuals to imagine and pursue an objective beyond their own well-being; it is the 'powers of higher potency and greater duration, of wider cosmic significance than the ordinary processes of life'.[38] In other words, cities' souls can give people a collective identity or a shared sense of togetherness that provides strength and confidence beyond mere survival – a feeling of connection or being part of a whole that lasts longer than you or your family. Cities remind us of how human civilisation, at its core, is not about meeting our animal needs but about sustaining something collectively valuable beyond one's life. That is how cities have evolved over centuries and generations – often outliving the destinies of nation-states (e.g., Baghdad, Jerusalem, Seoul) – packed with the hopes and desires of today's and yesterday's generations. This is clearly not a question of how many people reside in a designated territory or the population intensity itself.

How does a city develop its spiritual power? The short answer is interaction effects, and the historical records or physical monuments that engrave these effects as culturally significant in the minds of people. Cities are, ultimately, living museums that contain and continuously accumulate the historical layers of human interactions and subsequent events. Out of the ashes of these accumulated intense interactions (within a limited physical area), what surfaces is the 'scent' or 'atmosphere' that is infused into every bit of the city as physical urban heritages, customs, cultures, and habits. Ultimately, the secret behind cities' systemic endurance is their capacity to develop, store, and propagate archival records and knowledge on how their social groups and cultures have evolved over time. Hence, DeLanda uses the example of cities as social assemblages, the very complexity of which allows them to possess the quality of resilience. Cities, thanks to the interaction effects and transmission of semantic information across generations, have much longer lifespans than individual humans, often lasting for millennia.[39] In a similar vein, Mumford argued that:

> Through its monuments, written records, and orderly habits of association, the city enlarged the scope of all human activities, extending them backwards and forwards in time. By means of its storage facilities (buildings, vaults, archives, monuments, tablets, books), the city became capable of transmitting a complex culture from generation to generation, for it marshalled together not only the physical means but the human agents needed to pass on and enlarge this heritage. That remains the greatest of the city's gifts.[40]

Proven, then, is the potency of cities as representative containers of time, history, and evolution – of human civilisation. Given this, how does acknowledging the soul of a city – developed through interaction effects and their historical records forwarded onto future generations – help linking the environmental and the social?

My argument here is that a renewed focus on cities' historical relationship with physical geography settings (i.e., material surroundings) – through studying how our sense of collective cultural identity has been brewed in interaction with the physical landscape (in which we are all immersed) – can guide us towards integrating nature into the core of our everyday urban living.

Occupied with our desire to develop, progress, or compete, what we often forget is how the identity or soul of cities is formulated by our interaction with nonhuman surroundings or physical geographical/territorial settings. Indeed, urban development and planning have conventionally approached nature as a hindrance or barrier to be overcome by human ingenuity, believing that, with the right kinds of technological solutions and the perseverance of human will, we can change the course of nature (or ecological functioning) in a way that produces 'most profitable' outcomes conforming to the capitalist approach to land development. However, that trend is now changing, especially with the arrival of the Anthropocene. Climate irregularities and extreme weather events can easily wipe out human desire or will in 'one go'. Caring for the environment is no longer a benevolent action but a survival strategy – we simply cannot afford to ignore the feedback from ecosystem dynamics. As Haraway claims, citing Jason Moore at the World Ecology Research Network: 'cheapening nature cannot work much longer to sustain extraction and production in and of the contemporary world because most of the reserves of the Earth have been drained, burned, depleted, poisoned, exterminated, and otherwise exhausted'.[41] The Anthropocene marks the end of the refugia – an untouched utopia where we could run away from the mess we have made – as we now face or feel the consequences of our actions everywhere, such as extreme weather patterns and climate events that inevitably affect our daily socioeconomic activities.

Taking a step back from a reactive response to 'so what should we do right now?', constituting a deliberate direction or vision for the future legacy of cities requires a deeper reflection on historical trajectories – tracing stories of how cities have evolved into what they are today. As Mumford eloquently puts it, 'the prime need of the city today is for an intensification of collective self-knowledge, a deeper insight into the processes of history, as a first step towards discipline and control: such a knowledge as is achieved by a neurotic patient in facing a long-buried infantile trauma that has stood in the way of his normal growth and integration'.[42] Here, Mumford is talking about how cities should tap into the subconsciousness that pervades every future direction they take. And, unfortunately, this 'subconsciousness' has often been made up of our unwavering belief in technological solutions and human exceptionalism. This subconscious belief is what makes us disregard our organic partnership with our material, nonhuman surroundings:

Beneath its superficial regard for life and health lies a deep contempt for organic processes that involve maintaining the complex partnership of all organic forms, in an environment favourable to life in all its manifestations. Instead of regarding man's relation to air, water, soil, and all his organic partners as the oldest and most fundamental of all his relations – not to be constricted or effaced, but rather to be deepened and extended in both thought and act – the popular technology of our time devotes itself to contriving means to displace autonomous organic forms with ingenious mechanical (controllable! profitable!) substitutes.[43]

What we need, then, is an attempt to untangle this flawed subconscious attitude towards nature. Only when we recognise and rectify the underlying presumption behind our exploitive approach to the environment will we be able to rewrite the future of cities as 'an environment favourable to *life in all its manifestations*'.

When we think about it, cities' souls are surely not just a product of human interactions alone. How can we talk about cities' identities without the rivers, waterways, or topology – the physical settings that host human settlements? The development of certain architecture, transportation networks, or urban designs is severely influenced by their geographical availability and constraints. How do you talk about New Orleans' elevated houses and their architectural style without its exposure to flooding and tornado risks? How do you talk about Tokyo's predominant use of wood in construction and earthquake-resilient design without its frequent experience of earthquakes? How do you talk about Medellín's floating 'metro-cable' (gondola lift system) without understanding its topography and how communities have to reside in steep hills? The urban form or physical rendering of cities is often a direct by-product of its material, nonhuman surroundings – weather, topography, and other geographical specificities. The accumulation of physical interactions between human and nonhuman agencies is particularly apparent in the history of urban planning and development.

The agencies of nature or the environment are also present in the abstract ideas or identity around a city, especially with regard to waterways, streams, or rivers. As discussed in Chapter 4, Cleveland's city identity cannot be discussed without addressing its centuries-long relationship with the Cuyahoga River. Cleveland was established in 1796 in the intersection of the Cuyahoga River and Lake Erie, in the south of the Great Lakes – the world's largest surface freshwater reserve. The Cuyahoga has been at the heart of Cleveland's industrial development for a century, giving birth to the region's most prominent and profitable oil, steel, and chemical companies. The river 'provided access to iron ore and other materials, supplied water for cooling steel and manufacturing chemicals, and equally important, provided the most economic means of discarding wastes' by being an open sewer.[44] Eventually, the *consequences* of modernisation and human 'progress' (i.e., a decades-long ecological crisis) were crystallised through the dramatic fire event on the Cuyahoga River in 1969. The fire played a significant role in shattering Americans' subconscious attitude towards the environment, which saw nature as something to be utilised and consumed to the maximum. It was a painful realisation for Cleveland and the rest of America that human greed would ultimately come back to us as physical threats to our very material existence. After extensive media coverage of that fire, including in *Time* and *National Geographic*, the Cuyahoga obtained the mythical status of 'ecological sacrifice zone'.

Since then, the half-century-long process of clearing up the Cuyahoga has become the story of Cleveland, the city that inspired the nationwide environmental movement and subsequent federal-level government regulations, leading to the establishment of the Clean Water Act and Environment Protection Agency (EPA). The fire, the Cuyahoga, and the path towards redemption have built the urban character of Cleveland. The city has eventually taken ownership of its flawed history, placing it at the core of the city's collective identity and culture. This can be observed in its 2019 citywide campaign and celebration, 'River Reborn: Celebrating 50 years of Cuyahoga River progress',[45] which included an art exhibition and several public events that remind people of the river's winding history (see Fig. 5.1). The celebration also highlighted the city's new respectful relationship with water and its material/nonhuman surroundings.

Water is a source of life; waterways are a primary focal point of human settlements. They have always been there, and they will perhaps always be there. Compared to their historical existence, which can easily be traced back several centuries, the history of human settlements seems transient. Waterways watched us multiply, grow, evolve into larger social groups and entities, and eventually, become cities of high complexity. Hence it is perhaps not an exaggeration to say that every city has its own love-hate relationship with each waterway. You wanted to conquer it, but you realise you cannot –

Figure 5.1 An art exhibition commissioned by the Cleveland Museum of Art, as part of the 2019 citywide campaign 'Cuyahoga 50: Celebrating Our River, Igniting Our Future'. The exhibition included a new gunpowder painting by artist Cai Guo-Qiang, known for work that establishes an exchange between the viewer and the larger universe around them. Courtesy Cai Studio (picture taken by author). © Ihnji Jon.

it either comes back to you as a physical threat, causing severe flooding and water damage, or haunts you as a ghost of history and collective memory. In the case of Tulsa, the influence of the Arkansas River is present everywhere, reminiscing about the past, responding to the present, and imagining the future of the city – manifested as city design, flood risk management, and urban renewal (Fig. 5.3, 5.4). As discussed in Chapter 3, the city's extensive flood risk, caused by the river, has resulted in a network of stormwater reservoirs and flood-able zones transformed into parks and green spaces (e.g., Mingo Creek, Centennial Park, or River Parks – with bike/runners' trails along the river).

The city's relationship with the Arkansas River is also dictating the future vision of Tulsa. Arkansas River Development is one of the city's key projects in urban renewal and economic development, its controversy spanning

Figure 5.2   Cleveland is rebuilding a new relationship with its river. The Flats area, overlooking the Cuyahoga, is capitalising on the proximity to water and waterfront amenities on the now-restored river. © Ihnji Jon.

decades.[46] Since 2003, Tulsa County has been collecting a new portion of county sales tax, reserved for river corridor redevelopment. While the main purpose of the project is economic development, another rationale for the project is to enhance people's access to water. Waterfront areas along the river are seen as a 'beautiful water feature' that is not being properly utilised[47] – although River Parks, bike trails overlooking the river, allows public access to the water view, the river currently remains more or less a background that people are not necessarily interacting with. Proponents of the project argue that, although the development – which includes a new lower dam – may imply disruptions to ecological systems (e.g., bird habitats), it will also help the city rekindle its affection for the river and its heritage.

The fact of the matter is that people tend to care less about something that they do not have direct interactions with. It is only when they develop a genuine relationship with an entity or object – slowly built up by tactile, sensory experiences that becomes registered in their consciousness or core understanding of the world – that they actually start appreciating its exis-

Figure 5.3   Tulsa's complex relationship with the Arkansas River is prevalent in the city. The river was the beginning of human settlement in the city's history, the symbol of 'Tulsa' – the shortened version of 'Tulasi', meaning 'old town' in the Creek Nation's native language. Respecting waterways is a new way of celebrating the First Nations' territorial culture and its historicity, and yet at the same time, the river's frequent flooding and its devastating impacts on the nearby residential areas is a constant threat to the city. The city is trying to find a harmonious balance with nature, such as transforming areas with high flooding risk into flood-able parks and ecological protection zones (see Chapter 3 for more details). The picture was taken from the Arkansas River trail in Tulsa in July 2019. The area was flooded a month before, and one could still see the raised water level. © Ihnji Jon.

tence. The development plan therefore aims to enhance the recreational value of the Arkansas River, through building a new pedestrian bridge and potential kayaking facilities, which would then extend the existing ecological park (Gathering Place) to the other side of the river. This is projected to encourage people to nurture a new sense of care and affection for the river, which has always been at the centre of the city's transformation since its early days under the Creek Nation.

The story of Tulsa and its inseparable ties with the Arkansas River, similar to the story of Cleveland and its complex history with the Cuyahoga River,

Figure 5.4 Arkansas River and Zink Dam seen from the bike trail near Gathering Place (a new ecological park in Tulsa), taken in July 2019. During the historic flooding event that occurred two months before (late May 2019), the existing dams (Keystone and Zink) reached maximum capacity. With the city's ambitious vision of the Arkansas River Corridor Development project, there are now discussions around whether the city needs a new dam in this area. Environmental groups fiercely oppose this because of the potential threat to ecosystems and bird habitats near the river. Proponents, on the other hand, argue that a new lower dam, which would also serve as a pedestrian bridge connecting Gathering Place to the other side of the river, would make the river more accessible for people to enjoy and experience – cultivating a desire to care for the river in return. © Ihnji Jon.

demonstrates how the souls or identities of cities are constituted through each of their historical relationships and ongoing interactions with the physical geography or material surroundings of where they are located (see also Fig. 5.5 for the case of Cheong Gye Cheon in Seoul). Cities' identities or spiritual power (à la Mumford) can never be independent from the nonhuman agencies already in place, which came into existence long before human settlements. In that sense, cities are essentially material manifestations that embody co-constitutive relationships between the human and the nonhuman or the cultural and the natural. Tracing the formation

Figure 5.5   Cheong Gye Cheon is a restored stream in the centre of Seoul, South Korea. The restoration project attracted global attention; it is considered a key example of urban waterway restoration, as well as an urban renewal project that takes account of its heritage value. The history of Cheong Gye Cheon can be traced back to the Joseon Dynasty (1392–1910); despite its historical importance, it was once an eyesore and public health hazard because it was severely polluted with untreated sewage. After the Korean War (1950–1953), the government covered the stream with an elevated highway, as a part of an economic development plan. In 2003, with the new wave of celebrating urban heritage via 'place making', the city government decided to remove the highway and restore the stream to its present form. It was a complicated engineering process to rehabilitate the water back to the surface, since it had been severely polluted, with its trace mostly disappeared. Given such conditions, the project was not entirely 'natural', in the sense that engineers had to artificially pump the water from other sources just to have the stream take its course. All these controversies aside, the city government of Seoul capitalised on this moment as an opportunity to reinstate its relationship with water, placing the stream at the heart of the city's identity – its history is exhibited in Cheong Gye Cheon Museum. © Ji Eun Lee.

of the identity or soul of a city – rendered possible thanks to their degree of interaction effects (across different expressions of life, such as human/ nonhuman), backed by their capacity to store and disseminate archival knowledge – opens us up to new ways of appreciating and understanding our organic relationship with nature, where the social is not divorced from the environmental.

Injecting pro-environmentalist ideas via an abstract machine

So far, we have touched on how the characteristics of the urban as complex social entities – interaction effects, historicity, and evolution – help cities articulate effective linkages between the social and the environmental. In this final section, I will discuss how cities can inject their pro-environmentalist ideas via an abstract machine, using the powers of imagination, narratives, expressions, or poetic devices that can *inspire* people rather than forcing them to pursue environmentalism. This approach draws its theoretical insights from the aforementioned Deleuzean strategies of the postmodern left.

As discussed above, the Deleuzean political project is fundamentally against a top-down imposition of ethics or morality. While Deleuze was an avid advocate for the principles of freedom and equality, he would have fiercely objected to any centralised enforcement that negates the value of plurality and heterogeneity.[48] To be on the postmodern left is to possess an ultimate generosity towards 'the other', whose voices are not reflected in the currently dominant political discourses. The extent of immediate action, or how much we can 'get things done', is indeed an important aspect of a political project. But if we suppress the voices of the other in the process of doing so – through either hammering down essentialist morality or pro- jecting essentialist categories between us and them – it is not only unethical but also insufficiently future-forward to embrace the politics of possibility and the unknown. Such Deleuzean approaches to the postmodern left can be linked with the works of other political theorists who ardently prioritise openness and respecting heterogeneity as being the key principles of politi- cal projects going forward.[49]

How, then, do you introduce a new identity, societal vision, or potential direction of where we should be heading – in my case, pro-environmentalism – without disrespecting the existence of plural perspectives, life experi- ences, and different priorities? This has been the main question addressed throughout Chapters 3 and 4, in which I tried to explain broadly the ways that cities may go about this, through: (1) focusing on the physical or health threats of the Anthropocene moment (e.g., extreme weather, water and air quality); (2) talking about future generations and education for children (e.g., species extinction and the educational value of nature); and (3) linking 'green' with specifically local concerns or worries (e.g., the job creation potentials of green infrastructure and industries). Such strategies capitalise on the rise of new materialism, in that they place emphasis on tangible feedback and the pragmatic benefits of going green. In a way, they can be considered 'cheat-sheet' tactics towards environmentalism, as one gets to incentivise pro-environment actions without converting people's stance on morality or political ideology.

Even so, surely one can be more explicit about the purpose of their politics, movement, or the projection of normativity – what we *should* do. One interviewee in Tulsa, who works on promoting green buildings and architecture, mentioned that 'I know that, in the context of [the] political climate in Tulsa, we are afraid of being brushed off as "greenies". But I'm tired of being diplomatic about what we should do, or where we should stand. Climate change is here, right now'. How can one project this normativity without self-righteousness or a polemical attitude towards others? I would argue that seeing like a city,[50] or acknowledging complexity as the baseline of politics and governance, helps us pursue pro-environmental ideals while respecting the radical heterogeneity of different value systems and viewpoints on life. Warren Magnusson, in defence of plural democracy, salutes the openness and generosity of cities in embracing a pluralistic social order (as opposed to the imposition of state-driven sovereignty), which allows us to be more imaginative, rather than overly deterministic (everything or nothing!) or coercive (now or never!). As Magnusson puts it:

To see like a city is to recognise that political order is not something that can be fixed in any simple way. A political order is always in the process of being overcome, and challenges to it may arise from any quarter. In this context, the threat of adverse change provides the excuse for efforts to establish and maintain sovereignty. There is always a widespread desire for the certainty, fixity, security, and control that sovereignty promises, but it exceeds any need that sovereignty might serve. In the circumstances, it is well to be suspicious of any claim to sovereignty, on the grounds that it is likely to be as excessive as it is ineffective in relation to the securities it is supposed to provide. To see like a city is to accept a certain disorderliness, unpredictability, and multiplicity as inevitable, and to pose the problem of politics in relation to that complexity, rather than in relation to the simplicity that sovereignty seeks. To put it bluntly: to see like a city is to grow up politically. [51]

Cities are, thanks to the heterogeneity of peoples that they attract, nucleuses of cultural and political innovation. Given the diversity of races, cultures, languages, and customs – all wrapped up within a relatively narrow compass – it can be said that 'the complexity and the cultural inclusiveness of the metropolis embody the complexity and variety of the world as a whole'.[52] In such a context, if a new idea or proposition is to be introduced and tested in cities, it has to be creative, imaginative, and compelling enough to pertain to the widest spectrum of values and belief systems. Indeed, in this current historical moment of territorial inequalities and divisiveness, there have been criticisms regarding enclaves of urban elites and their left politics turning a blind eye to the consequences of internationalism (e.g., the exodus of local jobs, notably to China). But one should also acknowledge the capacity of those very urban elites to undertake self-reflection or reflexive critique, and, eventually, 'grow up politically', arriving at an understanding that not everything is a black-and-white issue that can be settled with a magic wand. One thing that is certain is that, because of the diverse backgrounds and vocations of the people they encounter and interact with in their everyday setting, urban denizens are often situated on fertile ground in terms of cultivating the spirit of openness that is sympathetic to difference (i.e., the ability to lend an ear to the other, or to put themselves in someone else's shoes). Remaining open to acknowledging and valuing the radical heterogeneity of peoples, their life trajectories, and divergent perspectives on what it means to 'live well' – even if our own logic fails to understand them 'rationally' – is the driver of future-forward coalition politics, or 'chains of equivalence',[53] for which cities are often a good ignition spot.

What, then, would be the best way of persuading someone, while remaining respectful of inevitable differences in life paths? And why might cities be particularly good at it? As noted above, cities develop their unique identities – what makes each city 'a city' – via interaction effects between extensively divergent sets of populations. This identity is referred to in different ways, one of which is 'city culture'. City culture can indeed be a result of government-led rules and regulations (e.g., urban hygiene and cleanliness in Singapore), but in general, broadly refers to a kind of mood, air, or atmosphere that has percolated into the subconsciousness of the city's residents – creating certain social norms or an unspoken agreement to act or behave in a certain way (e.g., tip culture, dress codes in public spaces, etc.). The pressure or motivation to follow these norms is not necessarily coming from strict policing or fines, but mostly from the sheer number of people who have been collectively performing them, as well as the amount of time people have spent doing this. It is, ultimately, a version of 'peer pressure' – because everyone is doing it, and they have been doing it for a long time, you may also have been doing it without any question, or you may decide to be part of it because you do not wish to be singled out.

There are different ways of creating this 'peer pressure', or a social/cultural norm that can seep into your subconsciousness to the point where you find yourself performing it as a member of the city (e.g., New Yorker, Parisian, Melbournian, Tulsan, Capetonian . . .). The very formulation of such a peer pressure moment can be considered *injecting a new identity through an 'abstract machine'*. There is no centralised mode of control, nor official reprimand/repercussions for your actions. Even so, the 'mood' of things, peoples, and surroundings makes you behave in a certain way or makes you want to behave in a certain way.

One way of doing this is through inserting an imperative that is strongly supported by facts, logic, and science – making it difficult for someone 'in their right mind' to deny this imperative, despite it being new and thus asking for some change in their behaviour. For instance, in creating a cultural momentum for more widespread climate/pro-environmental actions, I have argued here and elsewhere[54] that one should capitalise on the Anthropocene moment (i.e., the undeniable empirics of environmental degradation) in order to articulate effective political movements or policy actions. Undeniably frequent natural disasters and extreme climate events can help us formulate a collective dialogue around the limits of the 'soul-full' will of human agency, as well as the fragility of our dependency on nonhuman surroundings. In the Anthropocene – often represented by extreme climate irregularity events – we are constantly reminded of our dependency on ecosystems, since our bodily survival is often in the hands of nonhuman actants. This implies that, in the Anthropocene, pro-environmentalist normativity is not a moral imperative or an act of benevolence but a survival strategy that we clearly need to treat more seriously given the destructive and alarming feedback from ecosystems. The devastating summer bushfire season in 2020 in Australia (Fig. 5.6) has attracted colossal media attention and coverage, leading to a huge public turnout in congregations on the National Climate Emergency (Fig. 5.7, 5.8). This indicates growing public interest, concern, or even citywide consensus around the urgency of climate action. The pervasiveness of the smoke, together with the health risk it implies, erased geographic as well as temporal boundaries: the impacts of climate change were instantly felt in the city centre. What the fires made clear is that climate change is not something that is distant from everyday city living. And Melbourne, a cosmopolitan cultural capital of Australia, played a leading role in declaring the climate emergency as a cultural norm of our time.

However, relying on a logical imperative for action can turn at times coercive or judgemental. The world may be ending, but people may still want to retain their right to choose how they want to live or how they will spend their remaining time while they are here. Simone de Beauvoir once

Figure 5.6　Smoke haze in Melbourne during the devastating 2019–20 summer fire season (December to February) in Australia. © Ihnji Jon.

Figure 5.7   The line to enter the National Climate Emergency Summit, which took place 14 February 2020, a month after the colossal media coverage on the unprecedented fire season of 2020. © Ihnji Jon.

famously said that 'to exist is to dare to throw oneself into the world'. In fact, we are all forced into the world – 'exist!' was an order given to us by society the moment we were born. Regardless of religious orientations, 'live!' or 'stay alive!' has always been an undeniably canonical value that any society upholds. When we are born, every single one of us is asked to embark on a journey to find a (more or less) socially acceptable meaning for existence. In other words, we are all already given an unquestionable, universal norm 'to exist' without any choice about the condition we are born with. For many, that norm itself may already be too hard to swallow. You may want to shout 'OK, I will exist, but how I'm going to exist is my decision'. Just as we cannot tell someone with a terminal disease how to spend their limited time on this earth, it is not a simple matter to order someone 'to take care of the environment' just because the world is now ending. Their head may logically be thinking that doing so would probably be a rational choice for the sake of their family, society, humanity, or the earth system, but their

Figure 5.8 National Climate Emergency Summit on 14 February 2020 in Melbourne, Australia. The Melbourne Town Hall hosted the event; the Main Hall, where the first planetary session was held, was packed full. It was reported that the Summit attracted about 800–1000 participants each day for two days. © Ihnji Jon.

heart may divert them towards other different life choices and paths, such as pursuing a hedonistic lifestyle or prioritising the momentary instances of 'me, here, right now', not necessarily giving a second thought to how their very existence is connected with the other, their material surroundings, or any time frame beyond today or this month. As we saw in Chapter 4, pro-environment movements are often considered unabashedly 'white' or belonging to the privileged. People who have the resources to think beyond the next few decades are most likely to have the luxury to be a part of something beyond this month's survival.

What would be another way of cultivating a city culture, or injecting a message through an abstract machine, that does not rely on the logical imperative? Introducing and nurturing a new mood of doing something can also be addressed more creatively through arts and culture – touching someone's heart to induce action. Recently, there has been coverage on how 'Dreamers' in the US try to make their case using art to tell their stories:

141

When it's a story – a film, a dance, a podcast, a play, a painting, a song – we are more apt to understand human complexity better, to become united in our love and support of characters . . . So maybe, if the stories of the 'dreamers' become art, America will be better at loving them, too.

. . .

Mata, 28, is a grad student and dance teacher at the University of Maryland and part of a growing subgenre of DACA [Deferred Action for Childhood Arrivals programme; DACA] stories that are being communicated as art, rather than congressional testimony or political commentary.

A DACA opera in Texas; art installations at the border; DACA theatre camp in D.C.; Mata's dances in California, Minnesota and now D.C.; a podcast series in Colorado.

It's a last-ditch effort for some of them because the clock is ticking on the Obama-era executive order that gave them legal status here.

. . .

The stories, beautiful and raw, are art. And that, Wilson believes, will be the way to make change.

'It is almost always a politician, on either side of the debate, talking about immigration policies', she said. 'But that doesn't open people's hearts and minds'.[55]

Creative manifestations of new ideas, political perspectives, and marginalised voices – expressed through storytelling and narratives that can melt people's heart – can be a start in setting 'the mood' for change. And this is something that is currently happening. Actors, theatres, dancers, movie makers, music artists, journalists, writers, and novelists are together contributing to today's new collective narrative: 'ecology is hip'.[56] Upcycling for Mother Earth is a campaign often led by Hollywood celebrities, associating the slogan with dried flowers and neutral colours, such as ivory, beige, or subtle green. Such attempts to inculcate a message through poetic devices (e.g., stories, colours, imageries, films, rhythms, and movements) are, no matter how slow, effective in decoding the currently dominant system and replacing the collective subconscious or the 'software' of a society. Perhaps this approach to supersede the old software of the society with a new one is closer to the Deleuzean, 'abstract machine' version of conducting prefigurative politics: 'The issue is to produce the unconscious, and with it new statements, different desires: the rhizome is precisely this production of the unconscious'.[57]

The ultimate objective of this approach is, essentially, to 'nudge' or prompt a change in people's behaviour by creating 'the right kind of mood' or 'wave' that can whip up genuine emotional pulsation and connection. Take the *Fondation Cartier*'s 2019 art exhibition in Paris, entitled *Nous les Arbres* (direct translation: *We the Trees*). The exhibition tries to challenge and push the boundaries of how we perceive nature – through captivating images, sounds, stories, and narratives that can touch and affect our emotional qualities or how we feel about things.

> The exhibition Trees gives voice to numerous figures who, through their aesthetic or scientific journey, have developed a strong, intimate link with trees, thereby revealing the beauty and biological wealth of these great protagonists of the living world, threatened today with large-scale deforestation.[58]

By leaving us in awe of trees – with their immense historicity, the wonders of their evolution, and their 'intelligence' that transcends our limited cognitive capacity – an exhibition such as this can place someone in an emotional state of wanting to know and care about the natural world, without resorting to the fear-driven, coercive imperative of 'we have to protect nature or we'll all die'. Similar to the *New York Times*' Modern Love series – which is now rewriting the definition of how society defines or legitimises what 'love' is – what if we were to initiate a compelling narrative of urban politics and history that cannot be written without the agency of nature, or our everyday nonhuman surroundings?

Decoding and recoding the software, or the collective subconscious of our society, will require powers of imagination and storytelling in order to set the mood for a potential social change. If so, what makes cities particularly apt to act as generators of 'moods' that can switch on a desire for change? As a response to that question, I would like to conclude my argument by presenting two theoretical propositions on why cities can make great mood-setters for rehabilitating the human–nature relationship. First of all, cities are very experienced in nurturing new identities given the sheer extent of diversity and heterogeneity of their constituents, cities are used to forging a 'wholeness' of identity or soul without relying on one particular essentialist category (e.g., nationality, gender). In the process of building their own 'assembled', diasporic identity, cities have developed a unique quality of creating and disseminating narratives and discourses that can speak to the largest spectrum of different people's interests, desires, and concerns. Capitalising on such talents for injecting messages in a way that can be compelling to diverse groups, cities can kindle a collective emotional state that desires and hence drives a social change. For the purpose of my argument here, such 'change' would imply situating nature and the environment at the heart of our everyday socioeconomic affairs.

Second, and perhaps more important, one must not forget that what makes cities 'complex' is their physical graspability: their intense interaction effects come from the fact that the interactions occur within a designated physical boundary. This allows cities to possess tangibility and material presence. Cities are not an abstract concept of social entities – they exist in a real world and can be touched, felt, and experienced – hence the old saying, 'city air makes you feel free'. You can go out, stand in the middle of the crowd, and feel the air of anonymity and boundless possibilities. You can also stand in solidarity with complete strangers, feeling the air of togetherness, because you are connected with them through shared ideas and goals, not through blood ties. This is why cities' desires and activation for social change are not limited to languages, discourses, or linguistic articulations. While our ideas are articulated and circulated through language, a city's material presence (e.g., buildings, parks, trees, and the people who surround you) plays an important role in shaping how we together perceive the world or cultivate a collective desire for social change. If cities have always been the centres of social movements and progressive social campaigns, especially due to their physical tangibility and material presence as a social entity, couldn't they also become expressions of human society re-establishing the foundations of human–nature relationships, delivered by ecological urbanism projects, art installations, and cultural events that affect how we feel? Following the Deleuzoguattarian motto, 'expression is not a mere representation, but an intervention',[59] cities can inject a new message or identity via making use of their materiality,[60] thus overcoming the limits of logical imperatives (i.e., of pleading to our rational judgments). Again, for the purpose of my present argument, the message or identity that I would hope to inject would be our co-constitutive relationship with nature, or stories/histories of how nonhuman surroundings – rocks, rivers, streams, hills (i.e., physical geography) – helped mould cities into their current form.

CONCLUSION

This chapter focused on explaining how the 'complexity' of cities as social entities helps them to create more effective linkages between 'the social' and 'the environmental'. I focused on three key aspects of complexity, largely drawing from DeLanda's and other theorists' work on social assemblages as complex systems: (1) interaction effects that boil up a soul or wholeness identity within a particular social entity; (2) the role of time and historicity in evolution of social entities; and (3) introducing a new (subversive) identity while respecting the heterogeneity of the entity's constituents. Building on from these three aspects of complexity in social systems, I proposed why and how cities' complexity can help them in articulating the linkage between the social and the environmental. Three theses were set out:

(1) As centres of intensive material movements and interaction, cities can reinstate human dependency on nature through basic infrastructure (electricity, waste, water, sewer) systems. While pro-environment ideals are often brushed off as something for the privileged, every household is dependent on material resources that the environment provides. The inseparable coexistence and interaction effects between the social and the environmental can be highlighted via the more visible and pronounced presence of urban utility infrastructure.

(2) As representative containers of history and evolution of human civilisation, cities can lead the process of recognising the historically co-constitutive relationship between humans and their nonhuman surroundings. The development of city identity or 'spiritual power' – which attracts divergent populations – cannot be explained without the role of nonhuman agencies (waterways, hills, mountains, topography) and our interaction with them. Articulating the significance of nonhuman surroundings in urban design and planning can convince people to rethink their dichotomised understanding of the social versus the environmental.

(3) As comprehensive entities that celebrate difference and respect radical heterogeneity of peoples, cities can inject a new message or idea through

145

'abstract machines'. Avoiding coercive imposition or centralised control, this capacity can be used to introduce pro-environmental ideas and imageries by making them permeate the everyday lives of 'the urban'. These can be delivered via not only linguistic articulation but cities' material expressions that affect people's emotions and feelings.

In short, the complexity of cities (the intensity of interaction effects, the unpredictability of emergent/organic qualities, and their radically heterogeneous constituents) provides them with an ultimate advantage when it comes to developing more inclusive ways of linking the social and the environmental and going beyond the essentialist morality of protecting nature. By surpassing the limits of language and logic, cities have the potential to convince people to recognise interlocking destinies of the human and nonhuman – even those who are not initially interested in nature. It is hence my hope that this chapter has provided some guidelines for city planners, environment activists, and sustainability officers in communicating and disseminating their pro-environmental actions, thereby acquiring a wider range of supporters from diverse socioeconomic backgrounds.

6
Conclusion: Possibilities of the unknown, for the unknown

The diagrammatic or abstract machine does not function to represent, even something real, but rather constructs a real that is yet to come, a new type of reality. Thus when it constitutes points of creation or potentiality it does not stand outside history but is instead always 'prior to' history. Everything escapes, everything creates – never alone, but through an abstract machine that produces continuums of intensity, effects conjunctions of deterritorialization, and extracts expressions and contents.

– Deleuze and Guattari[1]

If you're automatically sure that you know what reality is, and you are operating on your default setting, then you, like me, probably won't consider possibilities that aren't annoying and miserable. But if you really learn how to pay attention, then you will know there are other options. It will actually be within your power to experience a crowded, hot, slow, consumer-hell type situation as not only meaningful, but sacred, on fire with the same force that made the stars: love, fellowship, the mystical oneness of all things deep down.

– David Foster Wallace[2]

Pragmatism finds certainty in its openness to contingency, its rejection of consolatory obfuscation, its repudiation of authoritarianism and its affective embrace of political possibility.

– Robert W. Lake[3]

Now that we are approaching the end of our journey together, I think I can fully disclose what motivated me to embark on writing this book. Its overarching message is that cities are a 'good scale' for enacting pro-environment actions in the Anthropocene, thanks to their physical graspability, intensity, and complexity. I have tried to transmit this message through a variety of

examples of how cities, as local sites experiencing climate change, are cultivating new strategies, discourses, and narratives on how to cope with crises
they often have no control over.

How does each chapter serve this message? The first chapter, 'Environment Politics Beyond Environment', sets the stage for my core argument on
why we should *re*consider our old approach to environmentalism. In doing
so, I provided a critique on the conventional 'green-only' environmentalism that segregates 'the environment' from everyday socioeconomic affairs.
In the second chapter, 'Why Cities? Towards a New Theorisation of "Scale"',
readers had an opportunity to engage with the 'politics of scale' literature
as well as 'new ecology' literature, which is currently at the forefront of
deciding who (or which geographical scales) should be considered responsible for enabling environmental action. The third chapter, 'Darwin vs. Tulsa:
How Cities Talk About "Nature" Without Saying the Word', discusses strategies of communicating environmental initiatives, especially with those who
hold different political ideologies or philosophies on life. Such strategies
were discussed as demonstrative examples of 'pragmatic environmentalism',
which draws its anti-essentialist roots from Spinozian ethics. The fourth
chapter, 'Cleveland vs. Cape Town: Can a City Aspire to be Green and Inclusive?', dives into the question of whether 'green' and 'equity' agendas can be
intertwined through cities' historical relationship with nature alongside the
presence of social actors who accentuate the distributive aspects of green
economy. The fifth chapter, 'Cities and Complexity: Linking "the Social"
with "the Environmental"', talks about why and how the complexity of cities
becomes an advantage in enacting environmental politics.

The truth of the matter is that I have become tired of the persistent discourse on how the world is coming to an end. Providing trenchant critique
on the status quo of the world is indeed the main task of academics. But at
the same time, I am concerned at how often and automatically we are sure
that the extractive logics of a capitalist system will run us over, leaving no
room for imagining a better future. Should we be robbed of our rights to
remain hopeful just because we happen to exist in this world? Hundreds of
thousands of babies are brought into this world every day without having
made the choice to be born. Does the fact that we are all pushed to survive
in the system we are born into make us a bystander to its oppressive effects?

Through this book, I have tried to express how we can still be hopeful
and imaginative about the world and a future yet to come. I have done this

by highlighting the agency of environment activists, urban planners, and other government officials who strive to deliver something positive (often going against dissenting currents around them). Indeed, the philosophies behind this approach are, as you may have noticed, heavily influenced by post-structuralist, post-hegemonic thoughts. In these I find possibilities of human agency and action beyond the confinements of recognised systems or institutionalised processes: 'causing runoffs, as when you drill a hole in a pipe; there is no social system that does not leak from all direction'.[4]

As I conclude this book in March 2020, the world has been struck with the COVID-19 pandemic crisis. Like the smoke haze that flooded the streets of Melbourne during the bushfire season a few months back, the Coronavirus percolates in the air we breathe and penetrates our everyday decisions. While the devastating socioeconomic effects of the virus, together with the difficulty of controlling its spread, remain daunting for everyone, one tentative silver lining thus far has been how the virus instigates new conversations on the fragility of human societies and our material interdependency on one another. Put another way, it tangibly reminds us of the fact that our own well-being can never be independent of others. The virus does not care for the artificial categories that we often use to exercise exclusive politics; 'The coronavirus shows in the end that life makes fun of the [national] borders, political entities, racial distinctions, that it mixes up everything, it assembles everything'.[5] And perhaps that is why it may prove to be the 'liberator' of a more inclusive politics that brings us back to the fundamentals of what it means to be human, providing a common ground on which the collective future of humanity – regardless of nationality, gender, race, and class – can be discussed and ventured forward. As Edgar Morin, a French philosopher and sociologist, eloquently puts it:

The virus reveals to us what was hidden in the compartmentalised minds formed in our education systems, dominant minds in the techno-economic-financial elites: the complexity of our human world in the interdependence and the intersolidarity of the sanitary, the economic, the social, and all that is human and planetary. This interdependence manifests itself through innumerable interactions and feedbacks between the various components of societies and individuals . . . The virus tells us that this interdependence should stir up human solidarity in the awareness of our collective destiny.[6]

Like the virus that permeates through our everyday life – literally like Deleuze and Guattari's metaphor of 'poison that spreads throughout one's body' or 'drop of wine in water' – no one can escape the matters of the environment that are ubiquitously present in every second of our bodily existence. Whenever we feel overly confident that our rationality and reason can transcend our material reality, time and again the ecologies of 'more-than-human' show us how much we are dependent on the 'material background' that we often take for granted. Such moments of realisation often come in the least expected moments, such as the COVID-19 pandemic that upended the status quo of our economic system, or irregularities in precipitation (e.g., drought, flooding) that emanate from excessive carbon emission (caused by human interventions). The unpredictability of 'more-than-human' ecologies can wreak havoc in our societies, discriminately affecting the weak and marginalised. At the same time, this very unpredictability is what motivates us to become *more conscious* of our ultimate vulnerability as physical beings. In a way, the uncertainty of such crisis moments can instigate new conversations on the fragility of human existence and our material interdependency on one another. It tangibly reminds us of the fact that our own well-being can never be independent from that of others; your privileged position may grant your own health care coverage, but unless *everyone* has equal access to health care, you will never be free from the risk of contracting the virus.

The climate crisis or a global health crisis, where abruptness and ungovernability often catch us off-guard, urges us to recognise our vulnerability as mortal bodies. In that sense, the unknowability of these crisis moments renders us sensitive to the 'relational ties' we all have, or the fact that 'my fate is not originally or finally separable from yours', realising 'something fundamental about the social conditions of our very formation'.[7] By making us intimately feel our physical vulnerability as humans, the unknown or ungraspable complexity of human/nonhuman interactions may offer the possibility of catalysing more inclusive politics. In fact, the political power of COVID-19 has become evident: with the effective paralysis of the global economy, national governments are now considering the deployment of universal income and other progressive policies to reinstate basic human rights and social values – measures often neglected during the 'ordinary' days of maintaining the capitalist status quo.

'Anthropocene' moments – such as the extreme weather events or the global health crisis, triggered by micro-beings that we can't even see with the naked eye – constantly remind us that we humans are not in complete control of our own destinies. The real political advantages of such crisis moments lie in the fact that they offer the very instances of: (1) realising our vulnerability as material beings, and subsequently; (2) coming together as a collective society to re-assess and re-establish what kind of values we stand for and how far we are willing to go in defence of those values. This is one aspect of the possibilities arising in the face of the unknown.

At the same time, this book also talked about something else: how can societies activate their society-wide agency for a collective action, especially in the face of such uncertainties and ungovernable moments? Would the top-down imposition of certain norms or social values become a more attractive mode of governance? It is indeed tempting to think so, especially in a global pandemic, exemplified by the COVID-19 crisis. It seems that top-down control, to a certain extent, has become inevitable in order to limit the spread of the virus. What is particularly distressing about the COVID-19 crisis is that people can transmit the virus without their knowledge; healthy individuals may not even feel the symptoms despite testing positive, and so can spread the virus which may end up affecting the weak and the vulnerable. Subsequently, several Asian and European countries have implemented strict movement bans, using military and other forceful measures to keep people indoors. Arriving at a collective action outcome – e.g., making everyone practice 'social distancing' – may benefit from the execution of top-down enforcement. Does this in any way imply the superiority of an authoritarian governance approach?

A complex systems approach, which this book defends, answers 'no' to that question. I wanted to write about the kinds of governance approaches that somehow manage to pursue collective values and spirit, specifically on the topic of 'how to be more kind to the planet we live in', while respecting different individual desires, ideological positions, and philosophies on life. In other words, although I wanted to convince everyone to be on board with my pro-environmentalist ideals – and the fact that we can never be independent of networks of nonhuman materiality – I did not want to achieve that through a coercive imposition of essentialist moral standards. To this end, I wondered if it is possible to persuade the mainstream public to undertake a project for the collective good, which may momentarily 'suppress' (or put a pause on) their individual rights to freedom or singularities of their desires? Historical studies on cities and localised urban politics have shown that this is possible. The classic example, used in Chapter 5, was Lewis Mumford's *The City in History*, which emphasises the 'spiritual power' of cities is nurtured only when citizens start pursuing a collective goal beyond their own well-being and individual survival. As for a public policy and planning perspective then, how do we cultivate a voluntary will among people to momentarily give up their singularity (à la Deleuze) for the sake of collective virtues and aspirations?

In the case of pursuing pro-environmentalism at a city-wide scale, I discussed several ways and levels this could be achieved. In some cases, people do not need to know that they are sacrificing. Similar to 'material participation' (featured in Chapter 3), pragmatic benefits (e.g., cost-effectiveness or convenience) of pro-environmental choices could usher people along the path of environmentalism without requiring them to consciously engage with the idea. Environmental activists, planners, and sustainable development professionals can lead this process of 'converting' non-environmentalism believers via insisting on the economic or everyday life rewards of energy-saving buildings or green infrastructure at the public policy level. Here, the environmentalist lifestyle is not a conscious choice, but people end up choosing it anyway if all buildings or urban designs are legally required to be carbon-neutral or water-saving.

In other cases, people can be charmed by the creativity and imagination of inventors, artists, and educators who successfully achieve an opportune and poignant articulation on: (1) how our survival is inseparable from nonhuman agencies and their ecological functioning; (2) how our thought processes or how we perceive the world is fundamentally affected by how we feel about our surroundings; and (3) how pro-environmental imageries are not necessarily about going back in time (i.e., the belief that the tension *between* our aspirations for human progress *versus* the environmental consequences of such progress can be mediated through the pursuit of excellence and innovation regarding the long-term sustainability of our time on earth). These messages can be introduced and permeate more effectively throughout the 'collective consciousness' of society, thanks to the work of discourse-generators who can take us beyond the mundanities of everyday life even in the most mundane situations. Artists, performers, and writers can help us access imagination in everyday life by awakening our sensibilities, or making us rethink how we feel about our everyday surroundings. Inventors, academics, and educators can instil the idea or spirit of hope that there are still things to be done, or that we can weather the unknown challenges ahead.

Finally, people can also be 'peer-pressured' to act or behave in a certain way, thanks to healthy civil society and political momentums propelled by activism, education, and collective awareness, resulting in the mobilisation of effective social movements that bear a longer-term cultural shift. The #metoo movement and youth climate activism have captivated global media and political discourse, creating a societal mood of society that does not tolerate certain behavioural choices. In today's societal mood, where supporting youth activism is considered a 'cultured' or 'woke' thing to do, what kind of parents can reject politics that aim to look after the future of their children? Likewise, in the aftermath of world-wide coverage of the #metoo movement, it is no exaggeration to say that there have been new developments in people's habits and comportments, with institutions and collectives becoming more conscious of instances that can be interpreted as sexual harassment or related unwelcome conducts. For such powerful political momentum and subsequent cultural change to occur, the existence of an open society and public trust in that openness is critical. Individuals should be able to speak their minds or mobilise social movements with the ideas they feel most pertinent to the collective betterment of their society.

In short, a complex systems approach to the pursuit of collective good – which in some cases asks people to change or sacrifice their 'default' setting of pursuing self-interest or individual desire/freedom – is essentially about respecting the heterogeneity of people's different life paths, perceptions, philosophies, and ideas about the world they live in. Should not a democratic society embody respect and celebration of difference, and find hope in the diversity that results from doing so? In the end, the Deleuzo-guattarian style of actualising the left's political agenda was founded in the very defence of heterogeneity over forced unity. As discussed in Chapter 5, Deleuze's future vision of the left was to encourage multitudes of assemblages and their expressions without a centralised, 'transcendent organising agent'. It would, after all, be unethical to suppress the right of marginalised individuals to express themselves in the name of forced solidarity or 'conforming to the standard'.

In a similar space of prioritising diversity over imposed unity, Laclau and Mouffe's post-Marxism tells us that the concept of 'working class' should not be perceived as an all-embracing monolithic category that determines one's (i.e., each constituent's) political agenda for good. In any categorisation or 'representation' that we attempt to make, there is always a segment of minority voices left out. For instance, the working class is composed of workers of older and younger generations, as well as of different racial and gender groups. What these different groups (within 'the working class') desire cannot be subsumed into one unilateral understanding of 'what the working-class wants'. Hence, in advocating for recognition of minority voices by dominant groups, contemporary political theorists argue ardently for plural democracy and the inevitability of agonistic conflicts among different social groups.[8] In fact, they consider the very existence of differences and conflicts as the ultimate attestation of a functioning democratic society.

So, if we accept the importance of upholding the values of pluralism for democratic societies, to what extent should diversity and heterogeneity of populations and their 'singularities' be respected? The COVID-19 crisis effectively questions the practical viability of plural democracy that today's political theorists hold so dear. The hanging balance between 'principles of freedom' and 'greater collective good' is basically what policy makers are at the time of writing struggling through in navigating the global health crisis, which is turning into an economic, social, and political crisis with soaring unemployment rates. This challenge is unprecedented, especially in the US where individual freedom is cherished in its national anthem. So then, how might we convince people to choose behaviours that support the greater collective good (i.e., urging people to 'shelter in place', preventing further spread of the virus) over behaviours that expressly prioritise individual rights to freedom?

A health crisis such as the COVID-19 pandemic presents us with the ultimate question underpinning this book: how could we as a society strike a balance between achieving a greater collective good *and* respecting hetero-geneity of different peoples' singularities and their uniqueness? Put another way, how can a society pursue the path of environmentalism without betray-ing the core principles of democracy and open society? Although this book has passionately made the case for a 'complex systems approach' that pri-oritises the value of pluralism (and openness towards others' life paths and perspectives), this author acknowledges the difficulty of executing such an approach under the extenuating circumstances of a crisis such as the COVID-19 pandemic, where a literal sense of life and death confronts us

every minute and every second. To what extent should the top-down imposition of norms be granted, for how long, and in what exact circumstances?

While this question encapsulates the existential crisis of Western democracy itself,[9] and is likely to remain central to future politics faced with
the uncertainty of the Anthropocene, I would like to conclude this book
by joining the discourse of writers who contend that the governance of
such crisis moments can harness the technical advantages of a functioning democracy. Josh Rogin, columnist at the *Washington Post*, argues how
democracies are better suited to protect public health through the example
of South Korea's response to the COVID-19 crisis:

> Some democracies are clearly not handling their responses well . . . Yet
> those are the faults of those governments, not of the open-society model
> writ large. In South Korea, authorities are reporting a steady downtick in
> confirmed coronavirus cases over the past week after a series of decisive
> actions. These measures focus on education, transparency, and mobilis-
> ing civil society – without resorting to Beijing's tactics of forcing millions
> into home detention, using minorities as slave factory labor or disappear-
> ing people who dare to criticise the government's actions.
>
> . . .
>
> South Korea's civil society has pitched in. Major events have been can-
> celled, church services have been moved online, and the government has
> persuaded citizens to stay away from Daegu – where the majority of cases
> are – without turning the city into a prison.
>
> Some of South Korea's measures have been controversial. For example,
> people who are confirmed to have coronavirus register their locations for
> sharing publicly, and a map of their past travels (without their names)
> is available for anyone wishing to avoid those spots. That may seem
> invasive, but it sure sounds better than having surveillance drones take
> people's temperature and spray disinfectant, as officials are doing in parts
> of China.[10]

While South Korea's choice of sharing location data publicly via a smartphone app – through which anyone can trace and avoid where COVID-19
positive cases are – has been met with severe criticisms on the arrival of sur-
veillance ('big brother') state, the other side of that coin is the emergence of

a formless mode of governance that maximises the merits of open society in lieu of physically forceful control: (1) open circulation of transparent information which establishes trust between government institutions and the public; (2) unrestricted media and space for open debates with guaranteed rights to freely raise and discuss social issues, keeping governmental actions in check; and (3) a healthy civil society, which can activate social mobilisation and collective action whenever necessary.

We live in a time where governance challenges are growing ever more complex, unpredictable, and wickedly ubiquitous in a way that is 'glocal'. Tracing the cause, effect, and pattern of their impacts does not always elicit a unilateral answer or solution. This increasing complexity, unpredictability and wickedness is increasingly propelled by our interconnected world. Would such dynamics signal a call for more closed or exclusive politics? The relative success of South Korea in curbing the COVID-19 pandemic proves the opposite. Instead of putting up more walls, South Korea's strategy has focused on readjusting the software of society, through information, education, and timely cultural shift. If the Anthropocene knocks on our door, with its legions that sneak in formlessly and all-pervasively – through the molecules of the air we breathe, the water we drink, the surfaces we touch – our response should likewise operate in a formless, software kind of way, permeating every bit of how our society functions, from institutional decisions to individual behavioural change. Devising a response can only be possible when we take on a 'complex systems approach' that is humble at its core – humble in that it not only accepts the unforeseeability of the future, but also avoids reductive assumptions on radical heterogeneity that keeps our societies vibrant and truly democratic.

This book used 'cities' as an example of how such an approach could be concocted, enabled by the complexity that the urban scale itself entails – as a physically graspable entity that hosts diverse populations in a denser, more connected place. Urban density is currently under attack in the aftermath of COVID-19,[11] but we should not forget that it is also a source of solidarity and politics of hope.[12] For instance, urban density can entail more social infrastructure, such as social ties and support networks, leading to more effective distribution of services to vulnerable populations.[13] If we all lived far apart from one another, the spread of the virus might have been slower, but the vulnerable may have been left even more vulnerable due to social invisibility, isolation, and abandonment.

More importantly, what is critical about the role of density is its contribution to plural democracy. Cities' diversity of populations and culture allows cultivation of an open-minded sensibility, forcing residents to physically co-exist with those who are radically different from them. Berman, using Baudelaire's poem ('The Eyes of the Poor'), captures the bittersweet reality of 'the urban' where the magic of *la nouvelle vie parisienne* meets 'the great saucer eyes'. 'How beautiful it is', exclaim the eyes of the poor, standing outside of the glorious new café, while the middle class, sitting on the terrace, find their stare 'unbearable'. The ironies and contradictions of urban life, according to Merrifield, is what 'upgrades and intensifies citizens' agora', a place where its physical openness invites the possibilities of unlikely encounters, being affected or affecting others, and out of it, the emergence of new citizenry and family.[14] As Berman puts it,

Figure 6.1   Ajay Jennings

Haussmann, in tearing down the old medieval slums, inadvertently broke down the self-enclosed and hermetically sealed world of traditional urban poverty. The boulevards, blasting great holes through the poorest neighbourhoods, enable the poor to walk through the holes and out of their ravaged neighbourhoods, to discover for the first time what the rest of their city and the rest of life are like.[15]

What makes this book truly unique is its effort to translate earthly politics – which have often been shrugged off as 'new age' counterculture movements – into a mainstream political movement that seeks a wider audience. The key ingredient in making this shift happen is the habit of tolerance towards 'the other', the characteristic of which cities are more apt to possess. To be a part of urban politics is to 'grow up politically'. This involves finding inventive and discerning ways to inject new ideas and identities, while being respectful of the differences of 'the other' that may not be one hundred per cent understandable or perceivable to you. That generosity, in embracing what's currently hard to know or understand – even within the entity of action or the place where you think you belong – is another possibility of the unknown that I wish the readers would take away from this book, since it will warrant more inclusive *and* democratic new ecology movements.

Postscript
Future directions for cities in the Anthropocene

In hopes of propelling new debate on the future role of cities in the Anthropocene, this postscript is organised around four questions that readers may find themselves asking, followed by my responses.

Question 1. Your discussions on Darwin, Tulsa, Cleveland, and Cape Town often end in a 'full-stop' – it feels like they do not go so far as to provide future directions for these cities. What can you say about their prospects moving forward?

As for Darwin, one of the most important assets that the region has is the strong presence of indigenous communities (Larrakia or 'saltwater people') and their rich cultural heritage.[1] I think there is a lot of potential in finding out how wisdom from First Australian culture can reshape the city's relationship with nature. In fact, when you go to the Museum and Art Gallery of the Northern Territory, there is an entire exhibit section dedicated to the impacts of Cyclone Tracy. It shows how aboriginal communities sensed the cyclone's arrival prior to the event by paying attention and actively listening to the feedback from nonhuman surroundings. As Lobo shows in her work,[2] Anthropocene moments – the abrupt shock of which reveals the limits of our modernised understanding of the world – can offer Darwin an occasion to more sincerely engage with the city's aboriginal heritage. Recently, the city launched a new project – 'Darwin City Deal' – which includes a variety of initiatives to promote and celebrate the culture of Larrakia Nation, including the development of the Larrakia Hosts Program ($2 million pledged by the Australian Government) and building a Larrakia Cultural Centre ($250,000 pledged by the Northern Territory Government).[3] I hope these projects do not simply reminisce about the past, but put forward more concrete aspirations about how local indigenous knowledge and practice (of 'paying

159

attention' to our natural surroundings) can contribute to the city's cultural shift towards new ecology.

Another good example of the Anthropocene moments becoming an opportunity to engage with aboriginal communities is 'carbon farming'.[4] Carbon farming is sustainable land management that initiates 'cool fire' in early dry season, before the hot fire that occurs in late dry season. Hot fires are more dangerous, generating more carbon emissions as well causing more damage to the land. The alternative is 'prescribed burning' or 'early grass seasons fire', another name for 'cool fire'. It originates from savanna burning projects, where ranger groups (with the help of traditional owners and scientists) plan, map out, and record the prescribed fires. There are significant environmental benefits to savanna burning. Through shifting the fire regime from late dry season to early dry season fires, savanna burning projects increase biodiversity, improve soil health, and cause a significant reduction in greenhouse gas emissions. The land rangers scientifically calculate the emissions saved by the 'cool fire' they executed (by comparing them against the emissions that would have occurred otherwise) and translate them into 'carbon credits' (one carbon credit unit equals one ton of carbon dioxide). The rangers can sell these units to the Australian government, which has approximately one billion carbon emission funds. They can also sell them to voluntary private buyers such as energy companies or airlines who purchase them for a higher price – because they can use this buying action as their marketing strategies. One of my interviewees noted that the climate crisis is what ultimately spurs the public to take an interest in indigenous carbon farming. As they put it,

> Climate change really drives what we do and carbon industry. With more increasing awareness on climate change, people realise that abating carbon emission does have economic value. We need to consider the cost of carbon emission in our economy, and reconfigure the ways [in which] our industries are set up. The cost of harming the environment has to be taken account of from the start. A lot of media coverage and discourses of politicians wrongly set 'economy' apart from 'environment', as if they are independent from one another. This is not true. Environmental impacts affect our economy and our health, and we have to include the cost of environmental damages when calculating industry budgets.

About Tulsa, one of the most positive things that I noticed was the influx of young professionals and families who come back from big coastal cities (e.g., New York) and now settle down in this new bustling town in the Midwest. The city, in its effort to reinvent its image from the 'oil capital of the world', welcomes this new workforce and the source of its vibrant economy. These young professionals are changing the city's atmosphere and mood about what's 'cool', as well as public opinions about how the city should be planned. They actively participate in young professional workshops and networking programmes,[5] where they talk about more sustainable, 'green' business operations in Tulsa as well as the positive change they want to bring to the city.

Another fascinating fact about sustainable development in Tulsa was the involvement of Cherokee Nation (a federally recognised first nation tribe) and their pioneering investments in renewable energy and electric vehicle use.[6] In 2017, Cherokee Nation became the first tribe in the state of Oklahoma (where Tulsa is located) to open a solar canopy car-charging station. The charging station provides about 58,000 kilowatt hours of electricity to the tribal complex. Their historical commitment to preserving the natural environment ties in well with their pursuit of green technology, as Chief Baker notes:

> Embracing solar panels and adding electric vehicles to our fleet is consistent with Cherokee Nation's leadership in clean-energy and footprint reduction . . . We have always been a good steward of the land, and this is another example of exceptional natural resource conservation, a legacy established by our ancestors.[7]

One of the stories that I failed to touch on in this book is remembering the history of Greenwood District in Tulsa, the 'Black Wall Street' where there were concentrations of Black businesses in the early 20th century. When I was visiting Tulsa, there was a big protest in the City Hall about its painful history and paths to reconciliation. The wound remains deep and still recent, and I could never do justice to this story by myself fleetingly mentioning it. But what I noticed was that the organisations like Typros (young professionals forum) or Sustainable Tulsa (promoting green businesses) were the magnets of racial diversity, much more so than when I attended some 'green-only' meetings (i.e. protecting nature for the sake of nature). This again repeats the theme of Chapter 4 where I emphasised the need for social actors to proactively articulate the convergence of green and equity values (based on local histories and materialities already-in-place), which is what anti-essentialist ecology should focus on going forward.

For Cleveland – my interviewees complained about how the 'shrink city' concept has become a stigma that the city now wants to be freed from. Particularly when it comes to creating economic opportunities for people, something Cleveland desperately needs, the idea that the city is 'shrinking' did not help. So, what is a better term? Take the Western Reserve Land Conservancy's programme 'Thriving Communities: Creating Healthy Cities'.[10] The organisation, as its name suggests, is primarily committed to nature/ land conservancy work. This doesn't usually concern urban areas, but since 2011 the organisation has taken on a new initiative to help revitalise urban centres. The Thriving Communities programme identifies/maps out the vacant lots in cities in Ohio, and works with communities to transform these abandoned sites into green neighbourhood amenities. Their rationale is that it's better to have people stay in already developed urban areas, rather than having them invade untouched natural reserves (often via new greenfield developments). Therefore, we should make existing urban areas healthier, safer, and better places to live. This argument adds another layer to the benefits of more compact urban development: 'making the already existing communities thrive' not only works for the city's aspirations for economic revitalisation (the kind that actually benefits the residents in the area), but also fits well with leaving the preserved lands intact. I think that this kind of partnership between land conservancy work (led by regional organisations and grant funding bodies) and healthy communities work (led by cities and neighbourhoods) has lots of potential in American cities hit by the foreclosure crisis.

One of the most realistic and pragmatic ways of pursuing a green agenda in Cape Town is the reimagining of urban infrastructure provisions. Given the continuously mushrooming new settlements in urban peripheries, it seems almost impossible to deliver utility services through a centralised infrastructure. Green tech actually facilitates these suburbs going 'off grid', which can become a source of empowerment for communities in terms of being in charge of their own electricity provision, consumption, and management. More importantly, how to fund this 'panacea' would likely be the key question for cities in emerging economies. GreenCape has been charting new ways of financing these alternative service provisions; its Alternative Service Delivery Unit is working on 'the design, facilitation and implementation of community-led [off-the-grid] service models that are financially sustainable, technically sound and socially inclusive'.[11] Matching the needs of informal communities with the business interests of companies seems to be at the heart of its sustainable funding flow, which remains critical for cities in the Global South where governments typically don't have large tax revenue reserves. Such a public-private partnership model can also be applied to other 'win-win' green tech projects, such as the waste-to-energy project in Addis Ababa (the capital of Ethiopia) that turns the city's garbage into 20 megawatts of power.[12]

African cities can be the next green tech capitals. Silicon Savannah in Nairobi, Kenya is a good example: a US$1 billion tech hub with 200 start-ups.[13] The reality of leapfrogging technologies is something that you truly feel when you visit Africa – I was surprised by the overwhelming presence of app-based mobile payment in Cape Town (e.g., SnapScan). 'Necessity is the mother of climate-change innovation', notes Aryn Baker, a journalist and correspondent based in Cape Town; transformative technologies are increasingly being born in Africa, where extreme circumstances give birth to the kinds of inventions that are ready for global deployment.[14] If green tech manufacturing can create jobs (see Chapter 4), why not invest in youth education so they can become the inventors of the technology itself? In this sense, Cape Town should embrace its soaring youth population as valuable assets and as a workforce, providing training and education opportunities that can help them realise their full potential. Indeed, the scope of such work spills over city boundaries and its responsibilities, but city governments can play a central role in making timely interventions through school programmes and development projects that are guided by the economic opportunities in green revolution.

Question 2. Chapter 4 (on Cleveland and Cape Town) underscores the power of localised environment politics, but it does not talk about how the stories of these two cities help in advancing existing debates on political ecology. Can you elaborate on what their experiences imply for the future of new ecology scholarship?

This is one of the key questions I struggled with, especially with increasing academic debates on the viability of more radical positionalities on 'growth' and 'development'.[15] One of the things I noticed in Cape Town was that, while white interviewees embraced the idea of 'going green', non-white interviewees were more concerned with the everyday life challenges such as instituting a city-wide sewage system or running water on tap (remember, one-fifth of Capetonians live in informal settlements). The tension between 'green' and 'social equity' was also pretty stark in Cleveland, where African American communities seem much less interested in questions of the environment as they battle with everyday neighbourhood violence. The timeline of their 'future' was entirely different from the timeline of the 'future' that we (pro-environment academic writers, including myself) often envision.

One of the key lessons I believe Chapter 4 provides is that we must not forget that a lot of environmental concerns are 'think-able' topics for us thanks to the privileges we often take for granted. Before resenting the fact that there are still people who don't understand the importance of the environment, we must ask ourselves: Do you worry about not having a working toilet? Do you worry every night that a family member or a neighbour might get killed by police? Do you worry about putting food on the table every single day? If the answer is no, then we must acknowledge the kinds of 'everyday privileges' that we have. Some of these privileges are so deeply engrained in our consciousness that we can't seem to imagine what life is like without the comfort of a safe, hygienic home that allows us the space to think beyond daily survival.

In the economically distressed neighbourhoods of American 'rust belt' cities or the Global South's informal settlements, as I mentioned in Chapter 4, 'economic development' is almost an imperative for those who still dream of a dignified human life. Of course, capitalist-driven growth and modernisation have caused devastating impacts on the environment and human society, such as predation on natural resources and the staggering level of economic inequality that threatens the very well-being of our society on the whole.[16] At the same time, I don't think one should deny the certain necessary aspects of 'development', or that some people may prioritise their everyday livelihood concerns (e.g. job opportunities) over much broader, longer-term questions on the environment. While I write about the desires that invoke new modes of human existence, it is my hope that new ecology scholars and activists can retain genuine curiosity towards the life experiences and opinions of those who may not share similar philosophies, rather than shutting them out as an incomprehensible 'other'. What we need is an *engaged* scholarship in which academics are genuinely interested in what's happening on the ground (in a particular physical location and a historic moment time), rather than finding comfort in the certainty of abstract (atemporal, ahistorical, a-contextual) ideals *vacuumed of* actual people, places, and things.

> Question 3. You have briefly touched on the impacts of COVID-19, but did not go into detail on what this pandemic means for cities. Can you say a little more about the role of cities in preparation for, in response to, or in recovering from a global pandemic?

The experience of the COVID-19 global pandemic has posed a lot of important questions for the future of cities, especially on urban density or 'compact urbanisation', which has been the anthem of sustainable development. The majority of this book, however, was written in pre-COVID-19 times, and is mainly about climate crisis. The pandemic, in the conclusion of this book, served more as a moment to collectively reflect on the material fragility and vulnerability we all share as humans (i.e., mortal bodies), which is similar to what happens in the wake of natural disasters. The conclusion's reference to a national scale action was mainly to highlight the difficulty of balancing 'respecting individual singularities' versus 'achieving public good' in plural democracy, which I think is central to this book's quest for 'environment politics beyond environment'. While I'm confident that cities can be leaders of new ecology politics (for the reasons I detailed in Chapter 5), I'm currently not in a position to say that they can also be pioneers in handling a sanitation crisis. I'm impatient to see how cities will recover from this unprecedented rupture in the months (if not years) to come, and urban historians, epistemologists, and practising architects will be able to offer more useful insights than I can at this time.[17]

That said, from the perspective of environment planning, I think cities can use this crisis to gain momentum in expediating some of the 'green' urban agendas that intersect with the interests of human health. In recovering from this global pandemic, there can be an enhanced appreciation of our access to urban oases and public green spaces. We may also find a pragmatic reason to develop neighbourhood-driven economies (via supporting local groceries and eateries) that reduce the need for unnecessary motor travel. Cities can more systematically orchestrate such initiatives at a scale that oversees different compartments in place. For instance, they can apply flexible land use for on-street parking sites, which can be redesigned and reinvented as green spaces or pedestrian-friendly areas. Also, when it comes to greening the city, cities can track and trace green spaces, their maintenance, and connectivity across different locations to ensure they are evenly distributed. Connected and evenly distributed green areas not only help the resilience of larger-scale urban forms in times of natural hazards (e.g., turning flood-prone areas into parks), but also to ensure equal public access to open green spaces. Furthermore, cities can support community development organisations and neighbourhood-serving local businesses, creating compact areas that cultivate place-based cohesion. Ensuring the socioeconomic health of these neighbourhood subsystems can render the city-wide system more resilient in times of crisis, not only in terms of social support but also in terms of reducing car dependency.

A post-disaster context often presents an occasion to ask ourselves what we truly value and what we are willing to forgo. In Christchurch, New Zealand, in the aftermath of the devastating earthquake in 2011, citizens were given a chance to discuss what buildings and city infrastructure they considered essential and valuable enough to be rebuilt and restored.[18] The post-COVID-19 condition may bring about a similar moment to reflect on what we absolutely need and what we can live without. Milan, Italy, as one of the first European cities to reopen after the attack from COVID-19, announced a set of city-wide actions to radically curb air pollution and congestion, including new cycle lanes, speed limits on private vehicles, and pedestrian/cyclist priority streets. I hope that similar debates and public sentiments (about the role of urban form and spatial organisation in improving our health) occur in cities around the world, imagining new ways of transportation as well as the degree of density cities wish to maintain.

Put another way, after the coronavirus, there will be a rise of value-loaded questions around what we stand for, which should be asked and answered within each of our unique local contexts. That's another reason why 'urban agora' is so important in the Anthropocene era, because the future of the human species hangs on our capacity to debate, constitute, and to be on board with a *collective* vision.

Question 4. The Actor Network Theory (ANT) has been criticised for its flattening of power and inability to explain why some actors are systematically excluded from the game. What is the contribution of 'new ecology' to the discussion of environmental justice?

I would respond to that question by focusing on these three aspects of 'new ecology' literature: (1) Its invitation to think of how human individuals and nonhuman agents are historically interdependent and entangled with one another; (2) Its usefulness in considering the co-constitutive relationship between the social and the technical (e.g., how 'users' of urban design or technologies make these better via their 'material participation'); (3) Its call for articulating more inclusive, generous, or 'humble' ways of interjecting your message or intention – without being too sure about their consequences (i.e. foregoing the modernist impulse to grab and control nature/your surrounding environment). While ANT camp and new ecology camp may agree with one another on the points (2) and (3), the emphasis on historicity and 'response-ability' that are embedded within one's situated surroundings – the point (1) – is what new ecology dialogues have reified through their stories or 'thick descriptions' (that cover different temporalities and capture the evolution of interaction effects *over time*).

I haven't been explicit about the new ecology's radical politics, but feminist geographers and new ecologists have proposed 'politics of care/care ethics' through which one can reject the atomised individual (agency) and the myth of 'boot-strapping'. By realising how each of our destiny has always been and always will be dependent on the surrounding environment and the materiality of 'life-sustaining' web, we can together project 'humanistic vision' that opens up the possibilities of unexpected synchronisation for 'a sustainable future' in-between the physical co-existence of different bodies. I believe that the 'solution' to the operational question of environmental justice has to be *found* in the intersections of technologies, physical environment, the economy, existing livelihoods, cultures, and customs in a specific place-based situation.

Notes

CHAPTER 1: ENVIRONMENT POLITICS BEYOND ENVIRONMENT

1. Gilles Deleuze and Felix Guattari, *A Thousand Plateaus*, trans. Brian Massumi (Minneapolis, MN: University of Minnesota Press, 1987, reprint in 2013 by Bloomsbury Revelations), p. 50.
2. One should note that an anti-essentialist approach to challenging the human/nonhuman dichotomy is pioneered by feminist political ecologists whose political standpoint began by dismantling the female/male dichotomy. See Donna Haraway, *The companion species manifesto: Dogs, people, and significant otherness* (Chicago, IL: Prickly Paradigm Press, 2003); Karen Barad, *Meeting the Universe Halfway: Quantum Physics and the Entanglement of Matter and Being* (Durham, NC: Duke University Press, 2007). Their radical positioning (in the context of urban planning) is well captured in: Donna Houston, Jean Hillier, Diana MacCallum, Wendy Steele, and Jason Byrne, 'Make kin, not cities! Multispecies entanglements and "becoming-world" in planning theory', *Planning Theory*, Vol. 17, No. 2 (2018), pp. 190–212.
3. See Baltimore's commentary presented by Welcoming America, a non-profit, non-partisan organisation and a supportive network for local communities taking pro-immigration initiatives on their own. www.welcomingamerica.org/learn/welcoming-refugees-paris-attacks
4. John Dewey, *Experience and Nature* (Redditch, Worcestershire: Read Books, 2008[1925]), p. 14.

CHAPTER 2: WHY CITIES?
TOWARDS A NEW THEORISATION OF 'SCALE'

1. Bruno Latour, *Politiques de la nature: comment faire entrer les sciences en démocratie* (Paris: La découverte, 1999); Bruno Latour, *Facing Gaia: Eight lectures on the new climatic regime.* (Hoboken, NJ: John Wiley & Sons, 2017a); Bruno Latour, *Où atterir? Comment s' orienter en politique* (Paris: La découverte, 2017b).
2. Donna J. Haraway, *Staying with the trouble: Making kin in the Chthulucene* (Durham, NC: Duke University Press, 2016); Donna J. Haraway, *The companion species manifesto: Dogs, people, and significant otherness* (Chicago, IL: Prickly Paradigm Press, 2007).
3. Anna Lowenhaupt Tsing, *The Mushroom at the End of the World: On the possibility of life in capitalist ruins* (Princeton, NJ: Princeton University Press, 2015).

4. Chad Zanocco et al., 'Place, proximity, and perceived harm: extreme weather events and views about climate change', *Climatic Change*, Vol. 149, No. 3–4 (2018), pp. 349–65.

5. Neil Brenner, 'The limits to scale? Methodological reflections on scalar structuration', *Progress in Human Geography*, Vol. 25, No. 4 (2001), pp. 591–614; Neil Brenner, 'Restructuring, rescaling and the urban question', *Critical Planning*, Vol. 16, No. 4 (2009), pp. 61–79; Erik Swyngedouw and Nikolas C. Heynen, 'Urban political ecology, justice and the politics of scale', *Antipode*, Vol. 35, No. 5 (2003), pp. 898–918.

6. For a summary of how 'politics of scale' dialogues have been influenced by poststructural critique, see Danny MacKinnon, 'Reconstructing scale: Towards a new scalar politics', *Progress in Human Geography*, Vol. 35, No. 1 (2010), pp. 21–36.

7. Roderick P. Neumann, 'Political ecology: theorizing scale', *Progress in Human Geography*, Vol. 33, No. 3 (2008), pp. 398–406.

8. See James McCarthy, 'Scale, sovereignty, and strategy in environmental governance', Antipode, Vol. 37, No. 4 (2005), pp. 731–53.

9. Adam Moore, 'Rethinking scale as a geographical category: from analysis to practice', *Progress in Human Geography*, Vol. 32, No. 2 (2008), pp. 203–25.

10. Mark Purcell, 'Islands of practice and the Marston/Brenner debate: toward a more synthetic critical human geography', *Progress in Human Geography*, Vol. 27, No. 3 (2003), pp. 317–32.

11. McCarthy, 'Scale, sovereignty, and strategy in environmental governance', p. 734.

12. See Judith Butler, 'Gender trouble, feminist theory, and psychoanalytic discourse', In Nicholson Linda J. (ed.) *Feminism/Postmodernism* (New York: Routledge, 1990), pp. 324–40.

13. Sallie A. Marston, 'The social construction of scale', *Progress in Human Geography*, Vol. 24, No. 2 (2000), pp. 219–42.

14. See Pol Bargués-Pedreny, 'From Critique to Affirmation in International Relations', *Global Society*, Vol. 33, No. 1 (2019), pp. 1–11.

15. Pol Bargués-Pedreny and Jessica Schmidt, 'Learning to Be Postmodern in an All Too Modern World: 'Whatever action' in International Climate Change Imaginaries', *Global Society*, Vol. 33, No. 1 (2019), pp. 45–65.

16. Tsing, *The Mushroom at the End of the World: On the possibility of life in capitalist ruins*, p. 278.

17. Matthew Paterson, *Understanding global environmental politics: Domination, accumulation, resistance.* (Basingstoke, Hampshire: Palgrave, 2001); Noel Castree, 'The geopolitics of nature', In J. Agnew, K. Mitchell, and G. Toal (Eds.), *A companion to political geography* (Oxford: Blackwell, 2003), pp. 423–39; Harriet Bulkeley and Michele Betsill, *Cities and climate change: Urban sustainability and global environmental governance* (London: Routledge, 2003); Miranda A. Schreurs, 'From the bottom up: local and subnational climate change politics', *The Journal of Environment & Development*, Vol. 17, No. 4

(2008), pp. 343–55; Karin Bäckstrand et al., 'The promise of new modes of environmental governance', *Environmental politics and deliberative democracy: Examining the promise of new modes of governance* (Cheltenham: Edward Elgar Publishing, 2010), pp. 3–27.

18. Elinor Ostrom, 'A multi-scale approach to coping with climate change and other collective action problems', *Solutions*, Vol. 1, No. 2 (2010), pp. 27–36; I. M. Buizer, B. J. M. Arts, and Kasper Kok, 'Governance, scale and the environment: the importance of recognizing knowledge claims in transdisciplinary arenas', *Ecology and Society*, Vol. 16, No. 1 (2011); Faith R. Sternlieb, Patrick Bixler, and Heidi Huber-Stearns, 'A question of fit: reflections on boundaries, organizations and social–ecological systems', *Journal of Environmental Management*, Vol. 130 (2013), pp.117–25; Alice Cohen and James McCarthy, 'Reviewing rescaling: Strengthening the case for environmental considerations', *Progress in Human Geography*, Vol. 39, No. 1 (2015), pp. 3–25.

19. Henri Lefebvre, *The production of space*, (Oxford: Blackwell, 1991); Haripriya Rangan and Christian A. Kull, 'What makes ecology 'political'? Rethinking 'scale' in political ecology', *Progress in Human Geography*, Vol. 33, No. 1 (2009), pp. 28–45.

20. Dominique Bourg and Kerry Whiteside, *Vers une démocratie écologique*, (Paris: Seuil, 2010).

21. Hugh C. Dyer, 'Climate anarchy: creative disorder in world politics', *International Political Sociology*, Vol. 8, No. 2 (2014), pp. 182–200.

22. Ibid., p. 182.

23. Hakan Seckinelgin, *The Environment and International Politics: International Fisheries, Heidegger and Social Method* (London: Routledge, 2005).

24. Dyer, 'Climate anarchy: creative disorder in world politics', p. 188.

25. ICLEI – Local Governments for Sustainability, founded in 1990 as the International Council for Local Environmental Initiatives, is a global network of cities, towns and regions committed to sustainable urban development.

26. Harriet Bulkeley and Susanne C. Moser, 'Responding to climate change: governance and social action beyond Kyoto', *Global Environmental Politics*, Vol. 7, No. 2 (2007), pp. 1–10.

27. Timothy Morton, *Hyperobjects: philosophy and ecology after the end of the world* (Minneapolis: University of Minnesota Press, 2013).

28. Latour, *Où atterrir*, p. 43.

29. Damien Cave, 'It Was Supposed to Be Australia's Climate Change Election. What Happened?' *New York Times*, 19 May 2019, www.nytimes.com/2019/05/19/world/australia/election-climate-change.html.

30. Aidan While, Andrew E. G. Jonas, and David Gibbs, 'From sustainable development to carbon control: eco-state restructuring and the politics of urban and regional development', *Transactions of the Institute of British Geographers*, Vol. 35, No. 1 (2010), pp. 76–93; Harriet Bulkeley and Michele Betsill, 'Revisiting the urban politics of climate change', *Environmental Politics*, Vol. 22, No. 1 (2013), pp. 136–54.

31. Neumann, 'Political ecology: theorizing scale'; Moore, 'Rethinking scale as a geographical category: from analysis to practice'; McCarthy, 'Scale, sovereignty, and strategy in environmental governance'; see also Neil Smith, 'Geography, difference and the politics of scale', *Postmodernism and the social sciences* (London: Palgrave, 1992), pp. 57–79.
32. Moore, especially, associates 'scale' with 'national identity' as a socially constructed category, noting the performative aspects of scales and how they cannot be essentialist or fixed a priori concepts – preferring 'matryoshka dolls' metaphor (as opposed to 'ladder' metaphor) on how scales in fact overlap or interact with one another (p. 217).
33. McCarthy, 'Scale, sovereignty, and strategy in environmental governance'.
34. Moore, 'Rethinking scale as a geographical category: from analysis to practice', p. 206; Michele Acuto, 'The new climate leaders?', *Review of International Studies*, Vol. 39, No. 4 (2013), pp. 835–57.
35. Harriet Bulkeley, 'Reconfiguring environmental governance: Towards a politics of scales and networks', *Political geography*, Vol. 24, No. 8 (2005), pp. 875–902.
36. Ibid., p. 897.
37. Helga Leitner and Eric Sheppard, '"The city is dead, long live the net": harnessing European interurban networks for a neoliberal agenda', *Antipode*, Vol. 34, No. 3 (2002), pp. 495–518; Joe Painter, 'Rethinking territory', *Antipode*, Vol. 42, No. 5 (2010), pp. 1090–1118.
38. Bulkeley, 'Reconfiguring environmental governance: Towards a politics of scales and networks'
39. Acuto, 'The new climate leaders?', p. 851.
40. Kevin Cox, 'Spaces of engagement, spaces of dependence and the politics of scale, or: looking for local politics', *Political Geography*, Vol. 17, No. 1 (1998), pp. 1–23.
41. David Chandler, 'Critiquing liberal cosmopolitanism? The limits of the biopolitical approach', International Political Sociology, Vol. 3, No. 1 (2009), pp. 53–70.
42. Nathan F. Sayre, 'Scale', In: N. Castree, D. Demeritt, B. Rhoads, D. Liverman (eds.), *A companion to environmental geography*, (Oxford: Blackwell, 2008), p. 100.
43. Nathan F. Sayre, 'Ecological and geographical scale: parallels and potential for integration', *Progress in Human Geography*, Vol. 29, No. 3 (2005), p. 277.
44. Stephen M. Manson, 'Does scale exist? An epistemological scale continuum for complex human–environment systems', *Geoforum*, Vol. 39, No. 2 (2008), p. 783.
45. Corey Lang, 'Do weather fluctuations cause people to seek information about climate change?', *Climatic Change*, Vol. 125, No. 3–4 (2014), pp. 291–303; Matthew J. Cutler, 'Seeing and believing: the emergent nature of extreme weather perceptions', *Environmental Sociology*, Vol. 1, No. 4 (2015), pp. 293–303; Corey Lang and John David Ryder, 'The effect of tropical

cyclones on climate change engagement', *Climatic Change*, Vol. 135, No. 3–4 (2016), pp. 625–38; David M. Konisky, Llewelyn Hughes, and Charles H. Kaylor, 'Extreme weather events and climate change concern', *Climatic Change*, Vol. 134, No. 4 (2016), pp. 533–47; Matthew R. Sisco, Valentina Bosetti, and Elke U. Weber, 'When do extreme weather events generate attention to climate change?', *Climatic Change*, Vol. 143, No. 1–2 (2017), pp. 227–41.

46. Mark Pelling and Kathleen Dill, 'Natural disasters as catalysts of political action', *Media Development*, Vol. 53, No. 4 (2006), p. 7; Jörn Birkmann et al. 'Extreme events and disasters: a window of opportunity for change? Analysis of organizational, institutional and political changes, formal and informal responses after mega-disasters', *Natural Hazards* Vol. 55, No. 3 (2010), pp. 637–55.

47. McCarthy, 'Scale, sovereignty, and strategy in environmental governance'.

48. Ibid., p. 745.

49. Tsing, *The Mushroom at the End of the World*; Latour, *Facing Gaia*; Isabelle Stengers, *In catastrophic times: Resisting the coming of barbarism* (Paris: Open Humanities Press, 2015); Haraway, *Staying with the trouble: Making kin in the Chthulucene*.

50. David Chandler, 'The death of hope? Affirmation in the Anthropocene', *Globalizations*, Vol. 16, No. 5 (2019), pp. 695–706; David Chandler, 'The Transvaluation of Critique in the Anthropocene', *Global Society*, Vol. 33, No. 1 (2019), pp. 26–44.

51. Bargués-Pedreny and Schmidt, 'Learning to Be Postmodern in an All Too Modern World: 'Whatever action' in International Climate Change Imaginaries'.

52. Stengers, *In catastrophic times: Resisting the coming of barbarism*, p. 61.

53. Latour, *Facing Gaia*, p. 275.

54. Latour introduces the invention of geotracking mechanisms that could trace the historicity of ecosystem functions – 'tracking space, marking plots, tracing lines' in the field of geography, geology, and geomorphology (2017a: 275).

55. See Will Steffen et al. 'Planetary boundaries: Guiding human development on a changing planet', *Science*, Vol. 347, No. 6223 (2015); their work on 'planetary boundaries' introduces an ecosystem-driven approach to define the most appropriate scale for addressing ecological crises; however, they admit that, because of their focus on ecosystem functions, their framework fails to provide practical guidance on navigating the sociopolitical issues of scale.

56. See Paul Chatterton, 'Building transitions to post-capitalist urban commons', *Transactions of the Institute of British Geographers*, Vol. 41, No. 4 (2016), pp. 403–15.

57. Elena M. Bennett et al., 'Bright spots: seeds of a good Anthropocene', *Frontiers in Ecology and the Environment*, Vol. 14, No. 8 (2016), pp. 441–8.

58. Bargués-Pedreny and Schmidt, 'Learning to Be Postmodern in an All Too Modern World: "Whatever action" in International Climate Change Imaginaries', p. 63.

59. J. Christopher Brown and Mark Purcell, 'There's nothing inherent about scale: political ecology, the local trap, and the politics of development in the Brazilian Amazon', *Geoforum*, Vol. 36, No. 5 (2005), pp. 607–24.
60. Patrick Devine-Wright, 'Think global, act local? The relevance of place attachments and place identities in a climate changed world', *Global Environmental Change*, Vol. 23, No. 1 (2013), pp. 61–9.
61. Latour, *Facing Gaia*.
62. The concept of 'Gaia' originates from 'Gaia Hypothesis' by Lovelock (1979), which emphasised that nature is a living, active organism rather than an inanimate object or background to be passively exploited; James Lovelock, *Gaia: A new look at life on Earth* (Oxford: Oxford University Press, 1979).
63. Latour, *Facing Gaia*, p. 280.
64. Donna Haraway, 'Situated knowledges: The science question in feminism and the privilege of partial perspective', *Feminist Studies*, Vol. 14, No. 3 (1988): 575–99.
65. According to Sloterdijk, the idea of the 'globe' is formed by our religious effort to follow the dream of total and complete knowledge of 'God'; Peter Sloterdijk, 'Spheres', *Volume II: Globes–Macrospherology* (South Pasadena, CA: Semiotext, 2014[1999]).
66. Latour, *Facing Gaia*, p. 104.
67. Zadist (in French, *Zadiste*) refers to a militant movement occupying a *ZAD* (*zone à défendre*, translated as 'zone to defend' – areas of ecological importance) to oppose a proposed development that would damage the environment.
68. Geneviève Azam, 'Écouter la terre pour réenchanter le monde: une écologie politique attentive', *Ecologie & Politique*, Vol. 56 (2018), p. 145.
69. Bruno Latour, 'An attempt at a' compositionist manifesto', *New Literary History*, Vol. 41, No. 3 (2010), pp. 471–90.
70. The recent urban climate action initiatives in Midwestern American cities empirically exhibit how the shared experiences of certain climate conditions can instigate policy change. Dubuque, Iowa is a great example: the city's frequent and severe experiences of flooding inspired its leadership to climate action. See Roy D. Buol, 'Dubuque is taking action on climate. Other Midwest cities and states should, too', *Des Moines Register*, 27 December 2018, www.desmoinesregister.com/story/opinion/columnists/2018/12/27/midwest-should-follow-dubuquelead-climate-change-action-renewable-energy-agriculture-water-quality/2387735002/.
71. Saskia Sassen, *The global city: New York, London, Tokyo* (Princeton, NJ: Princeton University Press, 2001); Saskia Sassen, *A Sociology of Globalization* (New York: Norton, 2007); Michele Acuto, *Global Cities, Governance and Diplomacy: The Urban Link* (London: Routledge, 2013a).
72. Sayre, 'Ecological and geographical scale: parallels and potential for integration'; Manson, 'Does scale exist? An epistemological scale continuum for complex human–environment systems'; Neumann, 'Political ecology: theorizing scale'.

73. Antoine Bousquet and Simon Curtis, 'Beyond models and metaphors: complexity theory, systems thinking and international relations', *Cambridge Review of International Affairs*, Vol. 24, No. 1 (2011), pp. 43–62.

74. Monica G. Turner, Virginia H. Dale, and Robert H. Gardner, 'Predicting across scales: theory development and testing', *Landscape Ecology*, Vol. 3, No. 3-4 (1989), pp. 245-52.

75. Cox, 'Spaces of engagement, spaces of dependence and the politics of scale, or: looking for local politics', pp. 20–21.

76. Manson, 'Does scale exist? An epistemological scale continuum for complex human–environment systems', p. 9.

77. Jim Glassman, 'From Seattle (and Ubon) to Bangkok: the scales of resistance to corporate globalization', *Environment and Planning D: Society and Space*, Vol. 20, No. 5 (2002), pp. 513–33; Helga Leitner, Jamie Peck, and Eric S. Sheppard (eds.), *Contesting neoliberalism: Urban frontiers* (Guilford Press, NY: 2007); Andrew D. Davis and David Featherstone, 'Networking resistances: The contested spatialities of transnational social movement organizing', in Walter Nicholls and Byron Miller (eds.), *Spaces of Contention: Spatialities and Social Movements* (London: Routledge, 2016), pp. 239–60.

78. David Alexander, 'Globalization of disaster: trends, problems and dilemmas', *Journal of International Affairs* (2006), pp. 1–22; Christopher B. Field et al., *Managing the risks of extreme events and disasters to advance climate change adaptation: special report of the intergovernmental panel on climate change* (Cambridge: Cambridge University Press, 2012).

79. Bulkeley, 'Reconfiguring environmental governance: Towards a politics of scales and networks'; Acuto, 'The new climate leaders?'.

80. Jackie Smith and Dawn Wiest, *Social movements in the world-system: The politics of crisis and transformation* (New York: Russell Sage Foundation, 2012); Giuseppe Feola and Richard Nunes, 'Success and failure of grassroots innovations for addressing climate change: The case of the Transition Movement', *Global Environmental Change*, Vol. 24 (2014), pp. 232–50; Lisa-Britt Fischer and Jens Newig, 'Importance of actors and agency in sustainability transitions: a systematic exploration of the literature', *Sustainability*, Vol. 8, No. 5 (2016), p. 476.

81. Anna Lowenhaupt Tsing, *Friction: An Ethnography of Global Connection* (Princeton, NJ: Princeton University Press, 2004).

82. Sayre, 'Ecological and geographical scale: parallels and potential for integration'

83. Ibid., p. 280.

84. LEED stands for 'Leadership in Energy and Environmental Design', an international green building rating system.

85. The ecological neighbourhood model is well captured in '*écoquartiers*' in the Parisian region (e.g., Ile-Saint-Denis' *écoquartier fluvial* and the Gare Ardoine area's *écoquartier resilient*), where the spatial organisation of a particular group

of blocks is specifically designed and arranged such that their functions are in accordance with ecological processes (especially for water management).

86. Zanocco et al., 'Place, proximity, and perceived harm: extreme weather events and views about climate change'; see also a recent report by Knickmeyer et al. (2019) on how personal observations of disasters influence people's perception on climate change politics – Ellen Knickmeyer, Hannah Fingerhut and Emily Swanson, 'Poll: Disasters influence thinking on climate change', The Associated Press-National Opinion Research Center for Public Affairs Research, 2019.

87. Benjamin, R. Barber, *If mayors ruled the world: Dysfunctional nations, rising cities* (New Haven: Yale University Press, 2013); Simon Curtis, *The Power of Cities in International Relations* (New York: Routledge, 2014).

88. Barber, ibid., p. 4.

89. Doreen Massey, 'Interpreting identities: Doreen Massey on politics, gender, and space-time', In *Power-Geometries and the Politics of Space-Time* (Heidelberg: University of Heidelberg, 1999), pp. 47–9 (emphasis in the original).

90. J. Scott Turner, *The Extended Organism. The Physiology of Animal-Built Structures* (Cambridge, MA: Harvard University Press, 2000); J. Scott Turner, *The Tinkerer's Accomplice* (Cambridge, MA: Harvard University Press, 2007).

91. Paul F. Downton, *Ecopolis: Architecture and cities for a changing climate* (Collingwood, Australia: CSIRO Publishing, 2008).

92. Ibid., p. 370.

93. Ibid., p. 372.

94. Turner, *The Tinkerer's Accomplice*, p. 6.

95. Magali Reghezza-Zitt, Territorialiser ou ne pas territorialiser le risque et l'incertitude. La gestion territorialisée à l'épreuve du risque d'inondation en Île-de-France [in French] [Coping with Floods in Île-de-France. Is the place-based approach in risk management still efficient when risk turns into uncertainty?]. *L'Espace Politique*, Vol. 26, No. 2 (2015).

96. Robert Freitag et al., *Floodplain management: a new approach for a new era* (Washington: Island Press, 2009).

97. Cathy Wilkinson, 'Social-ecological resilience: Insights and issues for planning theory', *Planning Theory*, Vol. 11, No. 2 (2012), pp. 148–69.

98. Alan G. Wilson, 'Ecological and urban systems models: some explorations of similarities in the context of complexity theory', *Environment and Planning A*, Vol. 38, No. 4 (2006), pp. 633–46; Alan G. Wilson, *Complex spatial systems: the modelling foundations of urban and regional analysis* (New York: Routledge, 2014).

99. Wilson, 'Ecological and urban systems models: some explorations of similarities in the context of complexity theory', p. 366.

100. Lewis Mumford, *The City in History: Its origins, its transformations, and its prospects (Vol. 67)*, (Boston, MA: Houghton Mifflin Harcourt, 1961), p. 113.

101. Bulkeley, 'Reconfiguring environmental governance: Towards a politics of scales and networks'; Acuto, 'The new climate leaders?'.

102. An earlier version of this chapter appears in Ihnji Jon, 'Scales of Political Action in the Anthropocene: Gaia, Networks, and Cities as Frontiers of Doing Earthly Politics', *Global Society*, Vol. 34, No. 2 (2019), pp. 163–85.

CHAPTER 3: DARWIN VS. TULSA

1. Damien Cave, 'It Was Supposed to Be Australia's Climate Change Election. What Happened?', *New York Times*, 19 May 2019.
2. Somini Sengupta, 'Australia's Politics May Be Changing With Its Climate', *New York Times*, 7 May 2019.
3. See Robert A. Beauregard, *Planning matter: Acting with things* (Chicago, IL: University of Chicago Press, 2015).
4. The State of Oklahoma, where Tulsa is located, has been a Republican-dominant state for decades. To learn more about the political atmosphere of Tulsa, see: Joshua Partlow, Annie Gowen, and DeNeen L. Brown, 'Tulsa mayor welcomes Trump despite rally controversy', *Washington Post*, 18 June 2020.
5. Alan Greenblatt, 'The City Preparing for Climate Change Without Ever Saying the Words', *Governing: The States and Localities*. November 2017.
6. David R. Godschalk, 'Urban hazard mitigation: creating resilient cities', *Natural Hazards Review*, Vol. 4, No. 2 (2003), pp. 136–43.
7. Ian L. McHarg, *Design with Nature* (Garden City, NY: John Wiley & Sons, 1992[1969]).
8. Jane Bardon, 'Letter from Scott Morrison raises questions about why the NT received GST top up', *ABC News*, 14 November 2018.
9. Gilles Deleuze and Felix Guattari, *A Thousand Plateaus*, p. 86.
10. Manuel DeLanda, *A New Philosophy of Society* (New York: Continuum, 2006).
11. Bruno Latour, *Facing Gaia* (Hoboken, New Jersey: John Wiley & Sons, 2017).
12. Isabelle Stengers, *In catastrophic times: Resisting the coming of barbarism* (Paris: Open Humanities Press, 2015).
13. Gilles Deleuze, *Spinoza: Practical Philosophy* (San Francisco, CA: City Light Publishers, 1988), p. 28.
14. Spinoza's Ethics, IV, appendix, chap. 13, cited in Deleuze, *ibid.* p. 26.
15. Ibid., p. 26.
16. Ibid., p. 26.
17. Ibid., p. 27.
18. Yvonne Rydin, 'The challenges of the 'material turn' for planning studies', *Planning Theory & Practice*, Vol. 15, No. 4 (2014), pp. 590–95; Robert A. Beauregard, *Planning matter: Acting with things*.
19. Noortje Marres, *Material Participation: Technology, the Environment, and Everyday Publics* (Basingstoke, Hampshire: Palgrave Macmillan, 2012).
20. See City of Tulsa, 'Stormwater Runoff: Slow It, Spread It, Sink it', *Save Our Streams* (2018) www.cityoftulsa.org/media/3317/rain-barrel-sheet.pdf.
21. Jane Bennett, *Vibrant matter: A political ecology of things* (Durham, NC: Duke University Press, 2010); Maria Puig de La Bellacasa, *Matters of care: Specu-*

lative ethics in more than human worlds (Minneapolis, MN: University of Minnesota Press, 2017).

22. Corey Lang and John D. Ryder, 'The effect of tropical cyclones on climate change engagement', *Climatic Change*, Vol. 135, No. 3–4 (2016), pp. 625–38.

23. Ellen Knickmeyer, Hannah Fingerhut and Emily Swanson, 'Poll: Disasters influence thinking on climate change', *The Associated Press-National Opinion Research Center for Public Affairs Research*, 2019.

24. See Isabelle Stengers, *In catastrophic times: Resisting the coming of barbarism* (Paris: Open Humanities Press, 2015).

25. Laurie Mazur, 'This is how we can tackle climate change, even with a denier in chief', *The Nation*, 12 December 2016; Alan Greenblatt, 'The City Preparing for Climate Change Without Ever Saying the Words', *Governing: The States and Localities*, November, 2017.

26. Ann Patton, 'A Tulsa Story: Learning to Live in Harmony with Nature', in J. Bullock, G. D. Haddow, and K. S. Haddow (Eds.) *Global Warming, Natural Hazards, and Emergency Management* (Boca Raton, FL: CRC Press, 2009).

27. Marres, *Material Participation: Technology, the Environment, and Everyday Publics*.

28. Beyond Zero Emissions, *The 10 Gigawatt Vision: How renewable energy can power jobs and investment in the Northern Territory* (2019), p. 6, https://bze.org.au/research/regional/repowering-nt/

29. Beyond Zero Emissions, *The 10 Gigawatt Vision: How renewable energy can power jobs and investment in the Northern Territory*, p. 14.

30. *Living Future* website, https://living-future.org/lbc/.

31. City of Darwin, *Establishing a Resilient Urban Forest for Darwin* (2018). https://darwin.nt.gov.au/council/about-council/publications-and-forms/establishing-a-resilient-urban-forest-for-darwin.

32. Ibid., p. 15.

33. Timothy Morton, *Hyperobjects: philosophy and ecology after the end of the world* (Minneapolis: University of Minnesota Press, 2013); Pol Bargués-Pedreny and Jessica Schmidt 'Learning to Be Postmodern in an All Too Modern World: 'Whatever action' in International Climate Change Imaginaries', *Global Society*, Vol. 33, No. 1 (2019), pp. 45–65.

34. Benjamin Oreskes, 'To block homeless shelter, San Francisco residents are suing on environmental grounds', *Los Angeles Times*, 10 July 2019.

35. J. Christopher Brown and Mark Purcell, 'There's nothing inherent about scale: political ecology, the local trap, and the politics of development in the Brazilian Amazon', *Geoforum*, Vol. 36, No. 5 (2005), pp. 607–24.

36. Mark Purcell, 'Urban democracy and the local trap', *Urban Studies*, Vol. 43, No. 11 (2006), pp. 1921–41.

37. Jane Wills and Robert W. Lake, 'Introduction: The power of pragmatism', in Wills J, Lake RW (eds.) *The Power of Pragmatism* (Manchester, UK: Manchester University Press, 2020).

38. Robert W. Lake, 2017a. 'Justice as subject and object of planning', *International Journal of Urban and Regional Research*, Vol. 40, No. 6 (2017), pp. 1205–20.
39. Pierre Charbonnier, 'L'écologie ne nous rassemble pas, elle nous divise', *Le Monde*, 15 May 2020, p. 25.
40. Bruno Latour, 'Le Covid comme crash-test', Libération, 14 May 2020, p. 21.
41. Alice Kadlec, 'Reconstructing Dewey: The Philosophy of Critical Pragmatism', *Polity*, Vol. 38, No. 4 (2006), pp. 519–42.
42. John Dewey, *Reconstruction in philosophy* (Mineola, NY: Dover, 1920[2004]).
43. This was the case for the French president Emmanuel Macron, who might have had good intentions in desiring to implement a carbon tax as soon as possible (given the climate crisis), and yet was met with ferocious opposition by the public who accused him of being a self-appointed elitist emperor (McAuley 2019).
44. Robert W. Lake, 'Justice as subject and object of planning', *International Journal of Urban and Regional Research*, Vol. 40, No. 6 (2017), p. 1219.
45. Richard Bernstein, 'John Dewey's vision of radical democracy', in *The Pragmatic Turn* (Cambridge: Polity, 2010).
46. Robert W. Lake, 'On poetry, pragmatism and the urban possibility of creative democracy', Urban Geography, Vol. 38, No. 4 (2017), pp. 479–94.
47. Manuel DeLanda, *A New Philosophy of Society* (New York: Continuum, 2006).
48. Robert W. Lake, 'Justice as subject and object of planning', *International Journal of Urban and Regional Research*, Vol. 40, No. 6 (2017), p. 1215.
49. John Dewey, *Reconstruction in philosophy* (Mineola, NY: Dover, 1920[2004]), p. 121.
50. Richard Rorty, *Philosophy and the mirror of nature* (Princeton, NJ: Princeton University Press, 1979), p. 377.

CHAPTER 4: CLEVELAND V CAPE TOWN

1. See Sarah Dooling, 'Ecological gentrification: a research agenda exploring justice in the city', *International Journal of Urban and Regional Research*, Vol. 33, No. 3 (2009), pp. 621–39; Isabelle Anguelovski, 'From toxic sites to parks as (green) LULUs? New challenges of inequity, privilege, gentrification, and exclusion for urban environmental justice', *Journal of Planning Literature*, Vol. 31, No. 1 (2016), pp. 23–36; Kenneth A. Gould and Tammy L. Lewis, *Green Gentrification: Urban Sustainability and the Struggle for Environmental Justice* (London: Routledge, 2016).
2. Jessica L. Urban, 'Interrogating privilege/challenging the "greening of hate"', *International Feminist Journal of Politics*, Vol. 9, No. 2 (2007), pp. 251–64; Sara T. Black, Richard A. Milligan, and Nik Heynen, 'Solidarity in climate/immigrant justice direct action: Lessons from movements in the US South', *International Journal of Urban and Regional Research*, Vol. 40, No. 2 (2016), pp. 284–98.

3. www.cleveland.com/datacentral/2019/09/poverty-in-cleveland-and-cuyahoga-suburbs-remains-above-pre-recession-levels-new-census-estimates-say.html.
4. www.clevelandfed.org/en/newsroom-and-events/publications/metro-mix/cleveland/mm-201908-cleveland.aspx.
5. www.cleveland.com/opinion/2019/09/clevelands-poverty-numbers-should-shock-us-all-into-advocacy.html.
6. http://www.capetown.gov.za/Media-and-news/City%20gives%20informal%20traders%20a%20hand%20up.
7. www.ci.uct.ac.za/news/review-research-evidence-child-poverty-sa.
8. www.investcapetown.com/wp-content/uploads/2019/04/CCT-EPIC-2018Q1-FINAL-20180702.pdf.
9. www.capetown.gov.za/Family%20and%20home/Residential-property-and-houses/Informal-housing/About-informal-housing.
10. Gould and Tammy, *Green Gentrification: Urban Sustainability and the Struggle for Environmental Justice*; Jennifer L. Rice, Daniel A. Cohen, Joshua Long, Jason R. Jurjevich, 'Contradictions of the climate-friendly city: new perspectives on eco-gentrification and housing justice', *International Journal of Urban and Regional Research*, Vol. 44, No. 1 (2020), pp. 145–65.
11. See Daniel A. Cohen, 'Water Crisis and Eco-Apartheid in Sao Paulo: Beyond Naive Optimism about Climate-Linked Disasters', in Spotlight On: Essays on Parched Cities, Parched Citizens. *International Journal of Urban and Regional Research* (2018) https://ijurr.org/spotlight-on/parched-cities-parched-citizens/water-crisis-and-eco-apartheid-in-sao-paulo-beyond-naive-optimism-about-climate-linked-disasters/.
12. Eric Swyngedouw and Nik Heynen, 'Urban political ecology, justice and the politics of scale', *Antipode*, Vol. 35, No. 5, 898–918; Nik Heynen, Maria Kaika, and Erik Swyngedouw, *In the nature of cities: urban political ecology and the politics of urban metabolism* (London: Routledge, 2006).
13. Julian Agyeman, David Schlosberg, Luke Craven, and Caitlin Matthews, 'Trends and directions in environmental justice: from inequity to everyday life, community, and just sustainabilities', *Annual Review of Environment and Resources*, Vol. 41 (2016), pp. 321–40.
14. Winifred Curran and Trina Hamilton, 'Just green enough: contesting environmental gentrification in Greenpoint, Brooklyn', *Local Environment*, Vol. 17, No. 9 (2012), pp. 1027–42.
15. Ibid., p. 1028.
16. Cohen, 'Water Crisis and Eco-Apartheid in Sao Paulo: Beyond Naive Optimism about Climate-Linked Disasters'.
17. 'Nature-based solutions' or 'biophilic' cities discourse has become increasingly popular as cities actively prepare for climate change and adaptation; See Timothy Beatley, *Biophilic Cities* (Washington, DC: Island Press, 2011); Harriet Bulkeley and Vanesa Castán Broto, 'Government by experiment? Global cities and the governing of climate change', *Transactions of the Institute of British Geographers*, Vol. 38, No. 3 (2013), pp. 361–75.

18. See Nella Van Dyke and Holly J. McCammon, *Strategic alliances: Coalition building and social movements* (Minneapolis, MN: University of Minnesota Press, 2010); Jenny Pickerill, 'Black and Green: the future of Indigenous–environmentalist relations in Australia', *Environmental Politics*, Vol. 27, No. 6 (2018), pp. 1122–145.

19. Black et al., 'Solidarity in climate/immigrant justice direct action: Lessons from movements in the US South'.

20. Ibid., p. 256.

21. Joe Curnow and Anjali Helferty, 'Contradictions of Solidarity: Whiteness, Settler Coloniality, and the Mainstream Environmental Movement', *Environment and Society*, Vol. 9, No. 1 (2018), pp. 145–63.

22. Lisa S. H. Park and David N. Pellow, *The slums of Aspen: The war on immigrants in America's Eden* (New York, NY: NYU Press, 2011); Monica Aufrecht, 'Rethinking "greening of hate": Climate emissions, immigration, and the last frontier', *Ethics & the Environment*, Vol. 17, No. 2 (2012), pp. 51–74.

23. John Hultgren, *Border walls gone green: nature and anti-immigrant politics in America* (Minnesota, MN: University of Minnesota Press, 2015).

24. Sara T. Black, Richard A. Milligan, and Nik Heynen, 'Solidarity in climate/immigrant justice direct action: Lessons from movements in the US South'.

25. Julian Agyeman, David Schlosberg, Luke Craven, and Caitlin Matthews, 'Trends and directions in environmental justice: from inequity to everyday life, community, and just sustainabilities'.

26. Sara T. Black, Richard A. Milligan, and Nik Heynen, 'Solidarity in climate/immigrant justice direct action: Lessons from movements in the US South', p. 288.

27. Mark Swilling, 'Sustainability, poverty and municipal services: the case of Cape Town, South Africa', *Sustainable Development*, Vol. 18, No. 4 (2010), pp. 194–201; David Simon, 'Climate and environmental change and the potential for greening African cities', *Local Economy*, Vol. 28, No. 2 (2013), pp. 203–17.

28. Swilling, 'Sustainability, poverty and municipal services: the case of Cape Town, South Africa'.

29. Simon, 'Climate and environmental change and the potential for greening African cities'.

30. Ernesto Laclau and Chantal Mouffe, *Hegemony and State Socialism: Towards a Radical Democratic Politics* (London: Verso, 1985).

31. William M. Griswold, 'Director's Foreword', *Cai Guo-Qiang: Cuyahoga River Lightning* (Cleveland, OH: Cleveland Museum of Art, 2019), p. 13.

32. Cleveland, as an old city, has a combined sewer infrastructure: a single pipe handles both sanitary sewage and stormwater. During heavy rain, this can cause discharge overflow to the environment, such as Lake Erie or a nearby system. NEORSD minimises such untreated discharges and maximises treatment.

33. Joanna P. Ganning and J. Rosie Tighe, 'Moving toward a shared understanding of the US shrinking city', *Journal of Planning Education and Research* (2018), pp. 1–14.

34. Edward McClelland, *Nothin' but Blue Skies: the Heyday, Hard Times, and Hopes of America's Industrial Heartland* (New York, NY: Bloomsbury Press, 2013); Brian C. Chaffin, William Shuster, Olivia O. Green, 'A tale of two rain gardens: Barriers and bridges to adaptive management of urban stormwater in Cleveland, Ohio', *Journal of Environmental Management*, Vol. 183 (2016), pp. 431–41.
35. The historical background on Cleveland's pursuit of environmentalism was provided by the Cleveland Museum of Natural History, which is home to Green City Blue Lake Institute that promotes sustainable city living in Northeast Ohio. Learn more at: http://gcbl.org.
36. Kuhuk Sharma, Nicholas T. Basta, Parwinder S. Grewal, 'Soil heavy metal contamination in residential neighborhoods in post-industrial cities and its potential human exposure risk', *Urban Ecosystems*, Vol. 18, No. 1 (2015), pp. 115–32.
37. Jeffrey S. Lowe, 'Limitations of community development partnerships: Cleveland Ohio and Neighborhood Progress Inc.', *Cities*, Vol. 25, No. 1 (2008), pp. 37–44.
38. The Urban Institute, *The Impact of Community Development Corporation on Urban Neighbourhoods* (Washington, CD: The Urban Institute, 2005); Norman Krumholz, W. Dennis Keating, Philip D. Star and Mark C. Chupp, 'The long-term impact of CDCs on urban neighborhoods: Case studies of Cleveland's Broadway-Slavic Village and Tremont neighborhoods', *Community Development*, Vol. 37, No. 4 (2006), pp. 33–52.
39. Chaffin et al., 'A tale of two rain gardens: Barriers and bridges to adaptive management of urban stormwater in Cleveland, Ohio'.
40. Slavic Village is registered as a member of EcoDistricts, a North American city-neighborhood network that promotes community development imperatives beyond market-driven development models. The network has three imperatives: (1) equity (putting the needs of vulnerable populations first), (2) resilience (capacity to recover from social, economic, and environmental stresses), and (3) climate protection (being on a pathway to carbon neutrality).
41. As a result, Cleveland has now been studied as a pioneer in ecology-for-the-shrinking-city approach, where green urbanism is applied as a way of addressing neighbourhood safety and public health issues of blighted communities – underlining the social and economic benefits of greening vacant lots. See Sean Burkholder, 'The new ecology of vacancy: Rethinking land use in shrinking cities', *Sustainability*, Vol. 4, No. 6 (2012), pp. 1154–172; W. D. Shuster, C. E. Burkman, J. Grosshans, S. Dadio, and R. Losco, 'Green residential demolitions: case study of vacant land reuse in storm water management in Cleveland', *Journal of Construction Engineering and Management*, Vol. 141, No. 3 (2015); Dustin L. Hermann, Kirsten Schwarz, William D. Shuster, Matthew E. Hopton, 'Ecology for the shrinking city', *BioScience*, Vol. 66, No. 11 (2016), pp. 965–73.

42. Sustainable Cleveland, *Cleveland Climate Action Plan 2018 Update: Building Thriving and Resilient Neighborhoods for All* (City of Cleveland, 2018), p. 10, https://drive.google.com/file/d/1Z3234sMp7S7MjaXvMgcZtcAaYs4x2oHE/view.
43. Ibid., p. 22, 30.
44. As I discuss further below, the west, scenic side of Cape Town is often occupied by white, affluent communities, while the non-white residents were forced to relocate to the eastern suburbs during the apartheid era.
45. Edgar Pieterse, From Current Challenges to Strategic Risk – Keynotes from thought leaders and an open discussion about the strategic risks facing African cities. Conference speech at Harare Innovation Days: NextGen Cities, 27–9 November 2019.
46. Steven Robins, '"Day Zero", hydraulic citizenship and the defense of the commons in Cape Town: A case study of the politics of water and its infrastructures (2017–18)', *Journal of Southern African Studies*, Vol. 45, No. 1 (2019), pp. 5–29; Lucy Rodina, 'Planning for water resilience: competing agendas among Cape Town's planners and water managers', *Environmental Science & Policy*, Vol. 99 (2019), pp. 10–16.
47. Abigail H. Neely, "Blame it on the Weeds': Politics, Poverty, and Ecology in the New South Africa', *Journal of Southern African Studies*, Vol. 36, No. 4 (2010), pp. 869–87.
48. Brian W. van Wilgen and Andrew Wannenburgh, 'Co-facilitating invasive species control, water conservation and poverty relief: achievements and challenges in South Africa's Working for Water programme'. *Current Opinion in Environmental Sustainability*, Vol. 19 (2016), pp. 7–17.
49. Neely, '"Blame it on the Weeds": Politics, Poverty, and Ecology in the New South Africa', p. 870.
50. However, more recent testaments, notably by van Wilgen and Wannenburgh, show the delicate challenges of balancing ecological and socioeconomic priorities, as the areas that need alien species removal and further job creation, respectively, do not always match. In those moments of conflict, they note, it is eventually the ecological intentions that suffer, as creating economic opportunities for the poor is more often prioritised (hence weighting job creation over ecological benefits).
51. The Nature Conservancy, *The Grater Cape Town Water Fund: Assessing the return on investment for ecological infrastructure restoration* (November 2018), p. 34, www.nature.org/content/dam/tnc/nature/en/documents/GCTWF-Business-Case_2018-11-14_Web.pdf.
52. A PBO is a unique organisation type in South Africa, a non-profit company whose main objective is to perform public benefit activities with altruistic or philanthropic intent. Local governments (such as the City of Cape Town) often collaborate closely with PBOs, especially on new or inventive policy solutions at an experimental stage. Given the limited budget/means, a local government may not be able to offer a new full city-scale policy at first; if so, the govern-

ment can delegate certain tasks to PBOs, which can run a trial version at a smaller scale (e.g., one neighbourhood).

53. Gina Ziervogel, Moliehi Shale, and Minlei Du, 'Climate change adaptation in a developing country context: The case of urban water supply in Cape Town', *Climate and Development*, Vol. 2, No. 2 (2010), pp. 94–110.
54. Lucy Rodina, 'Water resilience lessons from Cape Town's water crisis', *WIREs Water*, Vol. 6, No. 6 (2019), pp. 1–7.
55. City of Cape Town, Water Strategy (draft for public comments), 2019, www.preventionweb.net/files/63935_capetowndraftwaterstrategy2019publi.pdf.
56. Ibid., p. 3.
57. Ibid., p. 1. It should also be noted that the drought event instigated many conversations and policy attention on the role of civil society and bottom-up collective actions. The new strategy (City of Cape Town, 2019) also highlights the role of communities, social cohesion, and partnering with communities in times of crisis, encouraging 'increased social networks, volunteerism and active citizenry that results in Capetonians pulling together in times of shock' (p. 71). There is much more recognition of the importance of community participation and investment in capacity building.
58. Peter Luhanga. 'Electricity Tariff Hike Angers Cape Town Residents', *News24*, 1 August 2017, https://news24.com/SouthAfrica/News/electricity-tariff-hike-angers-cape-town-residents-20170801.
59. Edgar Pieterse, 'Epistemic practices of Southern urbanism', *IJURR Lecture, Annual Conference of the Association of American Geographers*, Los Angeles, April 2013, https://ijurr.org/lecture/2013-ijurr-aag-lecture-epistemic-practices-southern-urbanism-edgar-pieterse/.
60. GreenCape is a major PBO in Cape Town; it works closely with the city government, especially on the topics of renewable energy and the job creation potential of the green economy. Established in 2010, GreenCape primarily aims to promote the green economy in Africa through supporting SMEs and potential investors and providing policy and regulatory advocacy. What it covers as the green economy is divergent, including renewable energy, water and waste management, sustainable transport, and agriculture.
61. In addition, green technologies (e.g., solar panel installations, rain barrels, decentralised grey water management), if adequately subsidised, can also help reduce the cost of living, which is the major enticing factor (or selling point) for low-income households. Currently, Cape Town residents are eligible for subsidies on solar water heaters ('solar geysers'), but such technologies still remain out of reach for low-income populations (i.e., still too expensive even with the additional support).
62. 'Solar PV' refers to solar photovoltaic, a technology that converts sunlight into direct electricity by using semiconductors (i.e., solar panels).
63. 'Townships' often refer to the settlements in the Cape Flat, the eastern suburbs of Cape Town where the majority of lower-income communities reside.

64. 'Coloured' refers to mixed-race South Africans who are descendants of Khoisan, Black Africans, white settlers, and Asians.
65. Roberts M. Ebrahim, A. Ruiters, A. and R. Solomons, 'Atlantis, A Utopian Nightmare?' South African Labour and Development Research Unit, Working Paper No. 66 (1986), Johannesburg.
66. Etienne L. Nel and Archibald Meston, 'Transforming Atlantis, South Africa, through local economic development', *GeoJournal*, Vol. 39, No. 1 (1996), pp. 89–96.
67. The Atlantis SEZ is currently being managed by the Western Cape Tourism, Trade, and Investment Promotion Agency (WESGRO; a department within the Western Cape provincial government), in collaboration with the City of Cape Town, GreenCape, and the National Department of Trade and Industry.
68. The resident communities have participated in co-creating the SEZ's implementation plans, and in 2019, the Atlantis SEZ Community Stakeholder Network was created. The network (15 community members) serves as a conduit for communication between the project and the Atlantis community.
69. This information was obtained through a focus group discussion with the government personnel working on Atlantis SEZ project.
70. Youth unemployment in Cape Town is about 40 per cent, while the overall unemployment rate is close to 25 per cent (See Tab. 4.1).
71. See Mitch Rose, 'Landscape and labyrinths', *Geoforum*, Vol. 33 (2002), pp. 455–67; Vanesa Castán Broto, *Urban Energy Landscapes* (Cambridge: Cambridge University Press, 2019). For the capacity of 'space' to deflect the linear horizon of time, see Doreen Massey, *For Space* (London: Sage, 2005). For Arendt's reference to 'promise', see Hannah Arendt, *The Human Condition* (Chicago: University of Chicago Press, 1958/2018), pp. 243–7. The idea of us collectively generating heterogenous and scale-jumping 'storylines' comes from Robert W. Lake, 'Unbounding Virtue', a manuscript under review with *Progress in Human Geography*.

CHAPTER 5: CITIES AND COMPLEXITY

1. Edgar Morin, 'En finir avec les malheurs de l'écologie', *Libération*, 3 February 2020.
2. John Dewey, *Experience and Nature* (Redditch, Worcestershire: Read Books, 2008[1925]), p. 33.
3. Nathan F. Sayre, 'Ecological and geographical scale: Parallels and potential for integration', *Progress in Human Geography*, Vol. 29, No. 3 (2005), p. 277; Roderick P. Neumann, 'Political ecology: Theorizing scale', *Progress in Human Geography*, Vol. 33, No. 3 (2008), pp. 398–406; Adam Moore, 'Rethinking scale as a geographical category: From analysis to practice', *Progress in Human Geography*, Vol. 32, No. 2 (2008), pp. 203–25; Stephen M. Manson, 'Does scale exist? An epistemological scale continuum for complex human–environment systems', *Geoforum*, Vol. 39, No. 2 (2008), p. 783.

4. Neil Adger, 'Social and ecological resilience: are they related?', *Progress in Human Geography*, Vol. 24, No. 2 (2000), pp. 347–64.

5. David Chandler, *Resilience: The Governance of Complexity* (London: Routledge, 2014); Kevin Grove, *Resilience* (Milton Park: Routledge, 2018).

6. Anthony Giddens, *The Constitutions of Society* (Berkeley, CA: University of California Press, 1986).

7. Manuel DeLanda, *A New Philosophy of Society* (New York: Continuum, 2006).

8. Nicholas Tampio, 'Assemblages and the multitude: Deleuze, Hardt, Negri, and the postmodern left', *European Journal of Political Theory*, Vol. 8, No. 3 (2009), pp. 383–400.

9. Manuel DeLanda, *A New Philosophy of Society*, p. 57.

10. Ibid., p. 34.

11. AbdouMaliq Simone, 'The surfacing of urban life: A response to Colin McFarlane and Neil Brenner, David Madden and David Wachsmuth', *City*, Vol.15, No. 3-4 (2011), p. 363.

12. See Colin McFarlane, 'On context: Assemblage, political economy and structure', *City*, Vol. 15, No. 3-4 (2011), pp. 375–88. This marks an important shift in urban theory, which often considered 'local scales' performative and yet largely submissive puppets of global neoliberalism – as we discussed in Chapter 2.

13. Antoine Bousquet and Simon Curtis, 'Beyond models and metaphors: Complexity theory, systems thinking and international relations', *Cambridge Review of International Affairs*, Vol. 24, No. 1 (2011), p. 49.

14. Ibid., p. 53.

15. Gilles Deleuze and Felix Guattari, *A Thousand Plateaus*, p. 113.

16. Lewis Mumford, *The City in History* (New York, NY: A Harvest Book, 1961), p. 29.

17. Manuel DeLanda, *A New Philosophy of Society*, p. 59.

18. In my other work, I explore the lessons of Butler's gender performativity for building anti-essentialist political solidarity. See Ihnji Jon, 'Reframing postmodern planning with feminist social theory: Toward 'anti-essentialist norms', *Planning Theory*, Vol. 19 (2020), pp. 147–71.

19. Charles Tilly, *Stories, Identities, and Political Change* (Oxford, UK: Rowman & Littlefield Publishers, 2002).

20. Tampio, 'Assemblages and the multitude: Deleuze, Hardt, Negri, and the postmodern left', p. 390.

21. Ibid., p. 388.

22. Ibid., p. 393.

23. I delve into this particular topic in depth in my other work: see Jon, 'Reframing postmodern planning with feminist social theory: Toward "anti-essentialist norms"'.

24. Deleuze and Guattari, *A Thousand Plateaus*, p. 117.

25. Ibid., p. 164.

26. Erik Werner Petersen, 'Design as seven steps of deterritorialisation', *Nordic Design Research* (Nordes), No. 1 (2005) https://archive.nordes.org/index.php/n13/article/view/232/215; In *A Thousand Plateaus*, Deleuze and Guattari give an example of the works of writers, filmmakers, and composers whose work is in constant variation, while their message itself permeates through each and every variation (pp. 10, 114, 594).
27. Ibid. Peterson explains Deleuze's example of the Pink Panther as an abstract machine of consistence, which works towards absolute deterritorialisation.
28. Deleuze and Guattari, *A Thousand Plateaus*, p. 100.
29. See Mark Purcell, 'A new land: Deleuze and Guattari and planning', *Planning Theory & Practice*, Vol. 14, No. 1 (2013), pp. 20–38.
30. Jon, 'Reframing postmodern planning with feminist social theory: Toward 'anti-essentialist norms'.
31. Ihnji Jon, 'Deciphering posthumanism: Why and how it matters to planning in the Anthropocene', *Planning Theory*, Vol. 19, No. 4 (2020), pp. 392–420; see also Robert A. Beauregard, *Planning Matter: Acting with Things* (Chicago, IL: University of Chicago Press, 2015).
32. See Mohsen Mostafavi and Gareth Doherty (eds.), *Ecological Urbanism* (Baden, Switzerland: Lars Müller Publishers, 2016); Charles Waldheim, *Landscape as Urbanism: A General Theory* (Princeton, NJ: Princeton University Press, 2016).
33. 'Banlieue' often refers to large social housing developments (Habitation à Loyer Modéré; HLM) in the outskirts of Paris or other big city-metropolitan areas in France; the majority of these residents are of African origin, initially migrated for factory job opportunities in the 1970s. Since post-industrialisation of the French economy, these areas are often associated with chronic unemployment, poverty, and violence.
34. François Jarrige, 'L'histoire de l'énergie est le summum de l'histoire écrite par les vainqueurs', *Libération*, 12 February 2020 (covered by Nicolas Celnik). See also François Jarrige and Alexis Vrignon, *Face à la Puissance: Une Histoire des Énergies Alternative À l'Âge Industriel* (Paris: La Découverte, 2020).
35. The location of the company is withheld for anonymity.
36. See Lewis Mumford, *The City in History*, 'Chapter 2. The Crystalization of the City'.
37. Ibid., p. 29.
38. Ibid., p. 31.
39. Manuel DeLanda, *A New Philosophy of Society*, pp. 44–5.
40. Lewis Mumford, *The City in History*, p. 569.
41. Donna J. Haraway, *Staying with the Trouble: Making Kin in the Chthulucene* (Durham, NC: Duke University Press, 2016), p. 100.
42. Lewis Mumford, *The City in History*, p. 526.
43. Ibid., p. 527.

44. David Stradling, 'Why the Cuyahoga Goes Burning Through Our Dreams', *Cai Guo-Qiang: Cuyahoga River Lightning* (Cleveland, OH: Cleveland Art Museum Exhibition Catalogs, 2019).
45. 'River Reborn: Celebrating 50 years of Cuyahoga River progress', www.neorsd. org/riverreborn-celebrating-50-years-of-cuyahoga-river-progress/; See also: 'Cuyahoga 50: Celebrating Our River, Igniting Our Future' (June 19–23, 2019). www.cuyahoga50.org.
46. Wayne Green, 'Inhofe still supports funding for Arkansas River projects', *Tulsa World*, 19 November 2012.
47. Mallory Thomas, 'Big Changes Planned for Arkansas River in Tulsa', *News on 6*, 6 December 2019.
48. Tampio, 'Assemblages and the multitude: Deleuze, Hardt, Negri, and the postmodern left', p. 385. See also Paul Patton, 'Deleuze and democracy', *Contemporary Political Theory*, Vol. 4, (2005), pp. 400–13; William E. Connolly, *Pluralism* (Durham, NC: Duke University Press, 2005).
49. See Judith Butler, 'Gender trouble, feminist theory, and psychoanalytic discourse' (pp. 324–40), *Feminism/Postmodernism*. Linda Nicholson, Ed. (New York, NY: Routledge, 1990); Ernesto Laclau and Chantal Mouffe, *Hegemony and Socialist Strategy* (London: Verso: 1985, 2001). Butler argued that the future of feminist politics should embrace the shattering of the gender dichotomy (female/male), since that would open up new possibilities of coalition politics with other minorities. Similarly, Laclau and Mouffe suggested that we should embrace the radically unfixed social identities; they argued that left politics should go beyond a fixed notion of the proletariat, in order to expand the movement and become inclusive with other oppressed (plural) minorities that are currently not represented in mainstream politics.
50. Warren Magnusson, *Politics of Urbanism: Seeing Like a City* (London: Routledge, 2011).
51. Ibid., p. 120.
52. Lewis Mumford, *The City in History*, p. 561.
53. The idea originated with Ernesto Laclau and Chantal Mouffe, *Hegemony and Socialist Strategy*; see also Mark Purcell, 'Resisting neoliberalization: Communicative planning or counter-hegemonic movements?', *Planning Theory*, Vol. 8, No. 2 (2009), p. 159 for a very helpful unpacking of this concept.
54. Jon, 'Deciphering posthumanism: Why and how it matters to planning in the Anthropocene'.
55. Petula Dvorak, 'Dreamers speak to us through art', *Washington Post*, 18 February 2020.
56. Chris Reed, *Projective Ecologies in Design and* Planning, in Frederick R. Steiner, George F. Thompson, and Armando Carbonell (eds.) *Nature and Cities: The Ecological Imperative in Urban Design and Planning* (Cambridge, MA: Lincoln Institute of Land Policy, 2016), p. 327.
57. Deleuze and Guattari, *A Thousand Plateaus*, p. 18.
58. Retrieved from www.fondationcartier.com/en/exhibitions/nous-les-arbres.

59. Deleuze and Guattari, *A Thousand Plateaus*, p. 100; Deleuze and Guattari explains how the 'signifier' is not merely a form of representation of the 'signified' but also an active performer of the signified. When we have a message to tell someone (e.g., 'I'm sorry'), sometimes it is not just about the message itself but more about how you deliver it (e.g., an apologetic facial expression, tone of voice, the kinds of things that render your message sound sincere and genuine). As they put it, '[t]he signifier reterritorializes on the face. The face is what gives the signifier substance; it is what fuels interpretation, and it is what changes, changes traits, when interpretation reimports signifier to its substance. Look, his expression changed' (p. 133–4).
60. See also Keller Easterling (2014)'s work on the power of infrastructure space, which provides a set of empirical examples that supports Marshall McLuhan's dictum 'the medium is the message'. Keller Easterling, *Extra-State Craft: The Power of Infrastructure Space* (London: Verso, 2014); Marshall McLuhan, *Understanding Media: The Extensions of Man* (New York: McGraw-Hill and London: Routledge & Kegan Paul, 1964, 2011).

CHAPTER 6: CONCLUSION

1. Gilles Deleuze and Felix Guattari, *A Thousand Plateaus*, pp.164–5.
2. David Foster Wallace, 'This is Water: 2005 Commencement Speech to the Graduating Class at Kenyon College', https://fs.blog/2012/04/david-foster-wallace-this-is-water/.
3. Robert W. Lake, 'The Quest for Certainty', In: Jane Wills and Robert W. Lake (eds.) *The Power of Pragmatism* (Manchester: Manchester University Press, 2020), pp. 273–4.
4. Deleuze and Guattari, *A Thousand Plateaus*, p. 239.
5. Emanuele Coccia, 'Les virus nous rappellent que n'importe quel être peut détruire le présent et établir un ordre inconnu', *Libération*, 14 March 2020.
6. Edgar Morin, 'Ce que nous dit le coronavirus', *Libération*, 13 March 2020.
7. Judith Butler, *Precarious Life* (London: Verso, 2004), p. 23. Tronto and Lawson's care ethics that challenge the neoliberal discourse on individualism and its overestimation of self-sufficiency by compelling each of us to recognise the weakness in ourselves. Their point of entering politics is to embrace the vulnerabilities that we all share as individuals, communities, cities, countries, or as humans entirely. See Joan Tronto, 'Care as a basis for radical political judgements', *Hypatia*, Vol. 10, No. 2 (1995), pp. 141–9; Victoria Lawson, 'Geographies of Care and Responsibility', *Annals of the Association of American Geographers*, Vol. 97 (2007), pp. 1–11.
8. Chantal Mouffe, 'Deliberative democracy or agonistic pluralism', *Social Research*, Vol. 66, No. 3 (1999), pp. 745–58; Chantal Mouffe, 'Feminism, citizenship, and radical democratic politics', in L. Nicholson and S. Seidman (Eds.), *Social Postmodernism: Beyond Identity Politics* (Cambridge: Cambridge University Press, 1995), pp. 315–31.

9. See Robert J. Samuelson, 'This crisis is about democracy itself', *The Washington Post*, 23 March 2020.
10. Josh Rogin, 'Democracies can succeed against the coronavirus', *Washington Post*, 12 March 2020.
11. There has been a surge of news reports on the disadvantages of urban density in times of a pandemic, as it accelerates the spread of the virus. See Sabrina Tarvernise and Sarah Mervosh, 'America's Biggest Cities Were Already Losing Their Allure. What Happens Next?' *New York Times*, 19 April 2020.
12. It has been reported that, with the power of community activism, the favelas of Brazil are organising their own response, hiring ambulances, tracking cases, and collecting funds in the absence of Bolsonaro (national) government's support. See Marina Lopes, 'Neglected by Brazil's government, favelas battle the virus themselves', *Washington Post*, 11 June 2020.
13. See Emily Badger, 'Density Is Normally Good for Us. That Will Be True After Coronavirus, Too', *New York Times*, 24 March 2020.
14. Andy Merrifield, *The Urban Question* (London: Pluto Press, 2014), pp. 82–8.
15. Marshall Berman, *All That is Solid Melts into Air* (London: Verso, 1988), p. 153, as cited in Andy Merrifield, *The Urban Question* (London: Pluto Press, 2014), p. 88.

POSTSCRIPT: FUTURE DIRECTIONS FOR CITIES IN THE ANTHROPOCENE

1. One of my interviewees in Darwin remarked that there is a national policy/politics disconnection from the territory; 'we experience that the policies [implemented here] are often decided by the east coast cities [of Australia – e.g., Sydney, Melbourne]. They are detached from the realities of the NT [Northern Territories, where Darwin is located], where the 30 per cent of the populations are indigenous peoples'.
2. See Michele Lobo, 'Affective ecologies: Braiding urban worlds in Darwin, Australia', *Geoforum*, Vol. 106 (2019), pp. 393–401, among other similar works she wrote on Darwin.
3. To follow the progress of Darwin City Deal, please visit: www.infrastructure.gov.au/cities/city-deals/darwin/.
4. See The Nature Conservancy Australia, 'Indigenous fire revolution', 20 February 2020, www.natureaustralia.org.au/newsroom/indigenous-fire-revolution/; National Indigenous Australians Agency, 'Caring for country in North East Arnhem Land: Dean Yibarbuk', 8 May 2014, www.indigenous.gov.au/caring-for-country-in-north-east-arnhem-land; See also the works of Indigenous Carbon Industry Network in Darwin.
5. See more at Tulsa's Young Professionals network (TYPROS) website: https://www.typros.org.
6. To find out more, please visit: www.cherokee.org/our-government/secretary-of-natural-resources-office/sustainable-energy/.

7. John Klein, 'Cherokees look to the sun for energy with car-charging station', *Tulsa World*, 26 December 2017.
8. See Ian McHarg, *Design with nature* (Garden City, NY: John Wiley & Sons, 1992[1969]); Ian McHarg, 'Man and environment', In F. Steiner (ed.), *The essential Ian McHarg: writings on design and nature* (Washington, DC: Island Press, 2006), pp. 1–14; Ian McHarg, 'Ecology and design', In F. Steiner (ed.), *The essential Ian McHarg: writings on design and nature* (Washington, DC: Island Press, 2006), pp. 122–30.
9. Follow the project through this website: www.visiontulsa.com/economic-development/arkansas-river-development/.
10. For more information, please visit: www.wrlandconservancy.org/whatwedo/advocacy-and-research/.
11. For more information, please visit: https://greencape.co.za/content/sector/the-alternative-service-delivery-unit.
12. https://ramboll.com/projects/re/reppie-in-addis-ababa-ethiopia-first-waste-to-energy-facility-african-continent.
13. See Laura Mallonee, 'The Techies Turning Kenya Into a Silicon Savannah', *WIRED*, https://wired.com/story/kenya-silicon-savannah-photo-gallery/.
14. Aryn Baker, 'In Africa, necessity is the mother of climate-change innovation', *Time*, 23 September 2019.
15. See Corinna Dengler and Lisa Marie Seebacher, 'What about the global south? Towards a feminist decolonial degrowth approach', *Ecological Economics*, Vol. 157 (2019), pp. 246–52.
16. See Joseph E. Stiglitz, *The Price of Inequality*, (London: Penguin Books, 2012, reprint in 2013 with a new 'Preface to the paperback edition'), especially pp. 115–32.
17. For instance, see the report by Kim Tingley, 'How Architecture Could Help Us Adapt to Pandemic', *New York Times Magazine*, 14 June 2020, pp. 50–55.
18. See Morten Gjerde, 'Building Back Better: Learning from the Christchurch Rebuild', *Procedia Engineering*, Vol. 198 (2017), pp. 530–40.

Index

The Pluto Press Newsletter

Hello friend of Pluto!

Want to stay on top of the best radical books
we publish?

Then sign up to be the first to hear about our
new books, as well as special events,
podcasts and videos.

You'll also get 50% off your first order with us
when you sign up.

Come and join us!

Go to bit.ly/PlutoNewsletter

Printed and bound by CPI Group (UK) Ltd, Croydon, CR0 4YY

23/04/2025

14661021-0001